FOURTH EDITION

Laura Stamm's POWER SKATING

Laura Stamm

Human Kinetics

Library of Congress Cataloging-in-Publication Data

Stamm, Laura.
[Power skating]
Laura Stamm's power skating / Laura Stamm. -- 4th ed.
p. cm.
Includes bibliographical references.
ISBN-13: 978-0-7360-7620-3 (soft cover)
ISBN-10: 0-7360-7620-4 (soft cover)
ISBN-13: 978-0-7360-8624-0 (Adobe PDF)
ISBN-10: 0-7360-8624-2 (Adobe PDF)
1. Hockey--Training. 2. Skating. I. Title.
GV848.3.S7 2009
796.962'2--dc22

2009016093

ISBN-10: 0-7360-7620-4 (print)
ISBN-13: 978-0-7360-7620-3 (print)
ISBN-10: 0-7360-8624-2 (Adobe PDF)
ISBN-13: 978-0-7360-8624-0 (Adobe PDF)

Acquisitions Editor: Justin Klug; **Developmental Editor:** Leigh Keylock; **Assistant Editor:** Laura Podeschi; **Copyeditor:** Patrick Connolly; **Graphic Designer:** Fred Starbird; **Graphic Artist:** Tara Welsch; **Cover Designer:** Keith Blomberg; **Photographer (cover):** Bill Smith/NHLI via Getty Images; **Photographers (interior):** Bruce Bennett, Erik Hill, Jerry Liebman, and Neil Bernstein; **Visual Production Assistant:** Joyce Brumfield; **Photo Production Manager:** Jason Allen; **Art Manager:** Kelly Hendren; **Associate Art Manager:** Alan L. Wilborn; **Illustrators:** Accurate Art, Inc., Tim Offenstein, and Alan L. Wilborn; **Printer:** Seaway Printing

Human Kinetics books are available at special discounts for bulk purchase. Special editions or book excerpts can also be created to specification. For details, contact the Special Sales Manager at Human Kinetics.

Printed in the United States of America 20 19 18 17 16 15 14

The paper in this book is certified under a sustainable forestry program.

Human Kinetics
1607 N. Market Street
Champaign, IL 61820
USA

United States and International
Website: **US.HumanKinetics.com**
Email: info@hkusa.com
Phone: 1-800-747-4457

Canada
Website: **Canada.HumanKinetics.com**
Email: info@hkcanada.com

E4609

To my beloved family, always and still the inspiration and cornerstone of my life. To my beautiful grandchildren, our next generation. To the memory of my parents, by whose example I learned to reach for the sky.

To my extended family—hockey players, big and small, pro and peewee; parents; and coaches whom I've taught over these 38 years. You trusted that my programs would help you and your players to skate great hockey.

To the sport of ice hockey. It has enriched my life beyond measure. There is nothing else I could have done in life with such love, passion, and dedication.

To those whose lives I have touched in the teaching process. Please know that you have touched my life in return.

Just as I learned that there is no difference between teaching and learning, I also learned that there is no difference between giving and receiving.

To all Laura Stamm instructors. You underwent extensive and rigorous training to become certified to teach my power skating system. You now carry on the tradition. You have enhanced my system and have spread it around the world. You ensure that it will continue into the future.

To the hundreds of hockey players, coaches, and enthusiasts from around the world who submitted testimonials on my behalf upon my nomination for induction into the U.S. Hockey Hall of Fame. And with very special recognition to Stan Fischler and Lori Fremaint, who spearheaded the nomination process.

To all of you. You helped me fulfill dreams beyond imagination.

Contents

Foreword

I met Laura Stamm in 1985. The Los Angeles Kings had hired Laura to be a power skating coach for a few of their prospects. I was one of the fortunate ones to be part of that group. I clearly remember the week I spent with Laura. She taught me technical ways to improve and make me a better skater. Most important, she didn't try to change my style. I can honestly say that the one week I spent with Laura, as well as the follow-through I had with her, changed my career.

As important as speed was to get into the NHL back in 1985, today's game is much faster and quicker. In those days it was the key to success, and it is even more so now. While I only spent one week with Laura, I have kept up the exercises throughout my career.

I recommend this book to anyone who wants to play hockey and anyone who wants to get to a loose puck quicker than his opponent to score goals and help the team win. This book will also help players to improve their game and get to a level they thought they would never reach.

Read this book, carry it with you, and always go back to it throughout your career. It could make the difference between having a good career and a great career.

Luc Robitaille
NHL Hall of Famer

Preface

HISTORY AND LEGACY OF THE LAURA STAMM INTERNATIONAL POWER SKATING SYSTEM

When I was a youngster, there was no organized hockey for girls. I played on the ponds with my brothers and their friends. Ultimately, I became a competitive figure skater, then a figure skating coach. I taught at the ice rink where the New York Rangers held their daily practices. Loving hockey as I did, I spent many hours watching their practices.

The Rangers ran hockey schools at this rink each summer. In 1971, Rod Gilbert and Brad Park, the hockey school directors, asked me to teach "power skating" at the hockey school. Although I knew very little about power skating or about technique training methods for hockey skating, I jumped at the chance. At the time, I didn't realize that this would be the start of the Laura Stamm International Power Skating System.

Back then, very little was known about the science (biomechanics) of hockey skating or about the importance of skating technique. Before I started to teach, I was handed a one-page document titled "Power Skating." This document included some drills such as stops and starts; skate to the blue line and back; skate forward, turn around, and skate backward, hurrying back to the starting point; and skate the circles. Nothing on the sheet of paper addressed *how* to teach players to skate correctly.

The hockey school had three groups of players. The youngest player was about 8, and the oldest was about 18. I watched, stunned, as these boys raced around the ice, legs churning, going nowhere fast. It was instantly apparent to me that these players needed to learn *how* to skate! I stashed the sheet of paper and started experimenting. My brain reeled with ideas—ideas derived from a lifetime of studying skating and watching hockey players skate. I knew immediately that I was doing the thing in life that I was meant to do.

In the summer of 1973, Bill Torrey, general manager of the New York Islanders, phoned and asked me if I could teach a promising rookie named Bob Nystrom. Bob supposedly had a lot of promise, but to make the team, he had to increase his speed. After watching him, I thought that by improving his skating technique, he could definitely become faster.

In those days, professional hockey players did not use female instructors. So to spare Bob any embarrassment, we kept our training sessions private. We worked together from 6 to 7 a.m., 5 days a week, for 8 weeks. Bob didn't miss a day.

After being a questionable rookie, Bob wound up with a 14-year career in the NHL. In 1980, when the Islanders beat the Flyers in overtime in game 6 to win their first Stanley Cup, it was Bob who scored the winning goal—a crowning achievement!

In 1995, the Islanders retired Bob's number (23). In 1991, the team inaugurated the Bob Nystrom Award, which is given to the Islander who best exemplifies leadership, hustle, and dedication.

Bob's words of praise helped to launch my career. After initially wanting to keep our sessions secret, Bob subsequently told the world, "Without Laura, I wouldn't have made it to the NHL!" This led to jobs with several NHL and WHA teams, including the Rangers, Devils, Kings, and Whalers. Well-known graduates include Luc Robitaille, Steve Duchesne, Kevin Dineen, Doug Brown, Rob Niedermayer, Scott Niedermayer, Brendan Morrison, Ted Drury, Matt Carle, Brian Rafalski, and many others.

Radio and TV features followed. Then, in 1974, I was hired to teach at a summer hockey school in British Columbia. I established the school's power skating program, and I taught it for 18 summers. During that time, thousands of aspiring hockey players came through the program, and many went on to have long and successful careers in the NHL.

As time went on, hockey associations around the United States, Canada, and Europe hired me to teach their hockey players. Eventually, I focused on running my own power skating programs, and I developed training courses for instructors who wanted to teach my power skating system. To this day, Laura Stamm power skating programs are taught only by instructors who go through rigorous training to become certified Laura Stamm instructors.

I didn't know it when I first started teaching, but I was teaching the European method of skating without ever having seen European hockey. What started as bits and pieces eventually developed into a true system. After all these years, this system is still the model by which all other power skating programs are measured.

My philosophy of teaching remains the backbone of my system. Each skating maneuver is taught by first breaking it down into its many parts. As the parts become integrated, we add more elements and complexity to the skill. The goal is for students to master each maneuver so that they will skate correctly, powerfully, and quickly—with and without the puck—in game situations. My program syllabus is structured much like a pyramid. Students first establish a strong foundation, and the training includes ever increasing subtleties as players reach the top.

Hockey skating has come so far in these 40 years. The game is played at lightning speeds. Players circle and weave, give and go. Defenders rush as if they were forwards, and forwards go back to cover for the rushing defenders. Players who can't keep up have little chance of making it at the highest levels. And every hockey school, almost every rink, offers some form of power skating instruction.

I'm teaching my second, even third, generation of players. I still can hardly believe that I jump-started the careers of hundreds—maybe thousands—of pro players, spawned the development of an entire industry, and was the model for and often the teacher of an entire generation of power skating instructors who have followed in my footsteps.

Over the past few years, I have started to reflect on my life's work. I look back on some of the things I accomplished:

I invented many terms that are now commonly used by most of the hockey community: *C-cuts, V-diamond, pivot-push-pivot-return, X-push, toe flick.*

I received testimonials from numerous players and coaches in the NHL and elsewhere.

I taught and mentored many successful hockey and figure skating instructors. Some started their own organizations after learning from me or after teaching for my organization.

I pioneered work in the field of power skating instruction. Many instructors could not have had a career in this field had it not been for my pioneering work.

I wrote many articles addressing hockey issues, such as violence, hazing, spring tryouts, and proper training.

I taught many coaches who tell me that they still use my power skating system with their youth players today—years after they took my program or learned from me while assisting me on the ice.

I taught numerous individuals who became fabulous skaters at every level—NHL, minor league, college, and recreational players (and instructors too).

I often volunteered my services in order to help players who otherwise could not have afforded to play hockey or to pay to improve their skating.

As skill levels continue to increase, hockey becomes more and more exciting. I feel very fortunate to have been there early on, to have catalyzed the sport's development, and in the process to have influenced so many lives.

Skate great hockey!

Acknowledgments

This book has just one author, but it could not have been written without the help of many. I express deep thanks and gratitude to all those who helped me make this book a reality:

NHL players Doug Brown and Greg Brown, for your fabulous skating and unending support.

NHL player Brian Rafalski, for being the featured player on the cover of this book.

The other hockey players who graciously contributed time, energy, and skating ability: Gordon Campbell, Erik Kallio, Mark Pecchia, Louis Santini, and Richard Stamm.

Marshall Rule, for your expertise, knowledge, and lifelong friendship. You have been my mentor since even before the beginning of my career. Our intellectual battles continue to further my education in skating.

Photographers Neil Bernstein, Bruce Bennett, Erik Hill, and Jerry Liebman, for your excellent work and professionalism.

Leigh Keylock and Laura Podeschi, my editors, and Justin Klug, acquisitions editor, for working tirelessly to produce a book far better than would have been possible had I been deprived of your intelligence, dedication, and meticulous attention to detail.

Jack Blatherwick, Eric Steenburgh, and Dan Tuck, for contributing your time, insights, and scientific knowledge.

The Northford Ice Pavilion in Northford, Connecticut, and the rink staff, for your help and cooperation: Marty Roos, Perry Roos, Debbie Schmarr, and Bill Maniscalco.

Luc Robitaille, for writing the foreword to this book. Thank you for your kind words and continuing support.

In Memoriam: The late and great Herb Brooks, for whom I had the honor of working when he coached the New York Rangers, and from whom I learned so much.

Introduction

Wayne Gretzky once said, "If you can't skate, you can't play our sport; skating is an art." Yes, skating is an art. Ice hockey is also an art—a complicated art that is made up of many skills. Skating is the most fundamental and important skill. What Gretzky meant is that if you can't perform every hockey skating maneuver with speed, agility, power, quickness, and efficiency, you won't make it to the highest levels of hockey. Today's NHL stars fly down the ice at speeds unheard of even 10 years ago. Those players who are agile and *fast* dominate the game.

Hockey starts with the skates and legs. If players can't get from point A to point B instantaneously and efficiently, nothing else will work!

Skating techniques are based on scientific principles—force generation, circle physics, center of gravity, acceleration, momentum, and inertia. Many players don't realize that perfecting their skating technique is a long-term process. It takes years to become a great skater, just as it takes years to become a great player. Without dedication and lots of hard work in *every* aspect of the sport, it is almost impossible to get to the big leagues.

Jack Blatherwick, a colleague of mine and one of the most knowledgeable people in the field of biomechanics and conditioning, says the following: "Even with all the training devices available in hockey today, skating technique is still the single most important element. Kids need to be taught correct skating technique from the get-go so that by the time they are in their teens they will be able to skate without having to think about it." Training considerations for different age groups are discussed in more detail in the upcoming section.

Coaches like players who have fast feet. Fast feet are important because hockey is a sprint sport. But fast feet do not necessarily result in going fast. Because speed is a measure of distance traveled in time (miles per hour, feet per second), every time players move their feet (stride), they should cover significant distances. Some players move their feet fast but have improper and incomplete leg drive. These players may look fast, but they end up going nowhere fast. The goal is to move efficiently fast.

To help players achieve efficiently fast movement with correct technique, the most effective teaching method is one that has a systematic and integrative approach. Like all skill development, the teaching of skating technique should be structured like a pyramid—in other words, players first need to build a strong foundation. More advanced and intricate techniques are incorporated as players mature and as their abilities improve. The process that I adhere to is as follows:

First, teach players to skate correctly.

Then teach them to skate correctly and powerfully.

Then teach them to skate correctly, powerfully, and explosively.

Then teach them to skate correctly, powerfully, explosively, and quickly.

Finally, teach them to skate correctly, powerfully, explosively, and quickly—with the puck, under lots of pressure and in game situations.

The *last* element of skill development is speed. No one can learn a new skill or skating maneuver going fast. It's too much for the brain and body to accommodate. Players must learn to skate *correctly* before worrying about skating powerfully, explosively, or quickly—no matter how long it takes. And, when performing powerfully, explosively, and quickly, doing so *correctly* is still the number one priority. This combination is what makes efficiently fast skating so difficult.

My teaching methodology uses the senses (feeling, acting [doing], seeing [visualizing], and thinking [decision making] = FAST) in a process that involves multiple building blocks. This process takes time, patience, experimentation, and years of practice.

HOCKEY TRAINING FOR VARIOUS AGE GROUPS

When teaching and coaching, you must be aware of the needs of the age group and level of skaters you are working with. Young athletes have specific needs, and premature or overly intense athletic training can be harmful. Hockey programs for youngsters are often too intense—competitions are too numerous, seasons are too long, and the emphasis on winning is too great. Young children are pushed by parents and coaches to choose and specialize in hockey long before they are mature enough to do so.

Up to the age of 8, children should enjoy a variety of fun and stimulating activities. They should engage in many different movement activities; children in this age group need to develop a broad base of movement skills. Dancing, tumbling, and jumping are excellent activities. These youngsters have very short attention spans, so instruction should be unstructured and fun. Teaching should be short and simple; the best teaching strategy is to use "show and tell" methods. Structured practices provide no long-term advantages for children in this age group.

Intensive training and competition at too early an age will inhibit the development of balance, agility, and coordination. They also prevent youngsters from learning other sports and developing the varied motor skills necessary for maximum athletic performance in later years.

Between the ages of 8 and 10, children's postural and balance skills mature and become more automatic. These children are able to master some of the basic movements needed for organized sports; however, they still have short attention spans, and it is difficult for them to make the rapid decisions that are involved in complex sports. These children should participate in several sports in order to develop balance, agility, and coordination. Sports such as hockey, soccer, and basketball—as well as martial arts, swimming, tee ball, and lacrosse—are excellent choices if approached in a fun and balanced way. In hockey for this age group, fundamental skating skills can be introduced and practiced, but practices must be fun.

From ages 10 to 12 (prepubescence), children show great improvement in coordination, motor skills, and decision-making capabilities. In hockey, skating skills must now be strongly emphasized; skating techniques should continue to be emphasized and built on in the ensuing years. Players in this age group are now ready for some endurance and quickness training. They should engage in activities and drills that incorporate core strength, quickness, coordination, body awareness, balance, and rhythm. Fun and variety are still important, so these kids should be encouraged to participate in multiple sports.

From ages 13 to 16, athletes are able to incorporate complex skills, and they can integrate large amounts of information. They can focus appropriately, and their decision-making capabilities improve dramatically. These young people are ready to specialize in their sport of choice and to practice with true dedication and intensity. This is also the time of the adolescent growth spurt, which is the period of greatest and most obvious change in a young person's life.

Skill Training

Skating is an extremely complicated activity, and hockey is an extremely complicated sport. Skating moves are not natural to the human body; in fact, they're often the opposite of natural. Skating moves are numerous, intricate, and interdependent. Each hockey maneuver consists of many parts. Each part must be learned separately and then integrated into the whole move. Proper technique training is essential for players to become fast, powerful, explosive, quick, and efficient skaters.

As previously mentioned, I believe in the pyramid method—that is, building a strong foundation and working up from there to integrate and refine each part into the whole. When teaching young skaters, we have them learn the skill without the puck first. Once the skill can be performed correctly, we add the puck. As players mature, we focus on developing power, explosiveness, and quickness. Finally, we focus on applying the skill under pressure and in game situations. At the end of each practice, players should be allowed to skate fast and have fun without worrying about correct technique.

Skill (technique) training programs for young hockey players—and for beginning players of all ages—should include simple skating fundamentals done at a comfortable level. The focus should be on helping players develop comprehension, smoothness, and efficiency.

For players age 11 and up, skating technique must be combined with power, explosiveness, and quickness. Training should include some interval training (work–rest training). Whether workouts are for sprinting, strength training, agility, skating, or athletic attributes—such as balance, rhythm, and coordination—the workouts should include some interval training.

Long, slow training (without quickness training) has been shown to teach muscles to perform slowly. Therefore, slow-moving activities such as jogging, without some interval training, will not train quickness.

Note: Long-distance running needs to be carefully monitored. If young people overdo it or if they perform this type of running on hard or uneven surfaces, this can result in growth plate injuries, especially during the adolescent growth spurt.

Work (i.e., sprint) periods for all young players, including adolescents, should be short (a maximum of 15 seconds) in order to avoid the accumulation of lactic acid. Enough rest time for full recovery must be included between each work (sprint) period.

While players are still learning skating techniques, quickness training should be done mostly off the ice. This helps ensure that the quickness training does not interfere with skill development. Coaches must remember that developing players cannot learn, perform properly, or perform effectively when they're fatigued. These players need a healthy mix of work time and rest time. Exhaustion prohibits skill development. *Proper execution* is the key to learning any skill (only perfect practice makes perfect).

Strength Training

With prepubescent children, any strength training that is done should involve submaximal resistance, such as one's own body weight, light dumbbells, or medicine balls. Whole-body activities are the most important and beneficial, especially for improving core strength.

For skating, developing players should work on two-leg and one-leg strength training. When players strengthen their legs at a young age, this increases their chances of learning to skate correctly. Skating ability and leg strength (especially single-leg strength) are synergistic, so they should be developed at the same age. But the training should be fun.

Modifying Training During the Adolescent Growth Spurt

During the adolescent growth spurt (AGS), kids often lose coordination and skill. Core strength, postural stability, concentration, technique, explosive power, and foot speed are all affected. The AGS has a negative (but temporary) impact on the learning process in general.

During growth cycles, kids don't have the biological base of one-leg strength or muscular endurance that is required for getting into a good skating position. On-ice practices should focus on skill and technique rather than on power. Off-ice work should include two-leg and one-leg exercises for coordination, balance, and agility. Exercises that help improve core strength and postural stability are critical. Heavy strength and power workouts should be postponed until the muscles are stronger.

During puberty, players' training should include speed, quickness, and explosive power as part of all workouts.

On-ice work to improve skating. Players should continue to work on developing sound skating fundamentals. Skating technique should be incorporated into all practices.

Off-ice work to improve skating. Players should work on two-leg and one-leg postural stability. Players should do exercises for foot speed and explosive jumping (power) from a position of good knee bend with the shoulders and head up.

When this combination of training is used, players are being prepared to reach their skating potential.

The three to four years just after puberty are the most critical for developing foot speed and explosive power. However, players must continue training for technique, power, quickness, and foot speed during and after the AGS; many players lose these qualities during their periods of rapid growth. Patterns are fairly well defined by puberty. But if players have a solid base of skating mechanics and quick feet, the elements of explosiveness, quickness, and efficiency can be improved after puberty and for several years beyond.

Competition is an important part of a young person's development. Hockey is one of the great competitive sports. It can be an excellent training ground for teaching youngsters how to compete successfully in life's many competitive and challenging situations. However, the value of hockey depends on how it is conducted. Parents and coaches have a critical role in ensuring that development occurs in an intelligent, well-structured, and well-thought-out process. This process should teach positive life lessons, maximize each player's inherent potential, and provide a positive learning experience as the players mature.

COACHING GUIDELINES

For youngsters, skating is not the most exciting part of hockey. Kids want to play the game, not practice skating. The challenge for a coach or power skating instructor is to teach the skating mechanics in a way that makes them well understood, easy to remember, and fun to practice. Once players realize that their game is improving because their skating is improving, they become willing students. As players get more ice time—and as they get some experience playing on the power play or when the team is shorthanded—the connection between skating ability and ice time becomes obvious. Here are some ideas for keeping skill training effective and fun for young players:

- When possible, explain your plans for the practice session before going on the ice. Ice time has a way of flying by. If players know your plans beforehand, they will be ready to work immediately.
- Establish an effective talk skating ratio. Alternate short and frequent explanations with longer periods of skating.
- Remember that although each player's skating style is unique, certain skating principles are universal and must be adhered to. Make sure you teach and reinforce these principles.
- Don't expect instant success. It takes many years to become a finished skater.
- Keep youngsters skating as much as possible—they tend to get restless easily. Organize the ice with this in mind. Skate the entire length of the ice when the group is small, but skate from sideboard to sideboard when

the group is large. Use small-group stations when applicable. Try to sense when the group is becoming restless, and change the activity before you lose the group.

- Don't allow players to skate sloppily. Make them concentrate on skating correctly. Stop them if the skating disintegrates into sloppiness. Let them know that your goal is to take them out of their comfort zones.
- Finish practices with fun and high-quality skating. Even stops and starts can be fun if players are working on improvement instead of just on conditioning!

Suggestions for Incorporating Skating Technique Into Practices

Teach the fundamentals of skating technique early in the season.

- First month: Spend one-half of each practice teaching skating fundamentals. These should include forward stride, backward stride, crossovers, starts, turns, transition, and so on.
- Second month: Spend one-fourth of each practice reviewing at least one or two of the fundamentals.
- Third month: Spend one-fourth of each practice reviewing at least one or two of the fundamentals while using pucks.
- After the third month: Spend a few minutes of each practice working on skating technique, and keep reminding players of correct technique when they have the puck, even in scrimmages.

Note: Remind players to skate correctly during all practices (and eventually in games).

Suggestions for Incorporating Skating Moves Into Scrimmages

Create scrimmages or games that have skating technique as the focus. Specific skating maneuvers can be enhanced in these scrimmages by establishing rules such as the following:

- Player with the puck must take four or five forward strides before passing or shooting.
- Player with the puck must take four or five backward strides before passing or shooting.
- Player with the puck must do two or three forward or backward crossovers before passing or shooting.
- Player with the puck must do one or two pivots (tight turns) before passing or shooting.
- Player with the puck must transition (from forward to backward or from backward to forward) one or two times before passing or shooting.
- Player with the puck must spin around (360 degrees) one or two times before passing or shooting.

- Player (with or without the puck) must accelerate from slow to fast each time he enters the offensive zone.
- Player (with or without the puck) must start from a complete stop—using toe starts—before passing or shooting.
- Player with the puck must do two or three stops and starts before passing or shooting.
- Player with the puck must make at least two lateral moves before passing or shooting.
- Players must practice the give-and-go two or three times before shooting.
- Player with the puck must go through an obstacle course before passing or shooting.

You can also make up more rules—or let the kids make them up. This kind of creativity is what young players thrive on.

Suggestions for Incorporating Races Into Practices

Use races and prizes to stimulate the competitive spirit. But keep in mind that races are only helpful with players who have reached a certain skill level; races can be detrimental when players are just learning new skills. Players caught in the frenzy of trying to win will by necessity ignore technique. Races can include forward skating, backward skating, cornering, turning, agility maneuvers, and so on.

Suggestions for Monitoring Improvement

Time your players and keep a record of their progress on different skating maneuvers. This should include the following:

- Straight skating—forward and backward
- Explosive acceleration from a complete stop
- Stops and starts
- Lateral mobility (this can be done using two skaters—one as a forward and the other as a defender)
- Turns, transition, 360s, and so on
- Obstacle courses (these should include several different skating maneuvers and agility moves)

Points to Remember

- A coach or instructor should develop a philosophy of teaching and should adhere to it.
- Affection and discipline are not mutually exclusive.
- Teaching can sometimes be like pulling teeth, but insistence on high standards pays off. Whenever possible, learning should be fun, but sometimes players must be made to learn in spite of themselves.
- Inventiveness, creativity, and analytic thinking should be valued and encouraged. Screaming coaches stifle creativity and build pressure. Wayne

Gretzky was not the product of intimidation—he was given the freedom to feel, act, see, and think (FAST), as well as to create and make many mistakes along the way.

- Practice does not make perfect. Only *perfect* practice makes perfect. Therefore, coaches should encourage their players to practice perfectly.
- Coaches must commit to the long term. Eventually, the techniques will click and the players will skate great hockey!

FORMAT OF THE BOOK

Each chapter of this book is divided into two sections. The first section includes a detailed explanation of the skating maneuver being discussed. The second section includes drills that can be used to practice that maneuver.

The drills progress from the simplest to the most difficult. The book indicates which drills are appropriate for young and learning players and which are appropriate for more advanced and elite-level players. The skill levels for the drills are defined as follows:

Basic: These drills are geared to a range of players whose ability and background are fairly basic. This means they probably have been playing for only a year or two. Players in house leagues and youth competitive leagues as well as learning adults would fit into this category. The skating maneuvers covered are fundamental and very important to the proper development of hockey players. Pucks are used, but on a limited basis, because students need to focus on their skating skills without the added distraction of pucks and the complicated skills of puck control.

Intermediate: These drills are geared to players with more experience. Students may or may not have taken Laura Stamm power skating programs in the past, but they have more hockey experience than players at the basic level. The drills include intermediate skating maneuvers and a faster pace. Pucks are also included more often.

Advanced: These drills are geared to players with extensive experience and strong skating skills (high-level players). The drills include advanced skating maneuvers and a rapid pace. Pucks are used in combination with all skating maneuvers and drills.

The drills in this book can be combined. Here are some examples:

- Combine turn drills with knee-drop drills.
- Combine crossover drills with pivots.
- Use obstacle courses.
- Use a stopwatch to time players.

Drills alone do not make an accomplished athlete. The goal is to learn proper technique and to use drills designed for practicing and enhancing that technique. The purpose of this book is to help players and coaches achieve this goal.

Chapter 1

Skates and Equipment for Superior Skating

You wouldn't start a trip without a map and some plans. In the same way, you shouldn't start skating until you've considered and followed the suggestions in this chapter.

The most important piece of equipment for hockey players is their skates. The skates are instrumental in preparing players to develop the skating skills necessary for speed, agility, and power. The quality, fit, manner of lacing, sharpening, and maintenance of your skates all affect performance, so choose your skates wisely. A cheap pair of skates is a bad investment; buying boots big enough for a youngster to wear for a few years is penny-wise and pound-foolish. To skate well, skaters must have well-constructed boots that fit properly and that have properly sharpened blades made of well-tempered steel.

HOCKEY SKATES

Skate boots that are well constructed and that fit properly enhance performance; poorly constructed boots hinder performance. The function of a well-made boot is to support the feet firmly while still allowing skaters to perform intricate skating maneuvers.

Well-made boots have a reinforcing material in the instep area of the foot (counter area). The reinforcing material provides support for the arches and ankles as skaters lean their feet inward and outward. If boots are well made, it is not possible to squeeze the counter and ankle areas together. Top-of-the-line boots fit better, provide more support, last longer, and offer better protection against injury from pucks or sticks.

Note: Unless there has been a specific injury to the foot, weak ankles are generally a myth. If ankles cave in, the cause is usually boots that are ill fitting or have poorly constructed counters. Lack of good ankle support almost guarantees that correct skating will be difficult and even uncomfortable. Ankles that cave in cause pain!

Guidelines for Selecting Skates

Get fitted for hockey skates at shops that specialize in skating equipment. The employees at these shops are knowledgeable about different brands and models, and they can help you choose the skates that meet your specific needs. Here are some guidelines for selecting skates:

- Boot sizes differ from shoe sizes and also from one brand to another. Each manufacturer builds boots on a different mold; therefore, one brand might fit well, and another might not.
- Boots should fit like a leather glove—snug but comfortable—and should support the feet firmly. Toes should come up to the front of the boot but should not be pinched or curled up on one another. Boots should fit snugly at the instep and across the balls of the feet.
- To test the fit of the boots, lace them snugly—there should be a spread of 1.5 to 2 inches (3.8 to 5.1 cm) between the eyelets on the same row. If the laces are closer together than this, the boots are probably too wide for your feet, and your ankles will cave inward when skating. If the spread between the eyelets is more than 2 inches, the boots may be too narrow. If your heels slip or if you can lift them when you stand and lean forward, the boots are too long.
- When being fitted for boots, wear the same weight of sock as you will wear when skating. A sock of a different weight can change the fit. Thin socks are preferable because they allow the boots to hug your feet. Do not wear two pairs of socks because that disconnects your feet from the boots.
- If you wear corrective orthotics in your shoes, you might also wear them in your skates. They will improve your balance and performance. But remember that the size of the boots must accommodate the orthotics, so you need to bring them along when being fitted for new skates.
- Before putting your feet into the boots, unlace the boots most of the way. Trying to jam your foot into a boot that is three-quarters laced is an exercise in frustration—your feet just won't go in, and you'll think the boots are too small.
- Today's boots tend to be extremely stiff and difficult to break in. Players who skate hard and wear their skates for hours at a time on a daily basis prefer stiff boots because they last longer. But youngsters, small adults, females, and recreational skaters will have a difficult time breaking them in. These skaters should consider a brand or model that is a bit less stiff. Another option is to choose a good pair of secondhand skates. Since growing players outgrow their skates before breaking them down, these skates are often in excellent condition. It's far better to get good-quality used skates than poor-quality new skates. If you are getting secondhand skates, be sure the blades are in good condition and *not* sharpened down excessively. Many hockey shops carry secondhand skates, and many hockey organizations

hold skate swaps at the beginning of the hockey season. Once broken in, the boots should feel as though they are a natural part of your feet.

Lacing the Boots

Proper lacing of one's boots is essential to good performance. Many players lace them too tightly. This limits foot mobility and cuts off circulation, which in turn causes numbness and cramps in the feet. Boots should support the feet, not immobilize them as if they are in casts. Properly laced boots support the feet while allowing players to readily bend their knees and roll their ankles inward and outward.

The tightest area of lacing should be from a point above the ball of the foot to a point just above the ankle (figure 1.1). This is where the most support is required. The toe area and the area high above the ankles should be moderately snug. Some elite players prefer to lace the area above the ankles fairly loosely; some even choose to not lace the top set of eyelets. Do not wrap tape around your ankles. This inhibits foot mobility and is totally unnecessary.

I recommend that players place their shin pads inside the tongues of their boots rather than over the tongues. This allows more freedom for bending the knees. Just be sure the shin pads are long enough to come all the way down your legs. You don't want an exposed area where a puck or stick could find an unprotected spot.

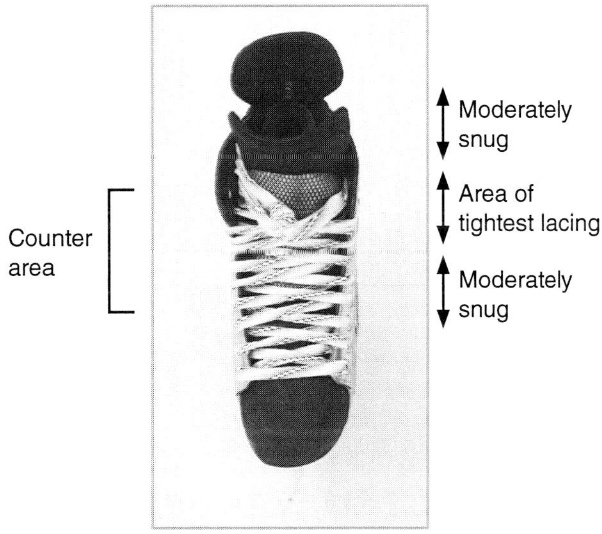

Figure 1.1 Correct lacing of the boot.

> **COACHING TIP**
>
> If laces are too tight at the top, bending your knees and ankles becomes difficult and uncomfortable. Snug is good; pain is not.

Tips for Breaking in New Boots

- Lace new boots *loosely* during the breaking-in process.
- Wear new skates at home—put the skate guards on and walk around in them for 30 to 60 minutes at a time. Some players like to wet their feet (with socks on), then put the skates on and walk around in them. Water acts like sweat; sweat breaks in the boots.

- Do not wear new skates for an important skating event or hockey tournament. Break them in during practices or at public sessions.
- Consider using your new skates on the ice for short periods and wearing your old ones for the rest of the session. The hope is to limit the uncomfortable breaking-in time and also to avoid blisters.
- Keep in mind that it's not uncommon to get blisters during the breaking-in process. This is one of the unfortunate realities that all players must deal with. If you feel a blister starting, take off the new boots or insert a second-skin material on the affected area. You can also cut a hole in a foam sponge to make a doughnut and place this over the affected area; this helps eliminate pressure between the boot and that part of the foot.

SKATE BLADES

Good hockey skates have high-quality blades made of heat-tempered steel that retain a sharp edge despite extremely rough use. Poor-quality blades nick and dull easily and have to be sharpened frequently. Some players buy their favorite blades separately and have these mounted on their boots.

Skate blades are only to be used on the ice. Off the ice, always wear skate guards, even when walking on the rubber mats in rink hallways and locker rooms. Never expose the blades to cement, steel, concrete, or wood surfaces, because they will get nicked and dulled. As mentioned, most high-quality boots also have high-quality blades, but there are several brands of blades. Regardless of the brand, new blades *must* be sharpened before you skate on them!

Blades rust easily. After getting off the ice, dry the blades thoroughly with a towel and put terrycloth skate guards on them. When you get home, take the guards off and air-dry the blades. Then put *dry* terrycloth skate guards back on the blades and put the skates back in your hockey bag. Never store blades in rubber skate guards; these guards retain moisture, and the blades will rust. When you're away from skating for long periods, store your skates without any guards on in a dry environment. You don't want to be that unlucky player who goes to the rink at the beginning of a new season, takes the skates out of the hockey bag, and finds they're totally covered with rust. No skating that day!

Blade Design

Each skate blade, from toe to heel, is designed with two knifelike edges separated by a groove in between (called the hollow) (figure 1.2). The function of the hollow is to expose the edges, enabling them to cut into and grip the ice more effectively.

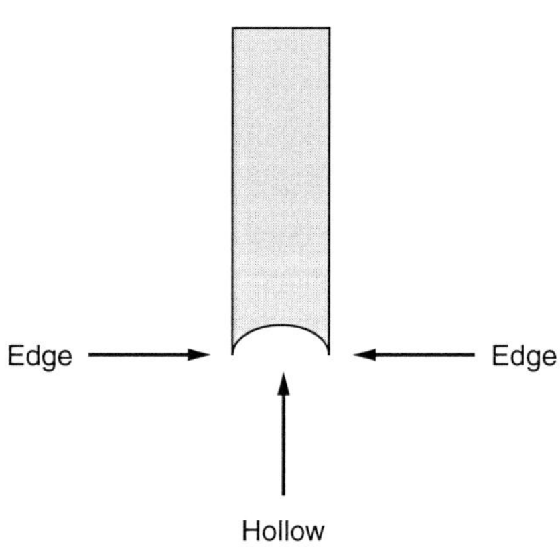

Figure 1.2 Cross section of the blade, showing the edges and the hollow.

The shape of the hockey skate blade is convex (curved). This curved shape is called the *rock*, or *radius*; the shape resembles a crescent moon or the legs of a rocking chair (figure 1.3). The rock of the blade allows the skates to curve so that players can maneuver in tight curves and circles. If the blades were long and straight like those of speed-skates, it would be difficult for players to weave, cut, or execute sharp turns.

Figure 1.3 Hockey blade, showing the rock.

Because they need to move in a straight line forward, backward, or sideways—rather than perform weaving or circular maneuvers—goalies' blades are almost straight instead of convex. Goaltenders also need blades that are fairly dull so they can slide sideways across the goal crease. Curved blades would also hinder a goalie's ability to make skate saves.

Sharpening the Blades

Blades should be sharpened when they no longer dig crisply into the ice, and they should be sharpened by an expert. Some pro hockey players sharpen their skates after every game; some even sharpen them after each period. However, this isn't necessary or even desirable for most nonprofessional players; excessive sharpening shortens the life of the blades. Here are some guidelines for sharpening blades:

- Blades can be sharpened so that the hollow is either shallow or deep. A deep hollow can make it difficult to execute a smooth, effective stop because the edges can grab the ice. Too shallow a hollow can make it difficult for the edges to dig into the ice.
- Children and small adults require sharper blades and a relatively deep hollow in order for the edges to dig into the ice. Heavier people can use less sharp blades and less of a hollow.
- Today, many high-level hockey players have their blades sharpened with a longer radius and a shallower hollow than in the past. A longer radius means more blade length is in contact with the ice, which in turn means that more distance is covered on each glide. A shallower hollow means the edges won't overly grab the ice; as a result, there is less friction against the ice during each glide (so more distance is covered on each glide). These two factors combine to enhance speed.
- Sharply rockered blades (shorter radius) allow for tighter turns, but the benefits of this do not outweigh the benefits of the increased speed that a

longer radius provides. Blades with a shorter radius also make balancing more difficult because there is less blade length in contact with the ice.

- When getting your skates sharpened, make sure not to have too much blade ground off from the very front or back of the blade. The front (toe) is needed for quick starts. The back (heel) is like the rudder of a ship; it is needed for stability.
- Ask the sharpener to hand stone the blades after each sharpening. This will guarantee smooth, finished edges.
- If the sharpener isn't careful, the radius (curve) of the blade may increase with each progressive sharpening. When this happens, too little blade will be in contact with the ice.
- Let the sharpener know precisely how sharp, how much hollow, and how much rock you want. Also tell the sharpener where you want the high point of the rock to be. Forwards generally prefer the high point of the rock to be just behind the middle of the blade; defenders prefer that it be just in front of the middle of the blade.

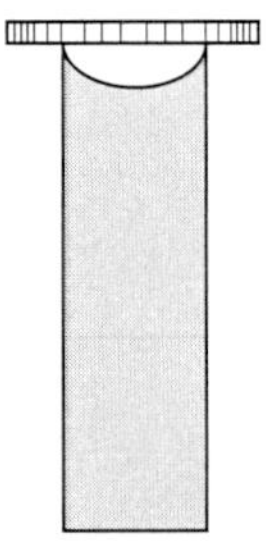

Figure 1.4 Blade cross section with level, properly sharpened edges.

If the blades are properly sharpened, the inside and outside edges will be level with each other. To test the accuracy of the sharpening, place a coin horizontally on the upturned blade. Study the angle of the coin. If it is perfectly level, the edges are even (figure 1.4). If the coin tilts to either side, the edges are not level and your skating will be impaired. Take the skates back for resharpening!

Some players make and keep a template of their blades. To do this, trace an outline of the blades after the first couple of sharpenings. After each sharpening, measure the blades against the template and make sure that they conform to it.

Remember, your skates are your most important hockey equipment. Choose them wisely and take good care of them.

Note: When practicing, playing a game, or performing the skating drills in this book, wear full protective hockey equipment: helmet, face mask or shield, mouthpiece, neck guard, shoulder and chest pads, elbow pads, pants, shin guards, and gloves. Keep the chin strap securely fastened at all times. In a fall, you need to rely on the helmet to protect you from a head injury!

Because skating drills require experimentation, falls are inevitable and should be considered as normal as breathing. By wearing protective equipment, you lower the risk of injury and also become accustomed to skating at your game weight.

EDGES

Every skate blade has two edges. The edges toward the inside of the boots are called the *inside edges* (figure 1.5*a*), and those toward the outside of the boots

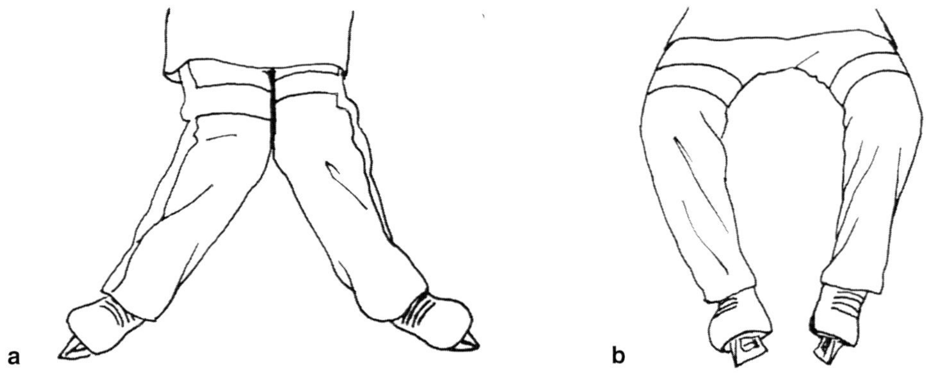

Figure 1.5 *(a)* Inside and *(b)* outside edges.

are called the *outside edges* (figure 1.5*b*). The edges have a specific purpose: to cut into the ice. In doing this, they perform two completely different and separate functions. One is to create motion (the power or pushing edge); the other is to establish direction (the gliding edge that travels on a curved path). Understanding how the edges function and how best to use them is key to all movement on ice.

Pushing

When used for pushing, the edges of the blades must dig into the ice to provide the grip that the pushing leg thrusts against for movement (power). If you push without first digging the edge into the ice, the skate will slip. You might attribute this to the ice being slippery, but the ice should *never* feel slippery. If you use the edges properly, they should be able to grip the ice strongly. Try to *feel* the edges cut into the ice. Even when gliding straight ahead on two feet, skaters incline slightly toward the inside edges for balance and stability.

Gliding

When used for gliding, the edges establish the direction of travel. Because blades are rockered, edges glide in a curved path. When gliding on the left forward inside edge (LFI), you travel in a clockwise direction. When gliding on the right forward inside edge (RFI), you travel in a counterclockwise direction. When gliding on the left forward outside edge (LFO), you travel in a counterclockwise direction. When gliding on the right forward outside edge (RFO), you travel in a clockwise direction.

When you are going backward, the directions are reversed. When gliding on the left backward inside edge (LBI), you travel counterclockwise. When gliding on the right backward inside edge (RBI), you travel clockwise. When gliding on the left backward outside edge (LBO), you travel clockwise. When gliding on the right backward outside edge (RBO), you travel counterclockwise.

Glide Direction	Edge
Clockwise	LFI, RFO, RBI, LBO
Counterclockwise	RFI, LFO, LBI, RBO

HOW THE SKATES AND BODY COORDINATE TO PRODUCE CURVES

A common misconception in hockey is that the skates should always be held straight up. When skates are held straight up, you ride simultaneously on the inside and outside edges (the flats) of the blades. Since the flat of each blade describes a straight line on the ice, you will travel either straight forward or straight backward. But you cannot glide on a curve nor grip the ice with the flat of the blade. You must use the edges—both for pushing and for traveling a curved path.

To get an edge to cut into the ice, lean the engaged boot so that the desired edge forms a sharp angle with the ice. To do this, press the engaged foot (the pushing or gliding foot) onto its side—this can be either the outside or the inside—and bend that knee in the same direction. Here are two important points:

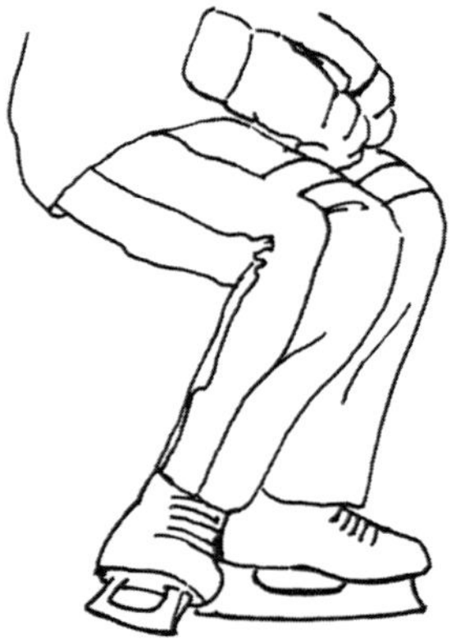

Figure 1.6 Pushing skate on a strong inside edge; 90-degree knee bend.

1. When the pushing skate is on an edge, the more the foot presses, the boot leans, and the knee bends, the more the skate will grip the ice and the greater the potential for thrust against the ice. An edge that digs into the ice at an angle of 45 degrees (when traveling fast) is the optimum cutting edge (figure 1.6).
2. When the gliding skate is on an edge, the more the foot presses, the boot leans, and the knee bends, the sharper the curve or circle will be. Try to achieve a knee bend of 90 degrees as measured between the thigh and shin of the gliding leg.

The skate alone cannot achieve the edge. The entire body coordinates to produce an effective pushing or gliding edge. To apply an inside edge, lean the boot, knee, and thigh toward the inside of your body (figure 1.7*a*). To apply an outside edge, lean the boot, knee, and thigh toward the outside of your body (figure 1.7*b*). The angle of your knee and thigh must line up above the skate so that all three (knee, thigh, and skate) describe the same angle to the ice. The rest of your body weight (hips, torso, shoulders) is balanced over the engaged skate and presses downward toward the ice to assist the edge in gripping the ice. If your body weight is not totally over the engaged skate, or if it does not press downward sufficiently, the edge will grip less effectively, the curve will be shallow, and balance will be impaired.

When skating on a curve or circle, remember the following:

- The faster you skate, the deeper the edge you must apply to the ice, and the more you need to bend your knees and press your body weight downward above the engaged edge.
- Centripetal and gravitational forces are at work; they must be equalized and in proportion to your speed in order for you to balance over the edge.

Figure 1.7 *(a)* Gliding forward on an inside edge (left skate); *(b)* gliding forward on an outside edge (left skate).

- The skate blade travels as if it were on the outside rim of a circle. The body rides slightly inside the rim. The lower body (skating foot, knee, thigh, and hips) presses toward the center of the circle; the hips always face the line of travel. The upper body (chest and shoulders) rests above the hips but still within the rim of the circle. If the upper body presses into the circle more than the lower body does, stability is jeopardized.
- Figure 1.8 shows the body position that is essential to effective forward movement on a curve. Expert hockey players frequently employ this position for difficult maneuvers such as tight turns, forward crossovers, or pivots.

Coaches often tell skaters to lean into the circle to obtain their curve. However, this advice often leads to the misconception that the entire body should lean (tilt) into the circle. Only the lower body (skates, knees, thighs, and hips) leans into the circle. The upper body (chest, shoulders, and head) does not lean; it should be essentially upright, with the shoulders level with the ice. Correct body positioning is one of the most important aspects of balance on skates. It must be mastered if you are to become a good hockey skater.

Figure 1.8 Body position for skating forward on a curve.

Chapter 2

Balance for Stability and Speed

Great hockey players have such great balance that they appear to be linked to the ice by a magnetic force. Players commonly take it for granted and overlook its importance, but balance is one of the most important aspects of hockey. Perfect balance is critical for all players. Balance enables players to skate with greater maneuverability and speed, perform high-velocity turns, execute explosive starts and stops, change direction quickly, shoot more powerfully, and deliver and withstand crunching body checks.

Many different balance situations exist in hockey; all of them should be mastered. Some players can balance well on two skates but not on one. Some can balance on one skate on the flat of the blade but not on an edge. Some can maneuver adequately when skating forward but not when skating backward. Others can balance well when skating slowly but not when skating rapidly (or vice versa), or they are competent when skating on counterclockwise curves but struggle when skating on clockwise curves (or vice versa). Still others skate well but have trouble recovering their balance and stride after a jump off the ice or a fall onto it.

Lack of balance when skating backward is a common and serious weakness. All players, not just defenders, should strive for excellent balance on backward skating moves. This will give them greater versatility in game situations.

Balance is controlled by proper weight distribution over the skates along with proper upper body positioning. Correct use of the back muscles is critical. Many players are unaware of how important it is to use the back muscles properly. While the legs are the engines and are used for power and motion, the back muscles are used to hold the upper body still—and balanced—above the moving skates.

Goalies need to have superb balance. They often need to fall to the ice to make saves and then quickly return to their feet. Balance, strength, and quickness are necessary for these instantaneous recoveries. Making a kick save without falling also requires excellent balance. Goalies who have not mastered balance often flop on all fours—not because they want to, but because they cannot stay on their feet. When this happens, they are slow to recover and are at the mercy of the opposition.

FALLING

Everyone falls! And all players need to learn two major things about falling—how to protect the head and how to get up.

You must prevent your head from hitting the ice or the boards. Padding usually protects the rest of the body, but even with a helmet, it is dangerous to hit your head. If you feel yourself falling forward, quickly lift your head and chin as high as possible and look up toward the ceiling to prevent your head from hitting the ice. This is called heads-up hockey (from USA Hockey). If you feel yourself sliding headfirst toward the boards, flip around so that your feet hit the boards instead. If you feel yourself falling over backward, tuck your chin into your chest to prevent your head from flipping back and hitting the ice.

The following drill will help teach you how to protect your head from hitting the boards: Start from one goal line and skate forward with speed. At the first blue line, fall flat forward (headfirst) in a Superman dive position, pretending that the red line is the boards. Just before reaching the red line, flip over quickly so that you are now on your back with your skates facing the red line (boards). Be sure to bend your knees, which will cushion the blow of your skates hitting the boards. Practice this over and over until it becomes second nature (figure 2.1, *a-b*).

Learning how to get up after a fall is challenging for beginning skaters. To practice getting up, do the following: After falling, get on all fours. Now put one knee on the ice and place the entire blade length of the other skate on the ice, directly under the center of your body. Press down against the ice with the flat of the blade and try to stand up. Be sure to keep your back straight during this process. After a few tries, you should be able to get up readily. See figure 10.2 on page 227.

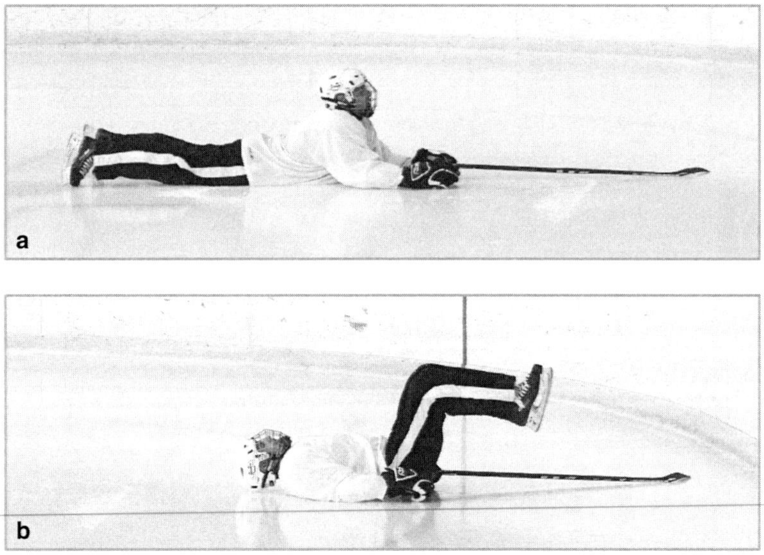

Figure 2.1 Protecting the head from hitting the boards.

BALANCE ON TWO SKATES

Balance on two skates is important in many different game situations—for example, when gliding slowly or when waiting for a pass or for a play to develop. It is also important when checking or being checked by an opponent. The following sections explain how to balance on the flats and edges while on two skates.

Balance on the Flats of the Blades—Skating Forward

In certain situations, players must glide forward on the flats of the blades—for example, when the play stops and players coast to a face-off circle. Here are some guidelines to follow when gliding forward on the flats of both blades:

1. Hold your skates about shoulder-width apart and bend your knees. In this position, you are stable and you can prepare to push off and skate forward (see chapter 4 for an explanation).
2. Hold your shoulders back. Maintain a vertical upper body position; use your back muscles to keep your back straight. Look straight ahead and keep your head and eyes up (figure 2.2). Slumping or looking down results in a loss of balance because it causes your body weight to pitch forward over the curved toes of the blades (figure 2.3, *a-b*). Holding the upper body still is critical for balance and control in skating.

Figure 2.2 Proper balance.

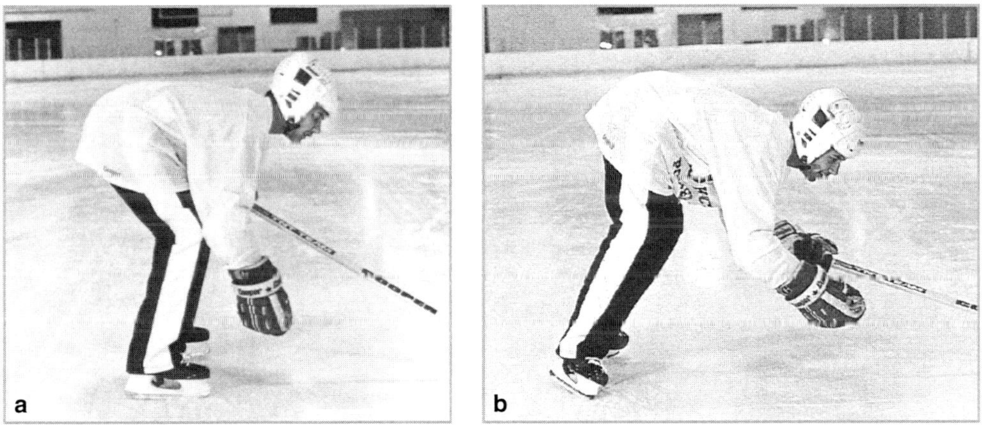

Figure 2.3 Result of slumping forward.

3. Keep your body weight on the back halves (middle to heels) of the blades.
4. Keep the skate blades in full contact with the ice. If you lift your heels off the ice, your weight will pitch forward over the curved toes of the blades. *Never* lean on your stick for balance or support. It is not a crutch or a third leg!

Balance on the Flats of the Blades—Skating Backward

The rules for forward balance on two skates also apply to backward balance; however, when skating backward, your body weight must be on the front halves (middle to front) of the blades—but *not* on the curved toes. Do not lean back. If your weight is over or behind the heels, you may fall over backward.

Balance on Two Skates on the Inside Edges

When gliding slowly forward or backward (i.e., to wait for a play or pass), keep the skates somewhat wider apart than your shoulders, with your knees flexed and both skates on the inside edges (figure 2.4). This stance provides excellent stability and thus is called the ready or stable position. You are prepared to move laterally, fake, check, or take a check. You are also prepared to push off and skate straight forward or straight backward. All you need to do is shift your weight onto the pushing skate and thrust off.

The more you dig in the inside edges and bend your knees, the more traction you will get into the ice, and the more stable you will be. If you are about to be checked and do not have time to do anything else, widen your stance, dig in the inside edges, and bend your knees as much as possible. In this position, you'll be much tougher to knock down.

Figure 2.4 Gliding in a wide stance on the inside edges.

Goalies almost always stand on the inside edges. Having good balance on the inside edges and knowing how to use these edges are extremely important skills for netminders.

Note: When a player is in the ready position, even minimal use of the inside edges is more beneficial than being on the flats of the blades.

BALANCE ON ONE SKATE

Except when you are in the ready or stable position, moving on skates is primarily a one-leg activity. In most maneuvers, only one skate is weighted at a time. This means that the body weight is totally committed to one skate. When you are pushing, your body weight is totally balanced over the pushing skate. After pushing, your body weight transfers so that it is totally balanced over the gliding skate.

Balance on one skate must be mastered for all skating moves—when skating forward, skating backward, crossing over, starting, stopping, or turning. You never know when you will be startled with a body check while on only one skate—for example, following a hard jolt—or when you will have to lunge, jump, evade, or leap over another player and land on one skate.

Learning skaters should first try to balance on the flat of the blade and then on the inside and outside edges. You will not be a proficient player until you are perfectly comfortable on one skate—whether skating forward or backward and whether skating on the flat or on an edge.

To balance on one skate, imagine that you are gliding on a tightrope. Imagine what would happen if your body weight moves forward and backward or from side to side. Imagine what would happen if the foot you are standing on is not centered under your body weight. These factors apply whether balancing on the flat of the blade or on an edge. To balance on an edge, imagine that you are gliding on a curved tightrope.

Balance on One Skate on the Flat of the Blade—Forward and Backward

To balance on the flat of the blade, you must have your body weight totally over the gliding skate; the full blade needs to be in contact with the ice. Concentrate your weight totally over the gliding skate, and press the blade against the ice so the skate cannot wiggle or move around (figure 2.5). Keep your hips facing straight ahead. If you lean to either side or lean forward or back, you may lose your footing—that is, you may fall off the tightrope.

Posture is critical for balance. Hold your shoulders back and use your back muscles to keep your back straight and still. Look straight ahead; keep your head and chin up. If your head and shoulders slump forward or if you look down, your weight will pitch forward over the curved toe of the blade, and you will lose your balance.

Figure 2.5 Proper balance on the flat of the blade.

Balance on the Inside Edge of One Skate—Skating Forward

Players glide, push, shoot, and check with the inside edges of the skates. Balancing on the inside edge is more difficult than balancing on the flat of the blade, but it is a key component of skating.

Figure 2.6 Gliding forward on the left inside edge.

To get on an inside edge, bend the knee of the working leg deeply, and lean the boot inward so the inside edge of the skate forms a 45-degree angle to the ice. Try to stand on the inside edge in this position. Impossible? Maybe at first. But with enough practice, you will be able to balance comfortably on a single edge. In fact, you will find it not only possible, but a vital prerequisite to skating.

To skate and balance on the inside edge of the left skate (LFI), lean the left boot, knee, and thigh strongly inward (toward the center of your body) so the inside edge cuts into the ice at a sharp angle (an effective edge angle at high speeds is 45 degrees, and it is accompanied by a 90-degree knee bend).

To glide forward on the inside edge, push with the right skate and leg, and glide forward onto the left inside edge (LFI). After the push, lift the right skate off the ice and hold it close to the left (gliding) skate (figure 2.6). Keep the left (skating) knee deeply bent; your body weight should be on the back half of the blade. Keep your hips facing the direction of travel (curve). You will curve in a clockwise direction. The more you lean the skate, knee, and thigh, the tighter the curve or circle will be.

Now do this on the right skate (RFI) by mirroring the previous procedure. You will now curve in a counterclockwise direction.

Note: This drill should also be applied when practicing the push of the forward stride.

Balance on the Outside Edge of One Skate—Skating Forward

Figure 2.7 Gliding forward on the left outside edge.

Balancing on the outside edge is initially more difficult than balancing on either the flat or the inside edge. Regardless of its difficulty, balancing on the outside edge is an essential aspect of skating on a curve or circle.

To skate and balance on the outside edge of the left skate (LFO), lean the left skate, knee, and thigh strongly to the left (toward the outside of your body) so that the outside edge cuts into the ice at a sharp angle (an effective edge angle at high speeds is 45 degrees, and it is accompanied by a 90-degree knee bend).

To glide onto the outside edge, push with the right skate and leg, and glide forward onto the left outside edge (LFO). After the push, lift the right skate off the ice and hold it close to the left (gliding) skate (figure 2.7). Keep the left (skating) knee deeply bent; your body weight should be on the back half of the blade. You will curve in a counterclockwise direction. The more you lean the skate, knee, and thigh, the tighter the curve or circle will be.

Now do this on the right skate (RFO) by mirroring the previous procedure. You will now curve in a clockwise direction.

Note: This drill should also be applied when practicing forward crossovers.

Balance on the Inside and Outside Edge of One Skate—Skating Backward

Skating and balancing on one edge when skating backward is just as important as when skating forward. The procedure is essentially the same as for forward skating, with two major differences:

1. Body weight must be on the front half of the blade (middle to front) rather than on the back half.
2. The direction of curve is opposite of the direction produced by forward edges. See the section on gliding in chapter 1 (page 7) for the directions of travel.

Note: The previous drills should be applied when practicing the backward stride and backward crossovers.

COACHING TIP

When gliding on edges, keep the shoulders level to the ice. Dropping the inside shoulder into the curve or circle is a common error. This tilts too much body weight into the circle, resulting in a loss of balance. When skating at fast speeds on a sharp curve or circle, it is safer to hold the inside shoulder slightly higher than the outside shoulder than it is to lower (drop) the inside shoulder into the curve or circle.

DRILLS FOR BALANCE AND STRETCHING

Balance should not be taken for granted. It is one of the first skills to deteriorate after a layoff (even a brief one). Many balance drills can also be used as warm-up and stretching drills. When used in combination with warming up, these drills should be done as the first moves of the day. Muscles require the opportunity to warm up and stretch gradually. If ice time is limited, stretching drills should be done off the ice; however, in this case, they will not help to develop better balance on the ice. Use balance drills in combination with warming up and stretching on the ice whenever possible.

Unless otherwise specified, the drills in this section can be done skating backward as well as forward. They are presented in a specific order that takes into account the ability of the skater as well as the need for gradual stretching.

Forward O Drill

All Skaters

This drill stretches the groin and inside thigh muscles. It also helps players improve their balance on the inside edges. In this drill, both skates are on the ice at all times. The skates move simultaneously out and in to create the letter *O*. This drill is especially helpful for beginning skaters.

Start with the skates on inside edges and in a V position—heels together and toes apart (figure 2.8*a*). Bend your knees, keeping your weight on the back halves of the blades. As you glide forward, move the toes of the two skates as far apart as possible. As the toes separate, straighten your knees (figure 2.8*b*). When both knees are straight, pivot the toes inward and draw them together (figure 2.8*c*). When the toes touch each other in an inverted V position, you will have completed one full circle, or the letter *O* (figure 2.8*d*). Now put the heels of the skates together in the original V position and repeat the maneuver.

Figure 2.8 *(a-d)* Forward O drill; *(d-a)* backward O drill.

Backward O Drill

All Skaters

This drill stretches the groin and inside thigh muscles. It also helps players improve their balance on the inside edges. In addition, this drill is often used to teach elementary-level skaters how to move backward.

The procedure is the reverse of the forward O drill. Start with the skates on inside edges and in an inverted V position—toes touching and heels apart. Bend your knees, keeping your weight on the front halves of the blades. As you glide backward, pull the heels as far apart as possible. As the heels separate, straighten your knees. When both knees are straight, pivot the heels inward and draw them together to form the letter *V.* When the heels touch each other in the V position, you will have completed one full circle, or the letter *O.* Now put the toes of both skates together in the original inverted V position and repeat the maneuver (see figure 2.8, *d-a*).

Upper Body Twists (Stretch for the Neck, Back, and Waist)

All Skaters

Glide on both skates, with your feet about shoulder-width apart. Hold the hockey stick behind your neck with a hand on each end of the stick, and twist (rotate) your waist and arms gently from side to side (figure 2.9, *a-b*). While twisting, reach your right elbow toward your left knee. Hold the stretch for approximately 10 seconds. Now reach your left elbow toward your right knee. Look toward the knee that your elbow is reaching for. Repeat slowly four or five times.

Figure 2.9 Upper body twists.

Balance on the Flats of the Blades (Back and Hamstring Stretch)

All Skaters

Glide forward on both skates, with your feet shoulder-width apart. Hold the hockey stick horizontally and fully extended above your head. Keeping your knees straight, reach the stick behind you and arch your back. Stay in this position for approximately 10 seconds. Still keeping your knees straight, bend forward and reach the hockey stick toward your toes. Keep your body weight on the back halves of the blades (figure 2.10, *a-b*). Hold the stretch for approximately 10 seconds. Repeat four or five times.

Do the same drill gliding backward; your body weight is now on the front halves of the blades.

Note: Keep the entire blade lengths in contact with the ice. If your heels come off the ice, you may fall forward over your toes. *Do not bounce;* bouncing may cause muscle pulls.

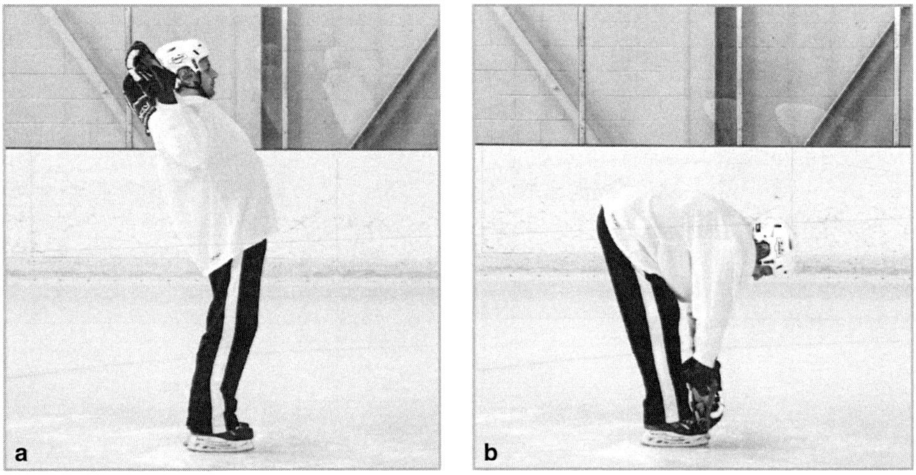

Figure 2.10 Hamstring stretch.

Balance on the Flat of the Blade—One Skate (Quadriceps Stretch)

Basic

Skate from the goal line to the blue line while holding the hockey stick horizontally at arm's length and at shoulder height in front of you. At the blue line, glide on the flat of the left skate and raise your right knee as high as possible toward the stick. Try to glide all the way to the far goal line before putting your right skate down. Repeat the drill, gliding on the flat of the right skate and lifting the left knee (see figure 2.5 on page 15). Raising the knee of the free leg gradually stretches the quadriceps (thigh muscles).

Many skaters are able to balance better on one skate than on the other. Give extra attention to the weaker skate in order to equalize the right and left sides.

Balance on the Inside Edge—One Skate (Quadriceps Stretch)

Basic to Intermediate

Figure 2.11 Balance on the inside edge (quadriceps stretch).

1. Glide forward on the RFI while holding the hockey stick horizontally at arm's length and at shoulder height in front of you. Raise your left knee up toward the stick as you glide. See how long you can glide on the RFI in this position before putting the left skate down. You will curve in a counterclockwise direction (figure 2.11).
2. Repeat the drill, gliding forward on the LFI in a clockwise direction.
3. Repeat the drill, this time gliding backward on the RBI and then on the LBI. When gliding on the RBI, you will travel on a clockwise curve. When gliding on the LBI, you will travel on a counterclockwise curve.
4. Glide a complete circle on the RFI and then on the LFI.
5. Glide a complete circle on the RBI and then on the LBI.

Note: Lean into the circle with only your lower body (skate, knee, thigh, and hips). Your upper body (chest and shoulders) should not lean (tilt) into the circle. If it does, too much weight will pitch into the circle, and you will lose your balance.

Balance on the Outside Edge—One Skate (Quadriceps Stretch)

Intermediate to Advanced

Figure 2.12 Balance on the outside edge (quadriceps stretch).

1. Glide forward on the RFO while holding the hockey stick horizontally at arm's length and at shoulder height in front of you. Raise your left knee up toward the stick as you glide. See how long you can glide on the RFO before putting the left skate down. You will curve in a clockwise direction (figure 2.12).
2. Repeat the drill, gliding forward on the LFO in a counterclockwise direction.
3. Repeat the drill, this time gliding backward on the RBO and then on the LBO. When gliding on the RBO,

you will travel in a counterclockwise curve; when gliding on the LBO, you will travel clockwise.

4. Glide a complete circle on the RFO and then on the LFO.
5. Repeat, gliding a complete circle backward on the RBO, then on the LBO.

Note: Lean into the circle with only your lower body (skate, knee, thigh, and hips). Your upper body (chest and shoulders) should not lean (tilt) into the circle. If it does, you will be off balance.

Forward Lateral Leg Stretch

Intermediate

Figure 2.13 Forward lateral leg stretch.

This drill helps players learn to bend one knee while stretching the other leg to full extension.

Glide forward on the flats of both skates. Then transfer your weight onto the right skate and glide on that skate. Bend your right knee deeply (90 degrees), and simultaneously stretch your left skate and leg straight out to the side until the leg is fully extended (figure 2.13). The toes of the left (extended) skate should line up with (be on the same horizontal plane as) the toes of the right (gliding) skate. Keep your back straight and your head up. Maintain this position for 10 seconds, and then change feet and stretch the other leg. Repeat four or five times. *Do not bounce.*

Backward Lateral Leg Stretch

Intermediate to Advanced

Perform the forward lateral leg stretch while skating backward. The drill is more difficult when performed backward, so this version is recommended for somewhat more advanced players.

STRETCHING DRILLS FOR BALANCE AND COORDINATION

The following stretching drills are multifaceted; they focus on improving balance and coordination. Some of these drills also focus on strengthening specific muscle groups used in skating.

Leg Lifts

All leg lifts should be done gently at first. The hamstrings, quadriceps, groin, and gluteal muscles must be stretched gradually and fully.

Basic to Intermediate

1. Glide forward on the flat of the left skate while holding the hockey stick extended horizontally at shoulder height in front of you.
2. Keeping the right leg straight out in front of you and parallel to the ice, see how long you can glide on the left skate (figure 2.14*a* on page 24).
3. Now glide on the right skate, lifting the left leg. Then try the same drill gliding backward.

Intermediate to Advanced

1. Leg lifts on edges. Perform the previous drill, but now glide on the outside and inside edges of the skates instead of gliding on the flats of the skates.
2. Leg lifts to stick. Glide forward on the flat of the left skate while holding the hockey stick extended horizontally at shoulder height in front of you. Lift the right leg up and try to reach with that skate to touch the stick (figure 2.14*b*). Repeat, balancing on the right skate and lifting the left leg. Now do this while gliding on the inside and outside edges.

Front–Touch, Side–Touch, Back–Touch

Intermediate to Advanced

The object of this drill is to stretch the lifted leg in all three directions. After each leg lift, the returning skate must actually touch the skate that is gliding on the ice. This touching of the skate helps to teach full leg recovery, which will be covered in later chapters.

1. Glide forward on the flat of the left skate while holding the hockey stick extended horizontally at shoulder height in front of you.
2. Lift the right leg up so that the right skate touches the stick (figure 2.14*b*). After it touches the stick, bring the right skate down until your skates touch each other (the right skate should not touch the ice).
3. Lift the same (right) leg out to the side and as high off the ice as possible (figure 2.14*c*). Then bring the right skate down until your skates touch each other (the right skate should not touch the ice).
4. Lift the same (right) leg straight behind you (figure 2.14*d*). Then bring the right skate down until your skates touch each other (again, the right skate should not touch the ice).
5. Repeat, gliding forward on the flat of the right skate and lifting the left leg.

6. Keep the lifted leg as straight as possible for optimum stretching. When lifting to the front, you stretch the hamstrings. When lifting to the side, you stretch the groin muscles. When lifting to the back, you stretch the quadriceps and gluteal muscles. Lift as high as is comfortable, but do not kick!
7. Repeat the drill, now skating backward.

Note: Since this is also a balance drill, remember not to let the skate that is off the ice touch the ice between lifts.

Figure 2.14 Leg lifts: *(a-b)* to the front, *(c)* to the side, and *(d)* to the back.

Plane Glide

Intermediate

Glide forward on the flat of the left skate while holding the hockey stick extended horizontally at shoulder height in front of you. Lift your right leg behind you. Keep the lifted leg straight and parallel to the ice. See how long you can hold this position without putting the right skate down on the ice. It is more difficult to balance with the free leg behind you than in front of you (see figure 2.14*d* for the proper position).

Advanced

Advanced players should perform the plane glide drill (forward and backward) gliding on the inside and outside edges instead of on the flat of the blade. Figure 2.15 diagrams the drill when skating forward and backward on the edges.

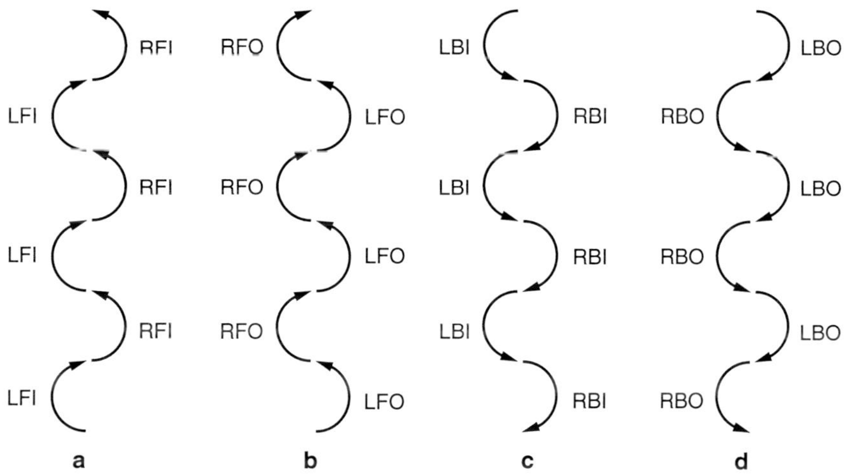

Figure 2.15 Plane glide on edges, alternating skates: *(a-b)* forward and *(c-d)* backward.

Groin Stretch

Intermediate

This drill is very important for stretching the groin muscles. It is also an excellent drill for improving balance, knee bend, and quadriceps strength. Although the drill is generally done skating forward, it can also be done skating backward; however, this is difficult, so it is recommended only for more advanced skaters.

Groin stretches must be done gently at first, and the intensity should be gradually increased. Since groin muscles are prone to injury, they must be thoroughly warmed up and stretched before hard skating (or before a game).

To perform the drill, glide forward on the flat of the right skate. Hold the hockey stick in the top hand with the stick blade on the ice in front of you.

Bend your right knee deeply, with your buttocks as close to the ice as possible. Keep your weight on the back half of the right (gliding) skate. Stretch the left leg behind you. Drag the inside of the left *boot* (not the blade) on the ice; the left skate should be in a turned-out position. Keep the blade of the extended skate off the ice (figure 2.16).

Maintain a vertical upper body position by keeping your shoulders back, your back straight, and your eyes and head up. Hold the stretch for at least 10 seconds. Now change feet; glide on the flat of the left skate and stretch the right leg. *Do not bounce.*

Repeat the drill four or five times. Gradually stretch the extended leg farther back as you feel the groin muscles stretch out.

Figure 2.16 Groin stretch.

Toe Touch

Intermediate to Advanced

This drill demonstrates the importance of keeping the entire blade length in contact with the ice.

Glide forward on the flat of the left skate; hold the hockey stick with just the top hand. Keep both legs straight. Stretch the right leg behind you, and lift it high enough that it is parallel with (horizontal to) the ice. Reach down with your free hand and touch the toe of the left skate. Repeat on the right skate. Keep your head up and your back straight throughout this drill. Repeat, now skating backward.

Note: Keep the entire blade of the engaged (gliding) skate in contact with the ice surface. If you allow the heel of the blade to come off the ice, your weight will pitch forward over the curved toes, and you may fall. Now do the drill skating backward. When skating backward, your weight is primarily on the front half of the blade. Again, you must be sure to keep the entire blade length in contact with the ice so that your weight doesn't pitch forward, causing you to fall.

STRETCHING DRILLS FOR BALANCE, COORDINATION, AND STRENGTHENING

Two-Foot Jumps

Basic to Intermediate

This is an excellent drill for developing quadriceps strength and knee bend, as well as for improving balance on the flats of the blades. Practice this drill skating forward and backward.

To perform the drill, glide forward on the flats of both skates. At the first blue line, jump up as high as you can and land on the flats of both skates. Continue jumping until you reach the far blue line.

Before each jump, bend your knees deeply so that you are coiled to jump. Jump as high as possible. Cushion the landing by deeply bending your knees as you land.

Keep your back straight and your head up as you land. Do not bend forward from the waist; doing so will pitch your weight over the curved toes of the blades. Be sure to land with the entire blade lengths (of both skates) in contact with the ice.

Repeat, skating and jumping backward.

One-Foot Hops

Intermediate to Advanced

This plyometric drill really works the quadriceps. It is excellent for developing the coiling mechanism that is essential for explosiveness. This drill also helps you develop the balance and recovery abilities that are necessary in game situations. Only one skate is on the ice throughout this drill.

To perform the drill, skate forward from the goal line. At the first blue line, lift one skate and begin hopping on the other skate. Continue hopping on the same skate until you reach the far blue line. When you get to the far blue line, skate to the far end.

Note: Before each hop, deeply bend the knee of the hopping leg so that you are coiled like a spring. Leap as high as possible. Cushion the landing by deeply bending the knee of the landing leg (figure 2.17, *a-c*, on page 28).

Coming back down the ice, hop on the other skate. Do the hops skating backward as well as forward, and be sure to hop equally on each skate. Keep your back straight; avoid the tendency to bend forward from the waist as you land (bending forward will pitch your weight forward over the curved toes). Look straight ahead and keep your head up. Be sure to land so that the entire blade is in contact with the ice.

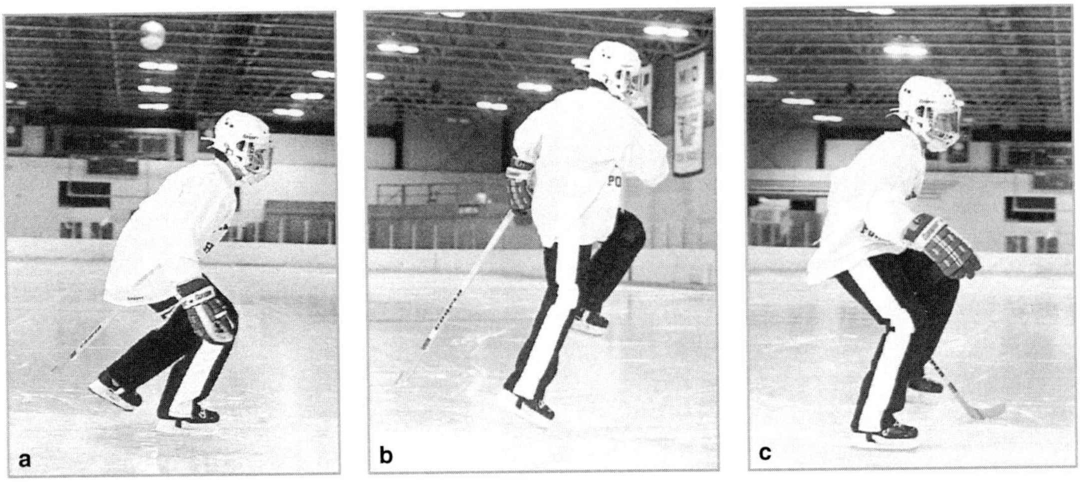

Figure 2.17 One-foot hops.

Shoot the Duck

Intermediate

Shoot the duck is an excellent drill for improving balance and coordination. It also strengthens the quadriceps, a major muscle group used in skating.

Glide forward on both skates. Squat down over your skates with your buttocks as close to the ice as possible. Put your weight over the right skate and lift the left skate off the ice, extending the left skate straight ahead of you. Glide for a few seconds. Then get up from this position *without letting the right (free) skate touch the ice.*

Repeat, now gliding on the left skate. Then repeat the drill gliding backward.

Keep your back straight. If you lean too far forward from the waist, you won't be able to bend your knee to sit low enough.

Advanced

Repeat the previous drill forward and backward, but while you are in the shoot the duck (or squatting) position, change feet continuously for the length of the ice.

Repeat the drill (forward and backward), now gliding on inside and outside edges.

Spread-Eagle Squat

Intermediate to Advanced

This drill helps improve balance and coordination, and it also strengthens the quadriceps.

Skate forward from the goal line. At the first blue line, turn sideways and face one sideboard. As you turn, bend your knees so that both skates face along the line of travel (they will face the sideboards) in a spread-eagle position (figure 2.18). See how long you can glide in this position before turning forward. Then skate forward to the far end.

Skating back down the ice, turn to face the same sideboards (you will now turn in the opposite direction). Then repeat the drill, skating backward.

Figure 2.18 Spread-eagle squat.

Forward Cross Lifts—Alternating Feet

Advanced

This drill (and the next one) helps players improve their ability to use the inside and outside edges. It also helps players improve balance, coordination, flexibility, strength, and body control. Perform the drill while holding the hockey stick horizontally, chest high, and fully extended in front of you.

Glide forward on the right inside edge; lift the left skate off the ice and behind you (figure 2.19, *a-b,* on page 30). Raise the left leg up and touch the hockey stick with the toe of the left skate while changing to the outside edge of the right (gliding) skate (figure 2.19*c*). Bring the left skate down onto the ice, crossed in front of the right skate and on its inside edge (figure 2.19*d*).

Repeat the procedure, now gliding on the left skate. Lift the right skate off the ice and behind you, raising it toward the stick. Change to the LFO as you lift the right leg; touch the stick with the toe of the right skate. Bring the right skate down onto the ice, crossed in front of the left skate and on its inside edge.

Keep repeating the drill for the length of the ice. Note that the direction of travel changes as the edges change.

Figure 2.19 Forward cross lifts.

Backward Cross Lifts—Alternating Feet

Advanced

Glide backward on the right inside edge; lift the left skate off the ice and behind you (figure 2.20, *a-b*) while holding the hockey stick horizontally, chest high, and fully extended in front of you. Raise the left leg up and touch the hockey stick with the toe of the left skate while changing to the outside edge of the right (gliding) skate (figure 2.20*c*). Bring the left skate down onto the ice, crossed in front of the right skate and on its inside edge (figure 2.20*d*).

Repeat the procedure, now gliding on the left skate; lift the right skate off the ice and behind you, raising it toward the stick. Change to the LBO as you lift the right leg up; touch the stick with the toe of the right skate. Bring the right skate down onto the ice, crossed in front of the left skate and on its inside edge.

Keep repeating the drill for the length of the ice. Note that the line of travel changes as the edges change.

Variation (Advanced)

This variation will improve your ability to use and balance on the outside edges.

Repeat the previous two drills. However, in this variation, the gliding skate always glides on outside edges—never on inside edges. Each time you cross over, the new gliding skate takes the ice on its outside edge instead of on its inside edge. See figure 6.18 on page 122.

Figure 2.20 Backward cross lifts.

Chapter 3

Force Application for Explosive Speed

Today's hockey is all about explosive speed. The sport is dominated by players who skate FAST—weaving, cutting, and changing direction on a dime. Players have unique styles, but all FAST skaters adhere to the principles of force application.

Every sport requires that force be applied correctly, powerfully, explosively, and with precise timing. The result is movement—of an object (puck, bat, ball, and so on), opponent, or oneself. Although the methods of applying force vary with each sport, the principles are essentially the same.

ELEMENTS OF FORCE APPLICATION

Every athletic motion requires a windup, release, and follow-through. Terms such as *coil, windup, release, follow-through, spring, drive, explode,* and *weight shift* (or *weight transfer*) are commonly used in the sports world. These are some of the elements of force application. They are also applicable to hockey skating.

To understand these elements, imagine a baseball pitcher's motion. The pitcher's backswing is an example of the windup or coiling action. The pitcher's throw exemplifies the release, follow-through, and weight transfer. The pitch itself demonstrates force applied explosively and timed precisely; the result is a ball that travels with precision and lightning speed.

The pushes of every skating maneuver can be compared to a pitcher's throw. Every stride requires a windup (coiling action), a release (application of force from the coiled position), and a follow-through (completion of motion)—along with accurately timed use of body weight (weight shift or transfer) during the push.

Skating requires an additional element that is not necessarily applicable in other sports—the return (recovery) of the pushing skate and leg. This element is important regardless of the skating maneuver being performed. After completing each push, the skate and leg must quickly return to center under the body in order to prepare for the next push.

Speed is defined as distance covered in time. In hockey, speed is measured by how far a series of strides carry the skater in a given time span. The time required for a single stride is approximated in fractions of a second. The distance covered on each stride depends on the correct, powerful, and precisely timed application of force. The time spent on each stride (leg speed or leg turnover) depends on how rapidly the player changes feet, which in turn depends on how quickly the free skate and leg return after each push. Since hockey is a sprint sport, players must move their legs very rapidly. However, correct, powerful, explosive, and complete application of force cannot be sacrificed just to move the legs rapidly.

Following is an explanation of the windup, release, follow-through, and return.

Windup

In skating, the windup corresponds to the backswing of a batter in baseball. The windup acts to coil the spring. The more coiling action, the more force available for the release. The coiling action is achieved by digging in the edge of the thrusting skate at a strong angle to the ice (approximately 45 degrees), strongly bending the knees (90 degrees), and pressing the body weight down over the gripping edge. This allows the edge to grip the ice strongly. Without a strong thrusting edge or without the body weight pressing down over the edge, a player will have no traction. The skate will slip and slide rather than cut into the ice.

Figure 3.1 The windup.

The deeper the edge digs into the ice and the more the body weight presses downward over the edge, the more grip is available for the upcoming push (release). Figure 3.1 shows the windup of the forward stride; the inside edge, the knee, and the body weight are concentrated over the pushing skate and are pressing strongly downward toward the ice. The player is prepared to push powerfully.

Release

The release is the actual thrust. The pushing skate and leg drive against the ice powerfully and explosively to move the skater. Many hockey players are unaware of just how hard their legs must push to get maximum speed.

During the release, the pushing skate and leg—with the body weight concentrated over them—push directly against the cutting edge, which is wedged solidly into the ice (figure 3.2, *a-b*). At the midpoint of the push, the body weight begins to shift from the pushing skate to the gliding skate; this shift is completed as the pushing leg approaches full extension.

Figure 3.2 The release.

Note: The timing of the weight shift is extremely important. Many players shift their weight prematurely. The result is that the skate loses its grip against the ice, causing a slip.

A general rule for pushing holds true for almost every type of skating maneuver: Each push must be executed so that the pushing skate pushes directly against the *entire length* of the blade, which is digging into the ice at an acute (approximately 45-degree) angle (figure 3.3, *a-b*). The pushing blade may face different directions depending on the specific maneuver and the speed at which that maneuver is done; however, the rule still applies. The skate and leg must exert force in a line perpendicular to that described by the pushing blade's length—in other words, perpendicular to the grip. Figure 3.4 shows the way the blade faces during various maneuvers and the proper direction of leg drive for each one.

You must push your entire weight against the gripping edge. The pushing skate and leg do the work, but the object is to **move yourself!**

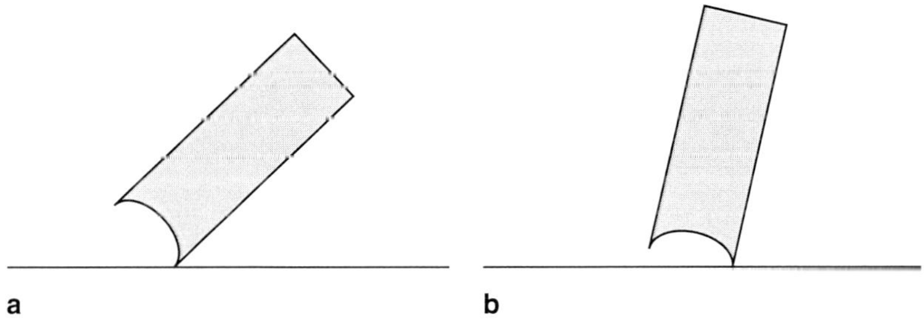

Figure 3.3 *(a)* A 45-degree angle of edge to ice sets up an effective thrust and allows the body weight to project low and forward; *(b)* a greater angle results in a weak push and causes upward body motion.

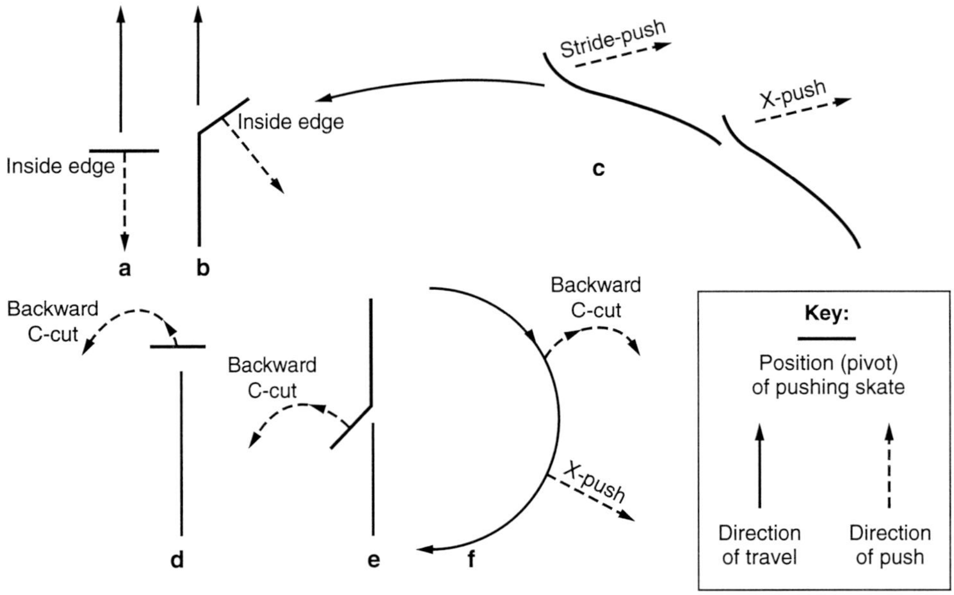

Figure 3.4 Pushing against the edge: *(a)* forward start, or traveling slowly; *(b)* forward stride, traveling faster; *(c)* forward crossovers; *(d)* backward start, or traveling slowly; *(e)* backward stride, traveling faster; and *(f)* backward crossovers.

Follow-Through

Thrusting the legs without following through is like swinging the baseball bat and then halting the bat midswing. In skating, incomplete leg drive results in a significant loss of power—and therefore a significant decrease in the distance covered on that stride.

Every push must finish with a proper follow-through:

- The pushing leg is fully extended away from the body with the hip, thigh, knee, ankle, and toe locked.
- The knee of the gliding leg stays strongly bent (90 degrees) as the thrusting leg extends.
- The push is finished only when the pushing leg is fully extended; the toe of the thrusting blade is just barely off the ice (figure 3.5, *a-b*).

Note: In backward skating, the pushing skate actually stays on the ice when fully extended.

Moving the legs too fast is a common error that prevents the legs from reaching full extension. Many players are encouraged to move their legs faster and faster. But each pushing leg *must* go through its full range of motion. The pushing leg must reach full extension on the push and must recover totally on the return. Players whose strides are incomplete have trouble reaching their potential for speed, and they tend to tire quickly. Their legs go fast, but they don't. I call this going nowhere fast.

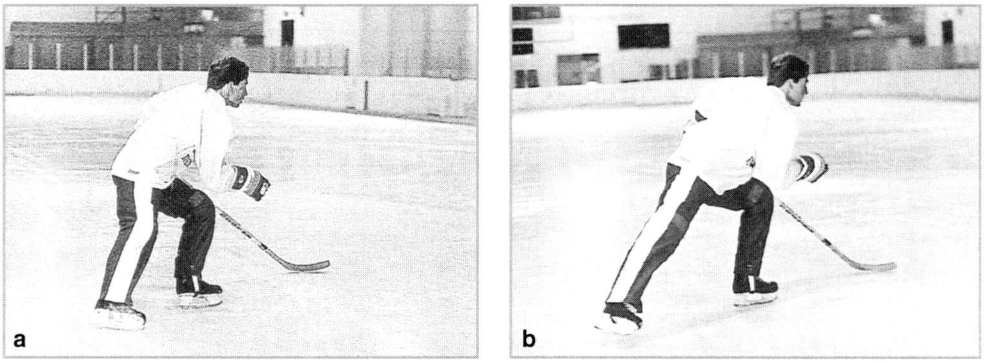

Figure 3.5 The follow-through.

The range of motion is different for tall skaters than it is for short skaters. In fact, the range of motion varies for each individual. You should first learn to push with complete leg drive for power; then you can practice this while trying to move your legs faster and faster. You may end up going faster with fewer strides.

COACHING TIP

Correct and powerful leg drive combined with rapid leg motion yields efficient speed.

Return

Leg speed depends on how quickly a player changes feet. This in turn depends on the complete and rapid return (recovery) of the pushing skate and leg—that is, how quickly the player returns the pushing skate and leg under the midpoint of the body. If the skate and leg do not return completely, the next push will be negatively affected.

After reaching full extension, the thrusting skate and leg return, retracing their outward path until the skate centers under the body. When the skate returns to this position, the other skate and leg are prepared to push effectively. The body weight is now situated over the skate that is preparing to push.

The returning skate stays close to the ice as it returns. In backward skating, the returning skate actually stays on the ice during the return. The higher the returning skate lifts off the ice during the recovery phase, the longer it takes to change feet.

Remember: Rapid leg turnover is critical for speed. Figure 3.6 *a* and *b* on page 38 show a low and complete return during the forward stride. Figure 3.6*c* diagrams the straight-line push and return of the forward stride.

Every return is exactly opposite to the preceding push.

- When skating forward, the pushing skate and leg push straight out; therefore, a straight-line path of return is most effective. A circular path takes longer, delaying the next stride.
- When skating backward, a circular path of return is necessary because of the circular (C-cut) push of the backward stride (see chapter 5 for details on the backward stride).

Figure 3.6 *(a-b)* Complete return during the forward stride; *(c)* push and return of the forward stride.

Note: The knee of the gliding leg must stay well bent during the return; this keeps the body weight low. Avoid popping or bouncing up between strides. Such pop-ups break forward momentum and cause a delay between strides.

TECHNIQUE DETAILS

The following technique details are essential for the effective performance of ALL hockey skating maneuvers.

Knee bend. Skating requires a deep knee bend, *both on the pushing leg and the gliding leg.* Measured between the thigh and shin, the angle of the knee bend should approximate 90 degrees.

Edges. The edges are used for two separate purposes. One is for pushing, and one is for gliding. We will refer to them as the pushing edge and the gliding edge:

- Pushing edge. Regardless of the maneuver or whether the player is skating forward or backward, the edge of the pushing skate (inside or outside) must dig into the ice at a strong angle. The ideal angle of the pushing edge to the ice is approximately 45 degrees (figure 3.7).
- Gliding edge. To skate in a straight line, a player must glide on the flat of the blade. To skate on a curve or circle, a player must glide on a strong edge (inside or outside). The edge used depends on the maneuver and the direction. When a player is skating on a sharp curve or circle (with speed), the ideal angle of the gliding edge to the ice is approximately 45 degrees (figure 3.8, *a-b*).

Figure 3.7 The pushing edge at a 45-degree angle.

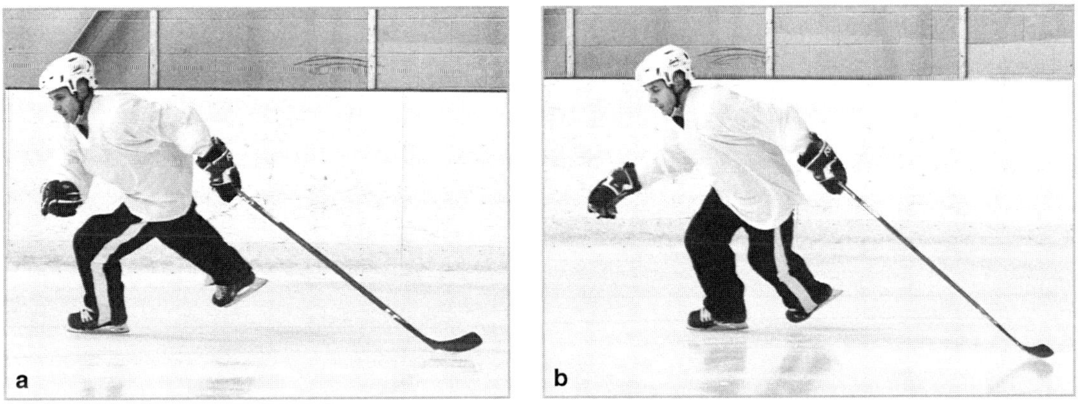

Figure 3.8 The gliding edge at a 45-degree angle: *(a)* outside and *(b)* inside edges.

Body weight and weight shift. Every stride consists of a push–glide sequence that involves a total transfer of body weight. The body weight must be totally (100 percent) above the working skate (sometimes the working skate is the pushing skate, and sometimes it is the gliding skate).

The push–glide sequence is applicable on every stride. When the working skate is the pushing skate, the *total* body weight is above the pushing skate (edge). During the push, the body weight transfers so that it is totally above the gliding skate (edge or flat). When the working skate is the gliding skate, the *total* body weight stays above the gliding skate during the entire glide and also as the gliding skate prepares to become the new pushing skate. Precise timing of these weight shifts is necessary for proper force to be applied effectively.

Center of gravity. The center of gravity is an imaginary circle approximately 3 inches (7.6 cm) in diameter that is located in the midsection of the body (just above the waist). I call the center of gravity the "power pack" or "battery pack" because to achieve power, every push must be initiated from beneath this center. If the skates are wider apart than this imaginary circle when a skater is initiating a push, power is sacrificed.

Leg drive and leg recovery. Every push must be executed to the full extension of the pushing skate and leg. The finish of the push is executed by the front of the pushing edge, which provides a final snap against the ice. After each push, the pushing skate and leg quickly return to a position beneath the center of gravity (power pack) to prepare for the next push.

Arm swing. When used properly, the arm swing increases momentum. The arms must move in line and in rhythm with the legs, as well as in line with the direction of travel. When a player is skating straight forward or backward, the arms move forward and backward (figure 3.9, *a-b*). When a player is moving laterally, the arms move laterally (figure 3.9*c*). When used improperly, the arm swing is a waste of effort.

Figure 3.9 Proper arm swing *(a)* when skating forward, *(b)* when skating backward, and *(c)* when skating laterally.

THE PUSHES OF HOCKEY SKATING

The pushes used in hockey skating are specific to the maneuver being performed. I have named each of these pushes to help players visualize and comprehend them more readily. The manner of executing each push is explained in the following chapters.

- The *forward stride-push* is the push of the forward stride. This push is always executed against the forward inside edge.
- The *backward stride-push* (backward C-cut push) is the push of the backward stride. This push is always executed against the backward inside edge (see chapter 5).
- The *forward X-push* is the second push of forward crossovers. This push is always executed against the forward outside edge (see chapter 6).
- The *backward X-push* is the second push of backward crossovers. This push is always executed against the backward outside edge (see chapter 6).
- The *forward C-cut push* is used in various agility maneuvers. This push is always executed against the forward inside edge (see chapter 4).

One other push exists, but it is not used often in hockey. This push is described in the windmill drill in chapter 9.

Chapter 4

Forward Stride for a More Aggressive Attack

How important is it for players to master the forward stride? Consider that the typical skater spends 85 percent of most hockey games skating straight ahead. Great players seem to float over the ice as if they were born with the gift of skating. Although a few players are truly natural skaters, most spend years perfecting their skating techniques.

Speed depends not only on rapid leg motion but also on correct and powerful use of the blade edges, legs, and body weight. A serious misconception is that skating fast simply means moving the feet fast. Too many players are taught to move their feet fast regardless of *how* they move their feet or whether they are following the principles of force application. These players move as though on a treadmill, working hard but going nowhere.

Speed is a measure of distance traveled in a specific time frame, such as miles per hour, or feet per second. Therefore, whether skating forward or backward, crossing over, turning, or starting, skaters must cover distance on every stride in order to go fast. In other words, you have to *go* somewhere.

All forward strides are technically alike. The amount of force exerted on each thrust and the techniques of leg drive, weight shift, and leg recovery do not vary. The basic difference between strides is the length of the glide—how much time is spent on the gliding skate before the next gliding skate takes the ice. For a skater to accelerate, glides must be short; but after the initial acceleration, the skater must maximize each glide. This will be discussed later in this chapter (see "Glide of the Forward Stride" on page 49).

As discussed in chapter 3, every skating maneuver must incorporate the elements of windup, release, follow-through, and return. The way that these elements are applied when performing the forward stride is explained in this chapter. The techniques of *all* hockey skating moves can be more easily applied after a player understands the techniques of the forward stride. Following is a detailed explanation of these techniques. The techniques are described for pushing with the right leg.

WINDUP

The windup takes place from a point centered directly under the body (center of gravity). The center of gravity is an imaginary circle—about 3 inches (7.6 cm) in diameter—located in the midsection (belly-button area) of the body. With youngsters I refer to the center of gravity as the *battery pack, power pack,* or *home base.* It is the place where each push must begin and end in order to achieve optimum power.

1. The windup starts with the feet close together and centered under the body; the toes are pivoted outward, and the knees are well bent (90 degrees). The feet and legs are in what I call the V-diamond position—the heels are together, and the knees are apart. The shape between the heels is a V; the shape between the ankles, knees, and thighs is a diamond. Figure 4.1*a* shows a wide V-diamond (used when starting or when skating slowly). Figure 4.1*b* shows a narrow V-diamond (used when skating fast).

Note: The V-diamond position is a critical position; it is integral to the execution of many other hockey maneuvers. (For more information, see chapter 9.)

2. With the knees still well bent, press the inside edge of the right (thrusting) skate into the ice so that the edge and lower leg form an approximate 45-degree angle with the ice.

3. Still keeping the knees well bent, place your body weight over the inside edge of the thrusting skate and continue to lower your weight (figure 4.2*a* on page 44). At this instant, the hips should be positioned above the pushing skate.

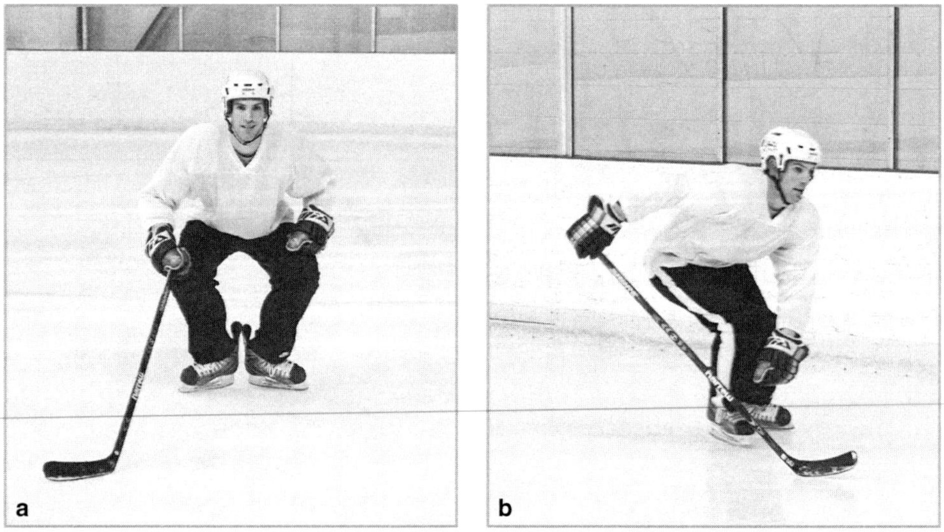

Figure 4.1 The V-diamond position: *(a)* wide V-diamond and *(b)* narrow V-diamond.

RELEASE

The release is the actual thrust of the pushing skate and leg directly against the inside edge—first to the back (opposite the direction of travel) and then out to the side. The precise direction of the push is determined by the turnout angle of the pushing blade (see figure 3.4 on page 36).

Note: When a player is skating forward from a complete stop, or skating very slowly, the turnout of the pushing blade to the ice (the direction the blade faces on the ice) is almost perpendicular to the direction (line) of travel. Since the push is *always* directly against the gripping blade (edge), the push will be opposite from the direction of travel. The angle of the pushing blade to the line of travel decreases as speed increases; at top speeds, the turnout of the pushing blade (and the direction of the push) is between 35 and 45 degrees from the line of travel.

1. Push directly against the grip, using the entire length of the inside edge to push. Start the push with the heel of the inside edge, and finish the push with the toe of the inside edge (figure 4.2, *b-c,* on page 44). This heel-to-toe push requires the use of the entire length of the rockered blade, and the body weight shifts from the back to the front of the inside edge during the push.

Note: In all skating maneuvers, controlling the body weight over the rockered blade is just as important as controlling the edges. When the body weight is distributed properly on specific points along the rockered blade, the player will have greater agility and maneuverability.

2. Although the leg performs the actual push, the goal is to drive the entire body weight against the blade edge that is gripping the ice.

3. The thigh muscles provide the main power in pushing. If they don't feel the strain of each push, they are not being fully employed. Coaches use various phrases to encourage players to push hard, including "explode off the pushing leg," "deliver a knockout punch," "go full throttle," and "gun the engine." Players get accustomed to pushing with a certain amount of force, believing it to be their maximum effort. However, most players are capable of pushing much harder. Experimentation is essential to developing a more powerful and effective push.

4. Pushing to the back and side against a strongly gripping edge sets up a powerful push. Pushing straight back in a walking or running motion does not provide an effective push. Pushing the leg straight back—and finishing the push with the front tip (tiptoe) of the blade—is one of the most common errors in skating. The reason for this error is that a forward–backward leg motion is a natural motion for the human body. But in skating, a straight backward motion, along with using the tiptoe of the blade to push, provides no traction and causes the blade to slip rather than to push against the ice. The following equations describe the skating motion and the walking or running motion:

Skating = out and in   **Walking or running = back and forward**

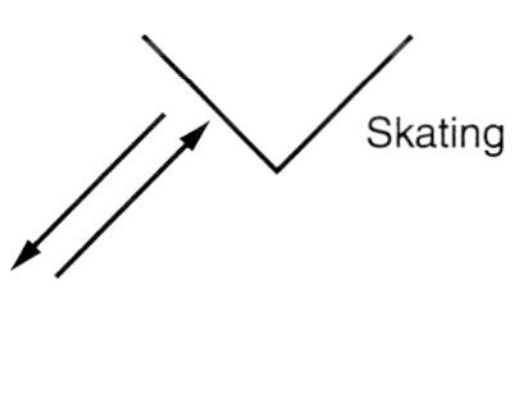

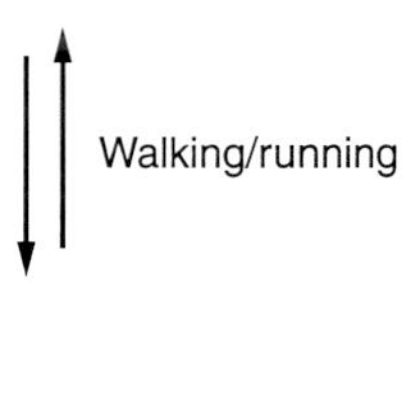

5. During the push (with the right skate and leg), the left skate takes the ice, receives the weight that is shifting from the pushing skate, and becomes the gliding skate. The transfer of weight onto the gliding skate takes place approximately halfway through the push (figure 4.2*b*). If body weight shifts too early or if it is not shifted forward and outward completely over the gliding skate, momentum and power are sacrificed.

6. The gliding skate must aim slightly outward as it takes the ice. Body weight must shift outward as well, and it must remain directly above the gliding skate for the duration of the glide. Toward the end of the glide, a transition to the prepushing phase needs to occur. In this phase, the gliding skate must be rolled onto its inside edge, and the body weight must shift inward and above the edge.

Note: Each glide has two changes in weight—an outward weight shift followed by an inward weight shift. (See "Glide of the Forward Stride" on page 49.)

(continued)

Figure 4.2 Forward stride sequence: *(a)* windup, *(b)* release, *(c-d)* follow-through, *(e)* return, *(f)* windup.

Figure 4.2 *(continued)* Forward stride sequence: *(g)* release, *(h)* follow-through, *(i-j)* return.

FOLLOW-THROUGH

The push is completed only when the pushing skate and leg reach full extension. Power is lost when skaters shorten this critical part of the push in an attempt to move their legs ultrafast.

1. Continue pushing against the inside edge until the pushing skate and leg reach full extension. Full extension means that the entire pushing leg—from hip to toe—is in a totally extended position at the completion of the push. The instant of the push when the pushing leg locks and the toe (front of the inside edge) snaps against the ice is called the *toe flick*. Snapping the toe against the ice at the finish of the push *must* correspond with the locking of the pushing leg; this combination gives the push its powerful finish (figure 4.2*d*).

Note: The longer the pushing edge stays in contact with the ice (continues to push), the more powerful that push will be.

2. As the pushing leg reaches its full extension and as the pushing skate leaves the ice, the pushing skate and leg become the free skate and leg.

3. The act of lifting the skate from the ice is a natural continuation of the push; this final instant of the push (toe flick) provides an additional surge of power and speed at the finish of the push. To achieve a toe flick, three things must occur simultaneously:

- The pushing leg—from hip to toe—must be completely locked and fully extended (figure 4.3*a* on page 46). There can be no crease behind the knee. A crease behind the knee indicates that the leg is not locked to its fullest.

- The toes of the free foot must be scrunched up, and the muscles of the foot must be arched tightly (figure 4.3*b*).
- The tendon guard of the free skate must press into the back of the extended leg at this instant of full extension.

Note: A properly executed toe flick has a distinct sight and sound: The sight is snow flying from the toe of the blade as it flicks against the ice. The sound is a *hrrush* at the finish of the push and as the skate comes off the ice.

4. While lifting the free skate off the ice, keep the free hip and knee in a turned-out position, and keep the toe of the free skate within an inch (2.5 cm) of the ice (figure 4.2*d* on page 44). Raising the free skate much higher than this raises the center of gravity, breaks forward momentum, and delays leg recovery. Toeing down, or finishing the push with the tiptoe instead of the inside edge of the toe (caused by loss of turnout), results in the heel kicking up in a walking or running motion (figure 4.4). This nullifies the toe flick.

Note: The joints of the hip, knee, and foot are connected. Therefore, if any one of them turns inward (to face straight forward or downward), all of them will turn inward. To finish the push with the skate and leg pushing outward, all these joints must be turned outward.

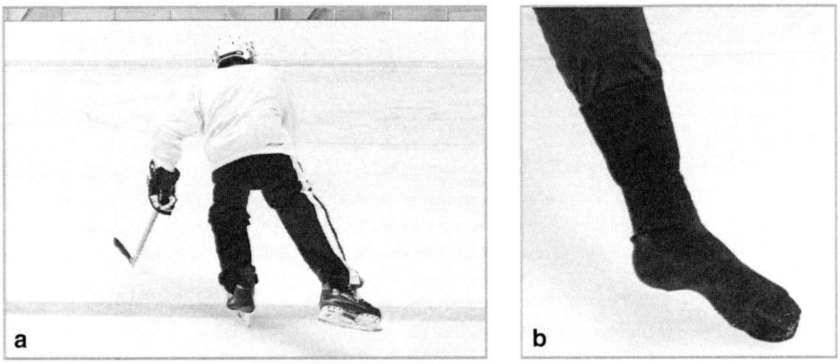

Figure 4.3 Toe flick: *(a)* proper form—the pushing leg is locked and fully extended; *(b)* the toes of the free foot are scrunched up.

Figure 4.4 Incorrect push.

5. As the pushing leg extends and becomes the free leg, keep the knee of the gliding leg well bent (90 degrees). If the gliding knee is straight or only moderately bent, the center of gravity will be too high, which hinders both stability and speed (figure 4.5*a* shows correct form; figure 4.5*b* shows incorrect form). The amount of knee bend of the gliding leg also determines the length of the push. Deeply bent knees allow for longer pushes; this maximizes speed and conserves energy. A deeply bent gliding knee is out ahead of that same toe.

6. At full extension, there should be a straight line of force from the shoulders, through the pushing leg, to the toe. At this instant, the proper body position for the forward stride is as follows:

- Gliding knee ahead of gliding toe
- Chest over gliding knee
- Hips facing straight ahead (facing the line of travel)
- Back straight
- Head up and eyes straight ahead
- Arms moving in line and in unison with the legs

Note: At top speed, the angle of the upper body (trunk) to the ice is approximately 45 degrees (figure 4.6).

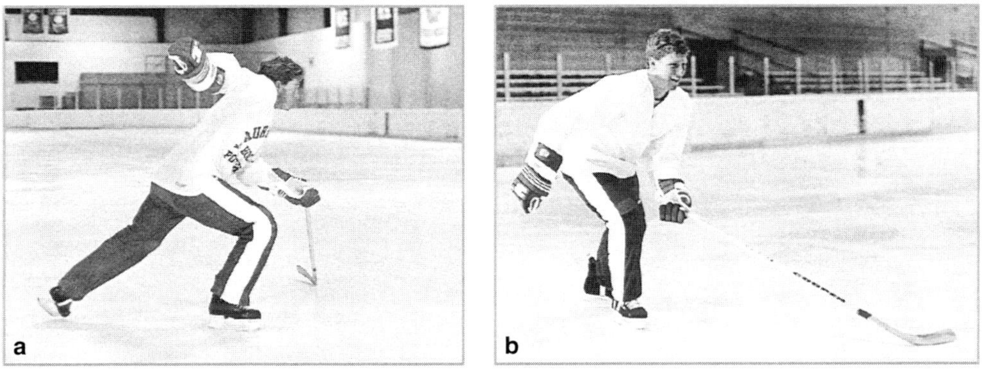

Figure 4.5 *(a)* Correct skating form—the gliding knee is bent strongly; *(b)* incorrect form—the gliding knee is not bent sufficiently.

Figure 4.6 The straight line of force and the alignment of the body at full extension.

RETURN (RECOVERY)

Too many players neglect to complete the return (recovery) phase. They take it for granted that the returning skate will come in by itself. However, what goes out does not automatically come in! This is a major cause of poor speed. After finishing each push, the skater must actually *pull* the free skate and leg back until they are centered under the power pack.

Because the skate and leg do not automatically return, this aspect of the stride (whether skating forward or backward) must be practiced as much as or even more than any other. The return of the free skate and leg coincides with a shift of the body weight over the inside edge of the gliding skate as it prepares to execute the next push.

Every return in hockey skating is the exact opposite of that specific and preceding push. Since the push of the forward stride is in a straight line outward, the return is in a straight line inward. The motion inward reverses the leg's outward path. The return must be quick and complete.

1. To return the previous pushing (now free) skate and leg, reverse the outward path. Pull the skate back under your body until it is directly under the center of gravity. Keep the skate within an inch (2.5 cm) of the ice as it returns (figure 4.2*e* on page 44).

2. During the recovery phase, keep the knee and toe of the free skate and leg turned out. This turned-out position allows the skates and legs to come together in the V-diamond position, prepared for the new push–glide sequence.

Remember: In the V-diamond position, the skates are close together while the knees are well apart.

3. Keep a deep knee bend on the gliding leg. Straightening the knee even a bit breaks forward momentum, slows the recovery, and delays the next push.

4. As the free skate and leg return, the free skate should momentarily meet the gliding skate in the V-diamond position and then immediately pass by it (about three-quarters of a blade length) to take the ice as the new gliding skate (figure 4.2*f*).

Note: On *all* skating maneuvers, the returning skate moves slightly ahead of the gliding skate (progresses) before taking the ice as the new gliding skate. The returning skate moves forward (or backward if skating backward) by approximately three-quarters of a blade length. This continuous progression of motion is an essential component of speed.

Execute the next push (with the left skate and leg) as follows:

1. If the recovering skate returns properly (in the V-diamond position), the gliding skate will already be prepivoted outward and prepared to push.

2. Dig the inside edge of the left skate into the ice (at approximately a 45-degree angle), and bend both knees deeply (90 degrees).

3. Place your weight over the left inside edge, and mirror the procedure of the windup, release, follow-through, and return described for the right leg (figure 4.2, *g-j*, on page 45). When you are once again gliding on the right skate, you have completed one cycle.

THE ONE-THIRD PRINCIPLE

The one-third principle illustrates how each part of the push affects the forward stride. Regarding power generation, think of the skate blade as being divided into thirds: the back third (heel), the middle third (middle), and the front third (toe). Power is generated equally by each part of the blade—one-third by the heel, one-third by the middle, and one-third by the toe (figure 4.7).

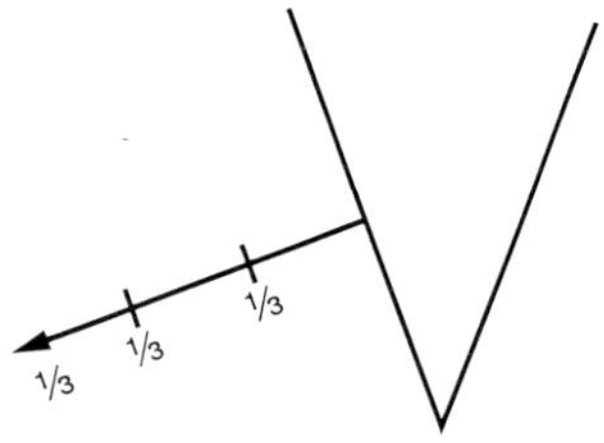

Figure 4.7 The one-third principle.

The first third of the push. The heel of the blade can generate power only when the pushing skate is directly under the center of gravity. If the skates are wide apart and outside the center of gravity when the skater begins to push, power will be lost on this third of the push.

The second third of the push. The middle of the blade generates power when the pushing leg is partially extended. Most players do get this second third of the push.

The final third of the push. The front third of the blade (toe) generates power on the final third of the push. This part of the push can only occur when the pushing leg is fully extended and when the toe of the inside edge pushes just before and as the skate comes off the ice (toe flick).

Wide-based skaters who also do not fully extend their legs or do not use the toe flick may lose up to two-thirds of their potential power on each push. These skaters work hard but accomplish little. Their legs go a million miles an hour, but they end up going nowhere fast.

GLIDE OF THE FORWARD STRIDE

Is the initial glide of the forward stride on the flat or on the outside edge of the blade? This question is often debated. Because of the curved pattern of the glide, the skate appears to glide initially on an outside edge. However, the outward curve may be a result of the outward direction of the gliding skate as it takes the ice from the V-diamond position—and the subsequent transfer of body weight outward over the blade.

If the glide actually does begin on the outside edge, the edge is minimal and of short duration. The skate changes almost immediately from the edge to the flat of the blade. The majority of the glide is on the flat. In preparation for pushing, the skater rapidly shifts the skate and body weight inward and above the inside edge.

Whether or not the initial glide is actually on the outside edge, skaters should try to skate as though it is, because an outside edge can *only* be achieved when the gliding skate takes the ice under the center of gravity. This requires the skater to return the free skate until it is completely centered under the power pack. Doing so encourages an efficient push, a precise weight shift from pushing skate to gliding skate, and forward motion in the desired direction, which is forward and outward from the V (figure 4.8*a*). Figure 4.8*b* shows strides that resemble railroad tracks. Railroad track strides are the result of incorrect and incomplete leg recovery. They create side-to-side (rather than forward) motion that wastes energy and inhibits forward speed.

Note: Although the stride is primarily forward, it is *not* straight forward as in walking or running. The direction of the glide is forward and outward. The angle outward comes from and is determined by the angle of the V.

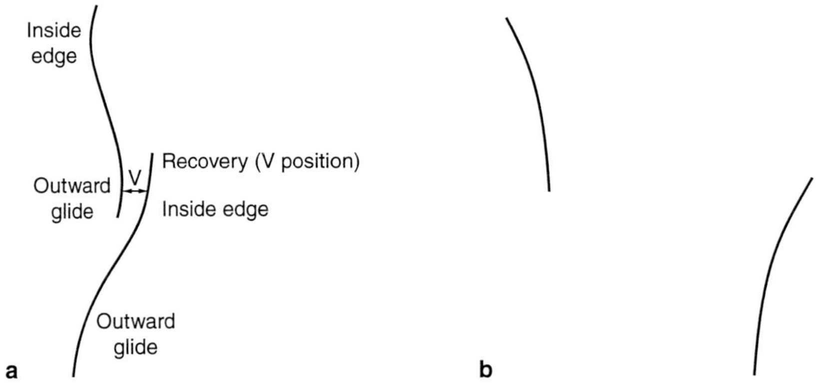

Figure 4.8 The glide of the forward stride: *(a)* correct—complete recovery with an outward and inward weight shift; *(b)* incorrect—incomplete leg recovery and a railroad-track stride pattern.

ARM SWING

Some skaters believe that swinging their arms vigorously makes them skate faster. Wrong! Speed in skating comes primarily from the legs. The arms provide rhythm and momentum. Although the arms do help to increase speed when used correctly, they are not the prime source of speed. The arms are never a substitute for the legs—they should be used in addition to the legs.

When game situations allow, players should hold their hockey sticks with just the top hand. This enables them to swing their arms properly and effectively for additional momentum and speed. The proper arm swing for the forward stride is forward and backward along the same diagonal lines as, and in rhythm with, the legs. Arms should match legs in terms of force, direction of movement, and range of motion. As in running, the right arm drives forward as the right leg drives back. Here are some additional points to keep in mind regarding the arm swing:

- Each arm-swing cycle finishes with one arm extended diagonally forward and the other extended diagonally back; the palms of both hands face upward. An imaginary line is formed between the right hand and foot and between the left hand and foot (figure 4.9*a*).
- The arms must *never* cross the midline of the body because this creates lateral motion instead of forward motion (figure 4.9*b*).

- The elbows must stay close to the ribs as the arms move forward and backward. If the arms move in a wide arc (elbows far away from the ribs), the arms are forced to swing from side to side, and they will cross the midline of the body. As mentioned, this creates sideways (lateral) motion rather than straight-ahead motion.
- Excessive churning of the arms is a waste of energy.
- The upper body must stay square to the line of travel during each arm swing. It must not twist from side to side. The shoulders should move easily and stay level with the ice.
- The arms and legs work in unison; therefore, full arm extension encourages full leg extension. A short, choppy arm swing encourages a short, choppy stride. Think of the windup for a softball pitch or bowling throw. A full backswing sets up forward motion on the throw. Similarly, in skating, a full backswing helps drive the body weight forward.
- Many players are taught to always hold the hockey stick with both hands. In general, this is sound advice; however, holding the stick in only one hand is advantageous in many situations. For example, in the following scenarios, holding the stick with both hands is unnecessary and even disadvantageous.

  Breakaways: In these situations, you need to skate at top speed. By pushing the puck out ahead and swinging your arms, you can skate faster. Skating while controlling the puck with the stick held in two hands is almost always slower than skating with the stick in one hand and swinging the arms.

  Breaking out or skating fast without the puck: In these situations, you try to get free, hoping to get into position to receive a pass. You should keep the hockey stick on the ice and create a target for your teammate to pass the puck to. When you hold the stick with both hands, you will probably swing the stick in the air, and you will be unable to

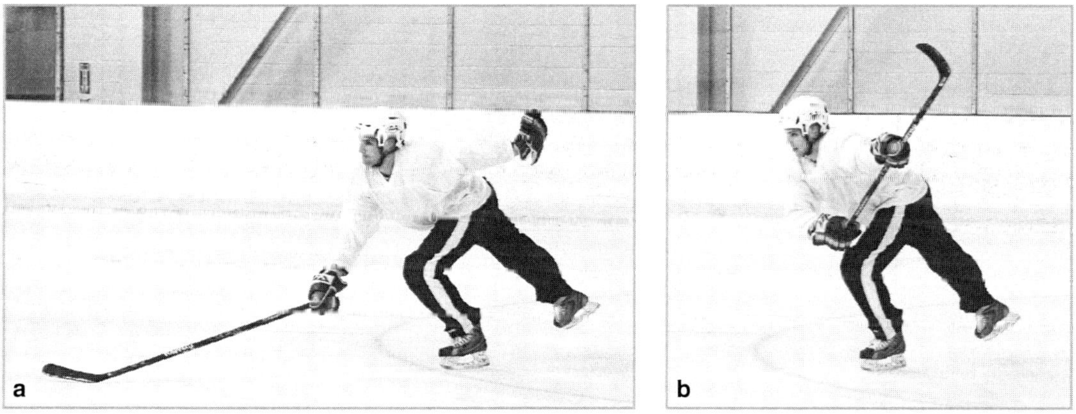

Figure 4.9 Arm swing: *(a)* correct—forward and backward; *(b)* incorrect—side to side.

create a target for the pass. In addition, if the stick is off the ice and the puck comes to you quickly, you might not be able to get the stick blade onto the ice quickly enough. As a result, you will miss the pass. This happens at all levels of hockey and often in critical situations.

Note: Holding the hockey stick with two hands while skating fast almost ensures that you will lift the stick off the ice and swing your arms from side to side. Hockey coaches call this pitching hay. I sometimes refer to this as cradling a baby.

Preparing to check an opponent: In these situations, holding the hockey stick with one hand and keeping it on the ice encourage a legal check. Holding the stick with both hands may encourage an illegal check—this commonly occurs when the checking player swings the stick in the air and ends up hitting the opponent with the swinging stick.

Practice skating forward at high speed while holding the hockey stick with just your top hand. Keep the stick blade on the ice. Skate fast, pushing the puck out ahead of you. Extend your arms fully as you swing them.

Note: The puck can be your best friend or your worst enemy. When you need to skate fast, the puck is your best friend only if you keep it well out in front of you. This allows you to bend your knees and angle your body well forward. If the puck is too close to your body, which is often the case when stickhandling, you have to straighten up and slow down in order to avoid overskating the puck. In effect, the puck blocks your forward motion. The rule for skating fast with the puck is as follows: *The puck goes first; you follow or chase it.*

Points to Remember

- Begin and end each push with the skates and legs in the V-diamond position.
- Keep your body weight low and angled forward for optimum forward motion.
- Keep the gliding knee well bent throughout each stride for speed and momentum.
- Push to the back and side, and push directly against the entire blade length of the inside edge. Note that some push to the back is always needed. You cannot move in one direction (forward) unless the push begins in the opposite direction (back).
- Begin each push with the pushing skate centered under the power pack. Finish each push with the pushing skate and leg fully extended.
- Prepare for the next push by returning that skate and leg to a point directly under the center of gravity.

Note: The combined movements described in the previous two points constitute the full range of motion of the pushing leg.

- When gliding, make sure the entire blade length of the gliding skate is on the ice. It is impossible to glide—or balance on the gliding skate—when only a portion of the blade is on the ice.

- Keep your hips square to the line of travel (facing straight ahead) and level with (parallel to) the ice.
- Look at the action and keep your head up. You must be able to see what's going on all around you. If you look down at the ice, you might get clocked (checked hard).
- Keep your head relatively still. Don't shake it from side to side.
- Keep your shoulders back, your chest up, and your back straight. If you hunch over, your upper body is as strong as a wet noodle. You can be easily knocked down.
- Once you can move your legs through their full range of motion correctly, practice doing this at progressively faster tempos.
- Goalies must master all skating moves. The forward stride is especially important for goalies. The techniques for pushing across the goal crease are the same as those used for the forward stride (figure 4.10, *a-c*).

Figure 4.10 Goalie using the forward stride across the goal crease: *(a)* release, *(b)* follow-through, and *(c)* recovery.

DRILLS FOR IMPROVING THE FORWARD STRIDE

The drills for improving the forward stride cover each segment of the stride. These drills progress from the simplest to the most complex. You should first practice these drills without a puck and then with a puck.

Note: Once the puck is introduced in a learning situation, skating technique usually deteriorates temporarily. In this book, skating comes first; making puck-handling mistakes is preferable to making skating mistakes. Be patient. *Skating correctly at high speed while carrying a puck is a skill that is honed only after years of practice.*

Windup Drills

The following drills help skaters improve the windup of the forward stride.

The Coil

Basic to Intermediate

This drill enables players to feel the amount of pressure required to dig the edge into the ice at an angle that allows them to push effectively. Players also feel the strain of maintaining that edge while the other skate is off the ice.

The drill is described for coiling on the right skate and preparing to push with that skate. Remember that the foot, skate, ankle, knee, and body weight must all work together to provide a strong cutting edge. Practice the drill equally on each skate.

1. Place the skates and knees in the V-diamond position—heels together and toes apart.
2. Dig in the inside edge of the right skate, and bend your right knee so that your skate, ankle, lower leg, and knee form a strong (45-degree) angle to the ice. The boot should lean halfway down to the ice.
3. Put all your weight on the right skate and lift the left skate off the ice.
4. Balance in place on the right inside edge. Apply strong inward pressure on the edge so that the edge angle does not change as you balance on it. The edge must not wobble from edge to flat, and the blade must not move around (figure 4.11).
5. Now do this while gliding on the forward inside edge of each skate (figure 4.12).

Note: This drill should also be performed backward when working on the backward stride (see chapter 5).

Figure 4.11 The coil drill: balancing on the inside edge.

Figure 4.12 The coil drill: player curving sharply on the inside edge.

1, 2, 3, 4, Push–Glide–Stop

Advanced

This drill improves a player's ability to coil effectively in preparation for pushing. It demands excellent balance and control. The drill is done in a specific rhythm: 1, 2, 3, 4, push–glide–stop.

1. Stand in place with your weight concentrated on the inside edge of the left skate.
2. Roll in the left ankle and bend the left knee. Keep your weight balanced totally on the left skate; now count to four.
3. After the count of four, push with the left skate and leg, and take one stride forward onto the right skate.
4. Stop.
5. Repeat the sequence on the right skate; balance on the inside edge for a count of four before pushing. Take one stride forward onto the left skate, then stop.

Repeat this drill several times. Remember to alternate pushing skates equally.

Windup, Release, and Follow-Through Drills

Because the release and follow-through of *all* skating maneuvers are inseparable, they should always be practiced together.

Note: Every push in the following drills should involve the proper technique for the push of the forward stride (the forward stride-push).

Flat to Inside Edge Drill

Basic to Intermediate

This drill is done skating at a slow to moderate pace; speed is not the goal. The idea is to develop the edging capability needed for an effective push, while at the same time practicing the actual forward stride-push. The action of going from the flat to a strong inside edge simulates that instant of the stride when the gliding skate rolls inward onto a strong inside edge in preparation for pushing. Be sure to practice the drill on each skate equally.

1. Glide forward on the flat of the left skate; the right skate is off the ice.
2. Keep all your weight on the left skate, with the right skate still off the ice. Now quickly roll the left ankle inward and bend the left knee so that the left inside edge cuts deeply (a 45-degree angle) into the ice. The sudden cutting of the left inside edge into the ice will form a sharp semicircular curve in the ice; you will curve clockwise (figure 4.13*a* on page 56).
3. When the left skate begins to curve sharply, push your left leg against the left inside edge (the forward stride-push) and glide forward onto the flat of the right skate.
4. Now quickly roll the right ankle inward and bend the right knee so that the right inside edge cuts deeply into the ice. The sudden cutting of the right inside edge will form a sharp counterclockwise curve (figure 4.13*b*).
5. When the right skate begins to curve sharply, push your right skate and leg against the right inside edge (the forward stride-push) and glide onto the flat of the left skate.

6. You have finished one cycle. Repeat the drill continuously—pushing with one skate and gliding onto the other skate—for the length of the ice. Figure 4.12 on page 54 shows a player curving sharply on the inside edge of the right skate.

Note: If the blade does not roll into a sufficient inside edge, the edge cannot cut into the ice. If this happens, the skate will have an insufficient grip, and it will skid as you attempt to push.

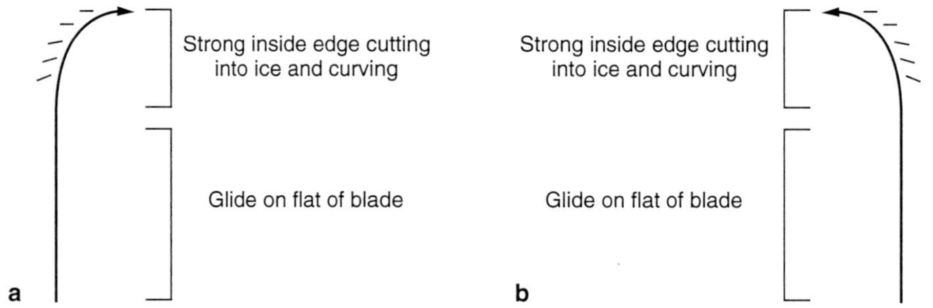

Figure 4.13 Flat to inside edge drill: *(a)* left skate and *(b)* right skate.

Forward Inside Edge Semicircles

Intermediate to Advanced

This drill helps players improve their skill at curving on forward inside edges. It requires skaters to use deep inside edges with strong knee bend, good body control, and excellent balance.

To perform the drill, skate forward from one goal line. Push off with the right skate and leg (the forward stride-push), and glide forward onto the inside edge of the left skate. Curve a complete clockwise semicircle (shape of the letter *U* or *C*) on the LFI. After completing the semicircle, push off with the left skate and leg, and glide forward onto the inside edge of the right skate. Curve a complete counterclockwise semicircle on the RFI. After completing the semicircle, push off with the right skate and leg, and once again glide forward onto the inside edge of the left skate. Skate continuous alternating semicircles for the entire length of the ice (see figure 2.15*a* on page 25).

Note: You *must* complete each semicircle before pushing onto the new gliding skate.

Release and Follow-Through Drills

The drills in this section will help skaters do the following:

- Develop an effective release and follow-through
- Improve the use of inside edges, knee bend, leg drive, and weight shift during the push
- Push more powerfully and effectively (the ultimate objective)

Snap–Stretch

Basic

On every forward skating stride, the muscles of the pushing leg—hip, buttocks, thigh, knee, ankle, and toe—must tighten at the very instant when the pushing leg is locked and fully extended. This tightening indicates that the pushing leg has reached its complete extension and that the toe can push against the ice to achieve the toe flick.

This drill teaches skaters the feeling of full leg extension. The drill is done while standing in place.

1. Stand in the V-diamond position with heels together and toes apart.
2. Bend both knees deeply, keeping your back straight (figure 4.14*a*).
3. Quickly straighten both legs so that both knees lock. Hold your legs in the locked position and feel the tightness in your leg muscles. There should be no crease behind your knees (figure 4.14*b*). This is how the pushing leg feels when fully extended.
4. Repeat the drill, but this time keep the knee of one leg bent (90 degrees) and snap the other (pushing) leg to the back and side until it is locked. Keep the inside edge of the toe on the ice when the leg is snapped at full extension. When locked, the leg is in the position of the fully extended leg during the forward stride (figure 4.14*c*). Keep the leg locked until you feel the tightness of the leg muscles and the amount of distance between the bent (gliding) and extended (pushing) legs. Be sure to keep the hip, knee, and toe of the pushing leg in the turned-out position. Repeat with the other leg.

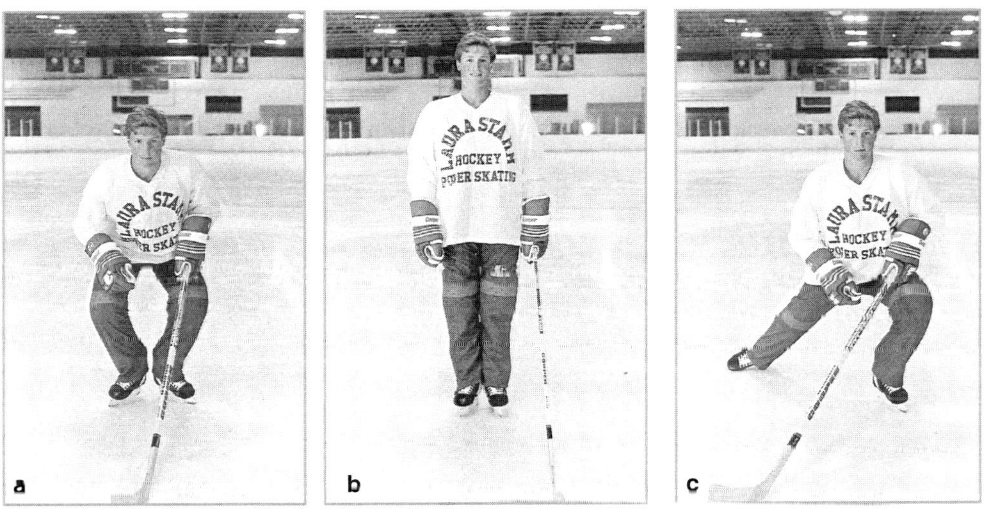

Figure 4.14 Snap–stretch drill: *(a)* body coiled in the V-diamond position; *(b)* legs in the locked position; *(c)* one leg bent, the other leg locked.

Bend–Extend

Intermediate

This drill enables players to practice keeping the knee of the gliding leg bent while the free leg is fully extended.

1. Start from the goal line and skate forward to the first blue line.
2. As you skate, incline your upper body forward so that your chest is lined up above the left (gliding) knee. Keep your back straight and your chest and head up.
3. At the blue line, push with the right skate and leg, and glide onto the left skate. Maintain a deep (90-degree) bend of the left (gliding) knee; the knee should be ahead of the toe. Thrust the right leg to full extension and hold it in this position—right knee locked; hip, knee, and toe turned out; and toe about 1 inch (2.5 cm) off the ice, with the tendon guard pressed into the back of the extended leg (see figure 4.6 on page 47).
4. Hold this position as you glide to the far blue line. When you reach the far blue line, resume skating to the far end of the ice. While skating to the far end of the ice, hold the hockey stick with just the top hand and swing your arms forward and back.
5. Repeat the drill as you skate back down the ice; push with the left skate and leg, and glide on the right skate.

Toe Flick Drill

Intermediate

1. Stand in the V-diamond position while facing and holding onto the boards.
2. Bend one knee deeply, and fully extend the pushing skate and leg.
3. Angle your upper body forward so that your chest lines up above the bent knee.
4. Lock and fully extend the pushing leg. The hip, knee, and toe of the extended leg should be turned outward.
5. Keep the toe (inside edge) on the ice, but lift the heel of the skate about 3 inches (7.6 cm) off the ice (figure 4.15*a*).
6. Curl your toes tightly and arch your foot so that the tendon guard of the boot presses into the back of the extended leg. *Note that this position is essential to achieving the toe flick.*
7. Flick the inside edge of the toe against the ice to lift the skate off the ice (figure 4.15*b*). Figure 4.15*c* demonstrates the incorrect position for the toe flick.

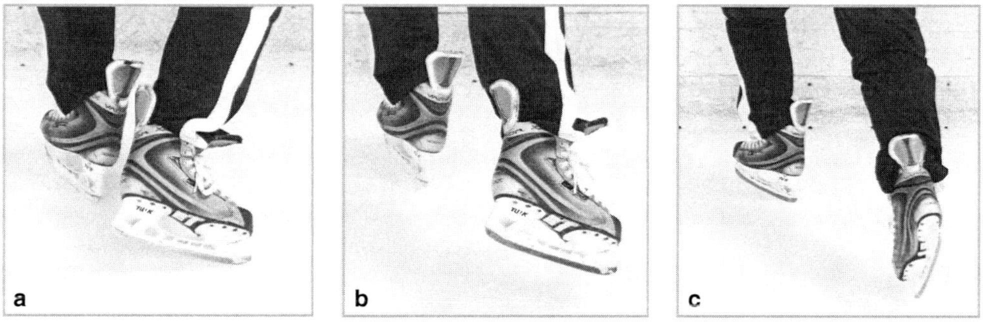

Figure 4.15 Toe flick drill: *(a)* toe on the ice; *(b)* toe flick; *(c)* incorrect position.

Advanced Toe Flick Drill

Advanced

For this drill, the instructor draws a curved arrow on the ice.

1. Stand in place on the ice in the V-diamond position.
2. With the left knee bent, fully extend the right leg so that the hip, knee, and toe of the right (pushing) leg are turned outward. The toe of the extended right blade should fit into the tip of the arrow.
3. Flick the toe into and against the arrow at the finish of the push and as the skate leaves the ice (figure 4.16).

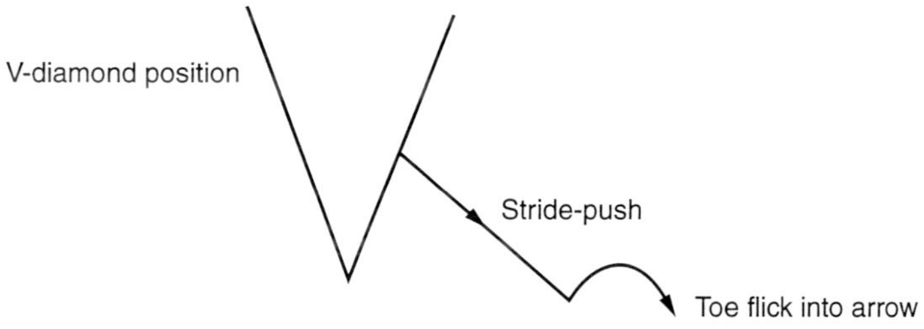

Figure 4.16 Advanced toe flick drill: flicking the right toe into and against the arrow.

Release, Follow-Through, and Return Drills

Snap–Click

Basic

On every forward skating stride, the muscles of the hip, buttock, thigh, knee, ankle, and toe of the pushing leg must tighten at the very instant when the pushing leg is locked and fully extended. This tightening indicates that the pushing leg has reached its complete extension and that the toe can push against the ice to achieve the toe flick. In addition to emphasizing the push, this drill emphasizes the V-diamond position for the return (recovery).

This drill is done while standing in place.

1. Stand in the V-diamond position (see figure 4.14*a* on page 57). With the knee of your standing leg deeply bent, snap the pushing leg out to the back and side until it is locked and fully extended (see figure 4.14*c*).
2. Return the pushing leg back under your body until that heel clicks against the heel of the standing skate. As your heels click, the skates and knees should take the V-diamond position. Be sure to maintain the turnout of the hip, knee, and toe through the return. Remember to return the leg on a path that exactly reverses its outward path.
3. Keep the knee of the standing leg well bent as the pushing skate and leg return and as your heels click together. Figure 4.17 diagrams the push–return sequence (straight out and straight in).
4. Repeat the drill, using the other leg as the pushing leg.
5. Keep repeating the drill in order to develop the correct return motion.

Note: Although the heels do not actually touch each other on the return of a normal stride sequence, they should be only about 1 inch (2.5 cm) apart.

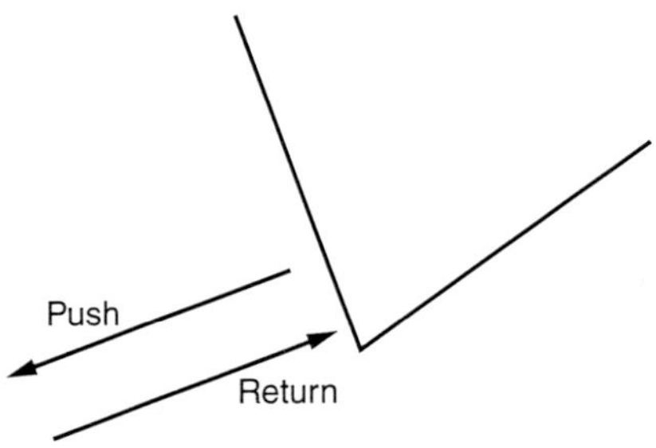

Figure 4.17 Push–return sequence.

Push–Click

Basic to Intermediate

Skate forward. On each stride, concentrate on returning the pushing skate so that your heels click together (magnetize) and your skates and knees are in the V-diamond position. Drive the pushing skate and leg directly against the inside edge, and return them along a straight line that retraces their outward path (see figures 4.2*f* on page 44 and 4.17).

The act of touching the heels together helps you develop the feeling of where your center of gravity is located—and the feeling of when your skates are directly beneath the center of gravity.

DRILLS FOR ALL THE ELEMENTS

The following drills combine training for all the elements of the forward stride: windup, release, follow-through, and return.

One-Leg Push

Basic

Most skaters are stronger and more coordinated on one side of the body than the other. As a result, one leg often achieves more power than the other. The goal is for both legs to become equal in power and effectiveness. This drill can help basic-level skaters accomplish this goal.

Skate forward across the ice, pushing only with the right skate and leg. To prepare for each push, dig the inside edge of the right skate into the ice (at a 45-degree angle), bend the pushing knee deeply (90 degrees), and concentrate your body weight downward and above the inside edge. Thrust powerfully and to full extension on every push. Be sure to finish each push with the toe flick. Return the free skate and leg to the V-diamond position under the center of gravity before pushing again.

Coming back across the ice, push only with the left skate and leg.

Variation (Intermediate)

Perform the previous one-leg push drill, but now use only four pushes to reach the opposite boards. Recover the free skate and leg rapidly and completely after each push to avoid excessive gliding. The goal is to build up speed on each of the four pushes—after each push, you should be traveling faster than you were on the previous push.

Drag–Touch

All Skaters

Drag–touch is one of my signature drills. It has been my favorite drill for 38 years. I created it early in my teaching career and have used it to improve the forward stride of thousands of hockey players, novice to pro. In all my years of teaching, I have never found another drill to be as perfectly suited for teaching the fundamentals and for helping players feel all the elements of the forward stride. Many of my former students (including professional players) still tell me that this is the best drill ever—that it helped them improve and fine-tune their skating more than any other drill did. Other coaches and power skating instructors also recognize how this drill is uniquely suited to helping skaters master the motions of the forward stride; many have incorporated the drill into their training regimens as well.

The drag–touch drill is a feeling drill—it helps players feel

- the leg muscles lock when the pushing leg is fully extended;

- the difference between a correct push and recovery sequence (skate and leg turned out) and an incorrect push and recovery sequence (skate and leg turned straight down);
- the toe flick (or lack of a toe flick);
- the correct straight-out and straight-in motions of the push–recovery sequence; and
- the difference between correct (out and in) and incorrect (back and forward) skating motion.

I call the drill drag–touch in order to abbreviate it. Its full name is drag your toes, touch your heels. Practice this drill properly and diligently. Once you can execute the drill correctly, the object is to skate the same way—except that you do not drag the toe at the finish of the push and you do not actually touch your heels after the return. This takes a long time and lots of practice to master.

Note: In this drill, the skater begins and ends every push in the V-diamond position. The toe of the pushing skate is on the ice at the completion of each push and during each recovery phase. The heels MUST touch each other in the V-diamond position after each return.

To perform the drill, push with the left skate and leg, and glide onto the right skate. Fully extend the left (pushing) leg, and drag the first 2 or 3 inches (5.1 to 7.6 cm) of the left inside edge (the toe) on the ice for about two seconds (figure 4.18*a*). Be sure that the tendon guard of the boot presses into the back of the leg during the drag phase. To drag the toe of the inside edge, the left hip, knee, and toe must be turned outward. If any of them rotate inward, the toe will be forced to point straight down at the ice (toe down, heel up), and you will drag the tiptoe of the skate in a walking or running position. This will result in the pushing leg slipping back.

After dragging the toe when the leg is at full extension, return the left skate back under your body. Bring the heel of the returning skate in until it *touches* the heel of the right (gliding) skate. Continue to drag the toe of the left skate on the ice as the heel returns and touches the heel of the right (gliding) skate. The skates should touch each other with skates and legs in the V-diamond position—heels together, knees and toes apart (figure 4.18*b*). Keep the knee of the gliding leg well bent as the free skate and leg return.

Note: For emphasis, I sometimes tell youngsters to magnetize their heels.

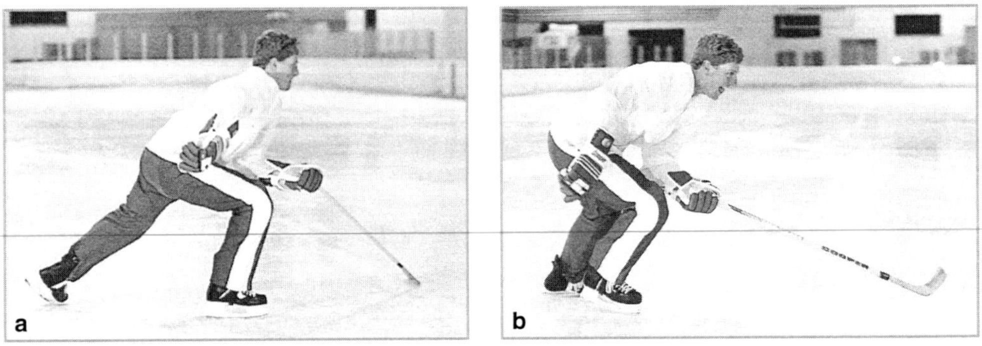

Figure 4.18 Drag–touch drill: *(a)* drag and *(b)* touch.

Repeat, pushing the right leg to full extension. When the right leg reaches full extension, drag the right toe for two seconds before bringing the right heel back to touch the heel of the left (gliding) skate. Skates and legs should once again meet in the V-diamond position.

The purpose of dragging the toes and touching the heels is to *feel* the difference between correct and incorrect execution at every instant of the push–recovery sequence. It's easier to feel what you are doing right and what you are doing wrong when the skates are on the ice than when they are off the ice.

Repeat this drill slowly until you can *feel* each segment of the forward stride and until you can distinguish between correct and incorrect execution at every step along the way. Then do the drill skating a bit faster.

Note: In regular skating, the toes should be no more than an inch (2.5 cm) off the ice at the finish of the push and as the skate returns. In addition, the heels should be no more than 1 inch apart at the completion of the return.

Two additional drills are used as progressions of the drag–touch drill: the stride–touch drill and the drag–touch, stride–touch, stride drill.

Stride–Touch

All Skaters

This drill is the second step in the progression for developing proper technique on the forward stride. It combines the regular forward stride-push with the V-diamond heel-touch recovery.

Finish each push as if it were a normal forward stride-push. Lift the fully extended skate so that the toe is within an inch (2.5 cm) of the ice; the tendon guard should be pressed into the back of the leg. Keep the returning skate within 1 inch of the ice. At the completion of each return, the heels must actually touch each other, with the skates and legs in the V-diamond position.

Drag–Touch, Stride–Touch, Stride

All Skaters

This drill is the third step in the progression for developing proper technique on the forward stride. The movement used in this drill is the actual forward stride.

Note: The only difference between the forward stride and the drag–touch drill is 1 inch (2.5 cm) of lift at the finish of each push and 1 inch of distance between the heels on each recovery.

For this drill, do not drag your toes or touch your heels. However, you should incorporate all the elements of the drag–touch drill in order to create an identically executed stride. When you complete the return of the free skate, the heels of the skates should be no farther than 1 inch apart, and the skates and legs should be in the V-diamond position.

Now skate fast, striving for perfect execution. Keep the skates close to the ice throughout each push–return sequence. Apply the techniques learned in the drag–touch drill; *these are the exact techniques of the forward stride.* Swing your arms properly and fully.

One-Leg Drag–Touch

Basic to Intermediate

Do the one-leg push drill (page 61), but now drag the toe (front of the inside edge) on the ice at the finish of each push. Skating across the ice, push each time with the right skate and leg. Drag the toe on the ice—with the heel about 3 inches (7.6 cm) off the ice—on each push. Press the tendon guard of the boot into the back of your leg on each push. Keep the toe of the blade on the ice as the heel returns to the V-diamond position. At the completion of the return, the heel of the returning skate *must* touch (make contact with) the heel of the gliding skate, with the skates and legs in the V-diamond position. Keep the knee of the gliding leg well bent during the return. Maintain the turnout of the hip, knee, and toe of the pushing leg during each push–return sequence.

Coming back across the ice, push each time with the left skate and leg.

RESISTANCE DRILLS

Resistance drills work on all the elements of the stride. The benefit of resistance drills is that they force skaters to dig deeply into the ice, to push extremely hard, and to recover correctly and completely.

Partner Resistance Drill

Basic to Intermediate

The object of this resistance drill is to feel the working of the edges, knees, legs, and body weight. The drill will also help you develop powerful leg drive and become accustomed to feeling the digging action of the blades before each thrust. Don't try to go fast. Concentrate instead on pushing correctly and powerfully.

1. Partner up with another player. Face each other and stand along the sideboards, holding a hockey stick horizontally between you.
2. The pushing player skates forward; the resisting (backward) skater resists the forward skater's movement by braking with a backward two-foot snowplow (described in chapter 8, page 176).
3. To move the resisting skater, the forward skater must turn both skates and knees into an exaggerated V-diamond position, with the knees well bent and with the inside edge of the pushing skate digging strongly into the ice. Body weight must be concentrated downward over the inside edge of the pushing skate.
4. Push hard, drive each push to full extension, and return each skate and leg to the V-diamond position to prepare for the next push.
5. Take turns pushing and resisting.

Variation—Resistance Drag–Touch (Basic to Intermediate)

Do the previous resistance drill using the technique described for the drag–touch drill to pull the resisting player across the ice.

The backward skater must provide enough resistance so the forward skater has to work hard to move, but not so much that the forward skater cannot move at all. The forward skater should be challenged to use correct edging, knee bend, leg drive, and body weight in order to move the resisting skater across the ice. As you push the resisting player across the ice, keep your shoulders back and your chest and head up (figure 4.19).

Note: When skating normally, use the same amount of edge, downward concentration of weight, and leg drive as when pushing a resisting skater.

Figure 4.19 Partner resistance drill.

Variation—Choo-Choo (Basic to Intermediate)

Instead of pushing a resisting player, you will pull a resisting player. Both skaters prepare to skate forward, holding onto their hockey sticks as shown in figure 4.20. The trailing player stands behind the pulling player and resists movement with a forward snowplow. The pulling skater must work against this resistance. Pull the resisting player across the ice using the forward stride. (The forward snowplow is described on page 171 in chapter 8.)

Figure 4.20 Choo-choo drill.

Variation—Choo-Choo on Knees (Basic to Intermediate)

Instead of resisting with a forward snowplow, the resisting player sits on his or her knees, positioned behind the front (pulling) skater (figure 4.21). Both players hold onto the ends of both of their hockey sticks. You, the forward skater, will pull the resisting player across the ice. Concentrate on using correct technique while pulling the resisting player across the ice. When you reach the opposite sideboards, switch so that the other player can now pull you across the ice.

Note: Both skaters must keep their heads up at all times.

Figure 4.21 Choo-choo on knees drill.

Variation—One-Leg Resistance Drill (Basic to Intermediate)

Perform the previous resistance drills, but use the same skate and leg to push as you pull the resisting player across the ice. When you reach the opposite sideboards, switch so that the other player can pull you back across the ice. Repeat this drill several times so that both legs will have the opportunity to be the pushing leg.

Resistance Drag–Touch

Basic to Intermediate

Perform the partner resistance drill on page 64 with this difference: Do the drag–touch drill as you pull the resisting player. Drag your toes and touch your heels in the V-diamond position on each push–recovery sequence. The tendon guard should press into the back of your leg at the full extension of each push.

Variation—One-Leg Resistance Drag–Touch (Basic to Intermediate)

Perform the previous resistance drills, but now use the same skate and leg to push or pull the resisting player across the ice. Come back across the ice, pushing with the other skate and leg. Drag your toes and touch your heels in the V-diamond position on each push–recovery sequence. The tendon guard should press into the back of your leg at the full extension of each push. Push equally with each leg!

Resistance 1, 2, 3, 4, Drag–Touch–Stop

Advanced

This drill enables skaters to work on all the elements of the forward stride—the windup, release, follow-through, and return. It demands great balance, power, and control. The drill is done in a specific rhythm: 1, 2, 3, 4, drag–touch–stop. Only one stride is performed at a time.

1. Partner up with another player. Stand at the sideboards, prepared to push the resisting (backward) skater as in the resistance drag–touch drill.
2. Roll in the ankle and bend the knee of the pushing leg, with your weight situated totally over the pushing skate. In this position, count to four.
3. After counting to 4, push once and take one stride forward. You should be able to move the resisting player.
4. At full extension, momentarily drag the toe of the pushing skate and then quickly return it so that the heels touch each other in the V-diamond position.
5. Stop.
6. Repeat with the other skate.
7. Alternate pushing legs as you push across the ice.
8. When you reach the opposite sideboards, switch positions with your partner; coming back across the ice, the other player pushes and you resist.

FORWARD C-CUTS

I created the term *C-cuts,* along with the drill, in 1971. It was described in my first book, *Power Skating the Hockey Way* (1977). The term *C-cuts* quickly became known and commonly used by hockey and skating coaches everywhere in North America. The C-cuts drill is still done at all my clinics. It remains one of my signature drills.

The C-cut refers to a push. I named the push a C-cut because in executing the push, the pushing skate scribes a cut in the ice that is similar to the letter *C* (a semicircular arc). The C-cut push is a very powerful push and is used in many hockey situations. It is used for backward as well as forward skating moves.

In executing a forward C-cut push, the pushing skate first drives to the back; it then curves out to the side until the leg is fully extended. Then it moves forward, and finally curves back to its starting position beneath the midline of the body to complete the C.

The C-cut drill incorporates numerous important skating and training fundamentals:

- Using inside edges to cut powerfully and forcefully into the ice in order to push.
- Pushing first to the back and then to the side rather than directly back.
- Training the body to experience a fully extended, straightened free leg and a maximum-effort thrust (rather than a partially extended leg and a weaker push).
- Training the gliding and pushing legs to work independently of each other (coordination). While the glide is a straight line forward and on a well-bent knee, the push is semicircular, and the pushing leg straightens (extends fully) at the completion of the push.
- Using the heel to begin each push of the forward stride. Too many skaters do not properly use the heel to begin each push. The C-cut push is executed specifically with the back half of the blade. The toe of the blade is *not* used in a C-cut push; *there is no toe flick!*
- Pushing to full extension. The push is completed only when the pushing leg is fully extended outward and away from the body. As always, full extension is based on a knee bend of 90 degrees on the gliding leg.
- Determining the difference in strength and coordination between the strong and weak leg in order to work on equalizing them.
- Conditioning the quadriceps. The C-cut drill employs the thigh muscles and forces them to work exceptionally hard.
- Preparing for more difficult maneuvers—such as tight turns, pivots, and bulling (see chapter 9)—that employ the forward C-cut push.
- Learning to execute the backward C-cut push of the backward stride. The push–glide sequence of backward C-cuts is exactly the reverse of forward C-cuts (see figure 5.3 on page 84).

Forward C-Cuts Drill

All Skaters

The forward C-cut maneuver is done with both skates on the ice at all times. The push forms an upside-down letter *C*. The push begins at the bottom of the C and ends at the top of the C. The drill is described for pushing first with the left skate and leg. It is diagrammed in figure 4.22. It is important to keep your back straight throughout this drill.

1. Glide forward on the flats of both skates, with your feet directly under your body.
2. Prepare to push with the left leg and to glide straight ahead on the flat of the right skate.
3. Keep your weight on the back half of the left (pushing) skate.
4. Bend your knees and dig the inside edge of the left skate into the ice; the pushing skate and knee should form a 45-degree angle to the ice. Concentrate your body weight over the inside edge and simultaneously pivot the left skate outward (toe facing out to the side) so that your skates approximate a right angle (heels together, toes apart). This is the windup of the forward C-cut push (figure 4.22*a*). You are now prepared to execute a C-cut push (figure 4.23*a* on page 70).
5. Cut (push) the letter *C* into the ice with the left skate; push first to the back, then out to the side until the pushing leg is fully extended (figures 4.22*b* and 4.23, *b-c*).
6. At the midpoint of the C-cut push, transfer your weight onto the right skate, which is gliding straight ahead on the flat of the blade.
7. Thrust powerfully and to full extension. Keep the pushing skate on the ice after the push is completed. The knee of the gliding leg remains well bent even when the pushing leg is fully extended.
8. After the left leg reaches its full extension, repivot the left skate inward. The left skate should now be pigeon-toed inward (facing the gliding skate). This step is necessary in order to return the skate to its starting position under your body (figures 4.22*c* and 4.23*d*).
9. Move the left skate and leg forward and then back into their starting position, centered underneath your body (figure 4.23*e*).
10. After the return, the skates should be side by side and centered under your body.
11. After returning, the left skate becomes the new gliding skate, and the right skate becomes the new pushing skate. Position your weight on the inside edge of the right skate, and prepare to cut a reverse and upside-down letter *C* with the right skate. Pivot the right skate (toe outward); push first to the back, and then out to the side until the right leg is fully extended. Then repivot the right skate inward (pigeon-toed position), and move the skate forward and then back into its starting position, centered under your body.

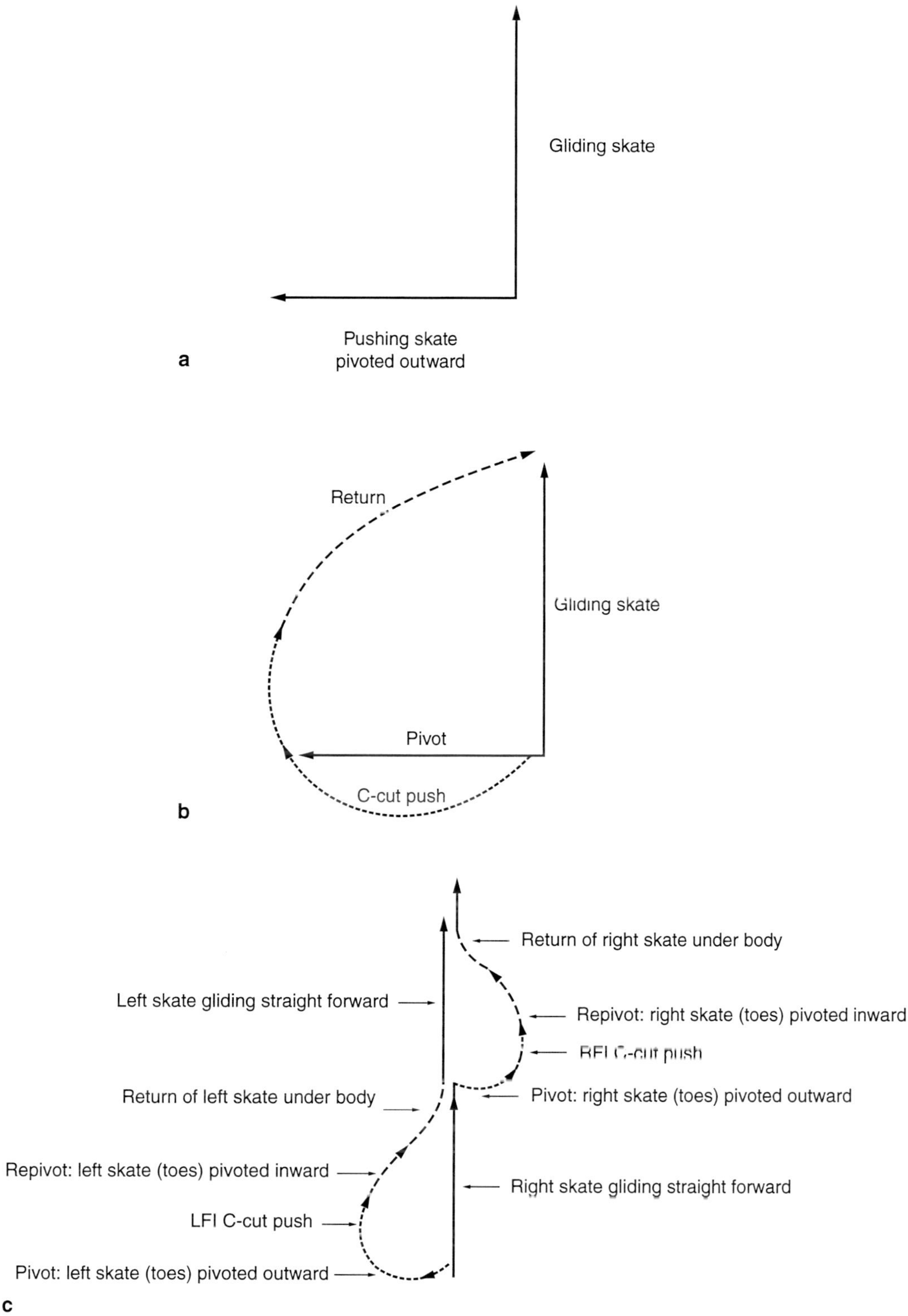

Figure 4.22 Forward C-cuts: *(a)* windup, *(b)* C-cut, and *(c)* full pattern of the forward C-cut.

Figure 4.23 Forward C-cut sequence: *(a)* pivot, *(b)* push, *(c)* full extension, *(d)* repivot, and *(e)* return.

Note: The forward C-cut push starts at the bottom end of the C. Push first to the back, then out to the side, then forward, and finally around and inward to the starting point under the center of gravity.

Remember: The pushing leg must be locked and fully extended out to the side at the midpoint of the C, but it must be coiled and centered under your body at the beginning and end points (which correspond respectively to the windup and return of each push). Keep the knee of the *gliding* leg well bent as you return the pushing skate and leg.

Points to Remember

- Keep the hips facing straight ahead (square). If the hips turn sideways or wiggle from side to side, you will skate like a snake, and forward motion will be impeded.
- The push is a C-*cut,* not a silent C. The skate must *cut* into the ice; you should hear the cutting sound. This indicates that your weight is over the pushing skate and that the inside edge is gripping the ice strongly. A well-executed C-cut is an extremely powerful push.

- The gliding skate must point straight ahead and glide on the flat of the blade as the pushing skate pivots, cuts the C, repivots, and returns. If both skates turn the same way, you will skate in a snakelike S formation; this will slow you down. Remember, the fastest way to travel between two points is in a straight line!
- The initiation of every push is opposite from the direction of travel. The forward C-cut push is first to the back, and then out to the side.
- The push is completed when the pushing skate and leg reach full extension. After this point and during the return, the skate no longer cuts into (pushes against) the ice, and power is no longer generated (or needed). The skate glides back to center under the body.
- Since the toe is not used for the forward C-cut push, there is no toe flick.
- When doing forward C-cuts from a stop or when traveling very slowly, the direction of the C-cut push is almost perpendicular to and opposite the line of travel. The angle of the push decreases with speed. At top speeds, the direction of the forward C-cut push is approximately 45 degrees from the line of travel.

Variations of Forward C-Cuts Drill

Forward C-Cuts Along the Lines (Basic)

Perform forward C-cuts across the ice, using the hockey lines as guides for the gliding skate. The gliding skate must travel straight forward along the hockey line as the pushing skate cuts each C-cut. At the completion of each C-cut push, the pushing skate must return and *touch* the gliding skate. As they touch, the two skates should line up with and be next to each other. See the pattern in figure 4.24.

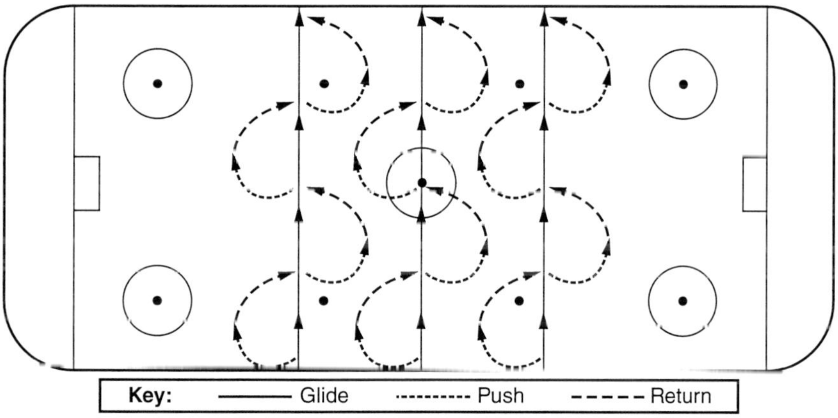

Figure 4.24 Forward C-cuts along the lines.

One-Leg Forward C-Cuts Along the Lines (Basic to Intermediate)

Perform the previous drill, but execute each C-cut push with the right skate and leg. Coming back across the ice, execute each C-cut push with the left skate and leg (figure 4.25). At the completion of each recovery, the returning skate must touch the gliding skate as in the previous drill.

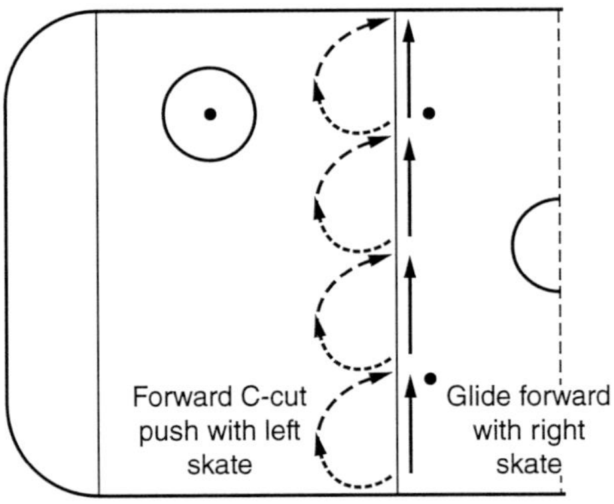

Figure 4.25 One-leg forward C-cuts along the lines.

Resistance Forward C-Cuts Along the Lines (Intermediate)

In this drill, you must stop after each return. Use the hockey lines as guides for the gliding skate. The gliding skate travels straight along the line as the pushing skate performs the forward C-cut. Pull a resisting player across the ice as in the choo-choo drill (described on page 65).

At the completion of each C-cut push, the pushing skate must return and touch the gliding skate. As the skates touch, they should line up with and be next to each other. After the skates touch each other, STOP! Now execute the C-cut push with the other skate and leg. *Be sure to come to a complete stop after each C-cut push.*

One-Leg Resistance Forward C-Cuts Along the Lines (Intermediate to Advanced)

Perform the resistance forward C-cuts along the lines drill, pushing each time with the right skate and leg. When the skate returns, it must touch the left (gliding) skate. As the skates touch, they should line up with and be next to each other. After the skates touch each other, STOP! Then do another C-cut with the same (right) leg and stop after the skates touch each other. Continue this until you reach the opposite boards.

Remember: After each return, come to a complete stop before doing the next C-cut push.

Coming back across the ice, do each C-cut push with the left skate and leg; stop after the skates touch each other.

Forward C-Cuts While Restricting the Arms (Intermediate to Advanced)

Perform forward C-cuts while holding a hockey stick horizontally behind your back—in the crooks of your elbows (figure 4.26). Do not let the stick move around. This variation eliminates the use of the arms and shoulders and forces the legs to do all the work.

Figure 4.26 Forward C-cuts while restricting the arms.

Forward C-Cuts Around the Ice (Intermediate to Advanced)

On the straightaways, perform alternating forward C-cuts; do a forward C-cut push with the left skate while gliding straight forward on the right skate, then do a forward C-cut push with the right skate while gliding straight forward on the left skate. To accelerate around the corners, do four or five consecutive forward C-cut pushes with the *outside* skate. The inside skate creates the curve by gliding continuously on its outside edge. See chapter 6 for information about curving on outside edges and the proper body positioning for skating curves.

Note: When you are skating counterclockwise around the corners, the right skate and leg do the C-cut pushes while the left skate glides continuously on its outside edge. When you are skating clockwise, the left skate and leg do the C-cut pushes while the right skate glides continuously on its outside edge.

Forward Shuffle Step

Intermediate to Advanced

The forward shuffle step is a very popular stickhandling move. The shuffle step is actually a preparatory move that is performed when players are faking or preparing to make a sudden move. It is called a shuffle step because the skates shuffle rather than push. These shuffle steps are actually mini-C-cuts, and the skates are always wide apart. Shuffle steps include only the first half of the C-cut—there is no return portion. As in all forward C-cuts, shuffle steps are done with the heels of the skates.

To perform the drill, start from the goal line and skate forward to the first blue line. At the first blue line, do a series of shuffle steps to the far blue line. At the far blue line, skate forward to the far goal line.

STRIDE TEMPOS: RAPID STRIDE VERSUS LONG STRIDE

All strides should be *full* strides. The difference between a rapid stride and a long stride is leg speed—in other words, the amount of time spent gliding. Rapid strides are comparable to those used in sprint running, when a sudden burst of speed over a relatively short distance is required.

The rapidity (tempo) of strides is determined by how quickly the skates and legs move and change as they push and recover. In hockey, this is referred to as *leg turnover.* The faster the legs change, the shorter the time spent gliding. Knee bend, edges, leg extension, and effort expended in pushing remain the same. The pushing leg must drive to full extension and return fully under the body even when leg motion is very rapid. In addition, the tempo of the legs during each push–return cycle should also be the same. Power is lost if one leg pushes fully and the other leg pushes only partially. The same is true if one leg moves rapidly and the other moves slowly.

Hockey often requires very rapid strides—for example, when starting explosively, accelerating from slow to fast, or bursting out on a breakaway. However, at certain times, slower leg speed is called for, such as when you have reached top speed and want to maintain it, or when you do not need to skate at top speed. In these situations, the legs move somewhat slower, but the strides are technically the same.

The following drills are designed for players who have attained a certain degree of competence on the forward stride—these drills are not appropriate for basic-level skaters. The main purpose of these drills is to help skaters develop correct technique at varying stride tempos and to help them develop balance and control at all stride tempos. Apply these drills to all skating maneuvers.

Long Glides

Intermediate to Advanced

As mentioned, all strides should be long, or full, strides; therefore, we will refer to long glides rather than long strides.

Skate three or four laps around the rink. Pick up speed on the corners using four or five forward crossovers. As you approach the blue line, use rapid strides. At the first blue line, push once with the right skate and leg and then glide on the left skate until you reach the red line. Keep the free leg fully extended until you reach the red line. At the red line, repeat the movement, switching feet and legs. Push once with the left skate and leg, and glide on the right skate, keeping the free leg fully extended until you reach the next blue line. The idea is to maintain speed and balance for the entire length of the glide. If you use the edges properly and push hard, you should be able to maintain speed on each glide.

When you reach the second blue line, use rapid strides to skate to the far end of the ice. Accelerate around the corners by doing four or five crossovers. When you are back at the first blue line on the other side of the ice, repeat the long glides. Move your arms diagonally forward and backward in line with and in rhythm with your legs. Keep the hockey stick on the ice, holding it with just your top hand. Reverse your direction around the rink and repeat the drill.

Remember: When doing drills that include the use of crossovers always alternate directions.

Note: Small skaters should use two strides from blue line to red line and two strides from red line to blue line.

Varying Stride Tempos

Intermediate to Advanced

Start from the goal line and skate forward for the length of the ice. Vary stride tempos as follows:

1. Between the goal line and the near blue line, take 8 to 10 rapid strides.
2. From blue line to blue line, take 4 strides.
3. Between the far blue line and the far goal line, take only 2 strides.

Maintain speed even when doing the very long glides. Push to full extension. Swing your arms diagonally forward and backward in line with and in rhythm with your legs. Keep the hockey stick on the ice, holding it with just your top hand.

The number of strides needed may vary. For example, younger players may need 12, 6, and 4 strides, respectively, from goal line to blue line, blue line to blue line, and blue line to goal line. Advanced players may need fewer.

Stride and Control

Advanced

This drill is excellent for improving balance and control on glides. It is similar to the drill for long glides.

Skate counterclockwise around the rink. Use four or five forward crossovers to accelerate on the corner. Immediately after coming out of the corner, skate to the near face-off circle; push once with the right skate and leg, and glide to the center red line on the left skate. At the red line, push once with the left skate and leg, and glide on the right skate to the face-off circle at the far end of the ice. Use powerful, rapid crossovers to accelerate on the corner, and then repeat the sequence. Keep the free leg fully extended during all glides. Try to maintain speed on the two long glides. Repeat the drill, now skating around the rink in a clockwise direction.

Because this drill involves using only two strides for the length of the ice (from near face-off circle to far face-off circle), it demands extremely powerful pushes and maximum acceleration around the corners. Balance and upper body control are essential. Smaller skaters may need to take four to six strides for each length of the ice. Again, the numbers are an approximation and depend on age and ability.

Note: This drill should also be used to practice forward crossovers. See chapter 6 for information about executing forward crossovers and the proper body positioning for skating curves.

Rapid Leg Tempos

Advanced

After you learn to push properly and powerfully, your legs may push effectively but not quickly enough. The challenge for every player is to develop powerful and rapid leg tempos while maintaining correct technique. As your leg speed increases, experiment using rhythms that put you temporarily out of control—first without a puck, then while controlling a puck. This is called *overspeed skating* and is an essential part of hockey training. Remember, correct technique plus rapid leg speed is the goal. One without the other is inadequate.

Note: All strides must be full strides. Work on increasing the tempo (rhythm) at which you move your legs while still moving your legs through their full range of motion. Remember: Leg tempo must not diminish the length of the stride.

Varying Leg Tempos

Intermediate to Advanced

To improve versatility, practice skating powerfully to many different tempos of music. This will help you skate rhythmically. Swing your arms in a diagonal motion forward and backward, always in line and in rhythm with the legs.

Leg tempo is different for each person. It varies according to one's body type and leg length. Short and tall players have completely different styles and leg tempos. If tall players move their legs too fast for their leg lengths, they reduce their ability to achieve full range of motion. Concentrate on developing powerful and rapid leg drive while still moving the legs through their full range of motion. Move your legs as rapidly as possible. But remember that leg tempo is unique to each individual and must accommodate your body type and leg length.

RESTRICTING THE ARMS

Restricting the use of the arms during stride drills helps emphasize and develop correct use of the legs, especially when skating with two hands on the stick and when controlling the puck. Too many players lose their stride when skating with the puck because they can't use their legs independently of their arms. The following drills restrict arm movement and train the legs to work independently of the arms.

Restricting Arms Drill 1

Intermediate to Advanced

Skate forward, holding the hockey stick horizontally behind your back (in the crooks of your elbows). Or, use no stick at all and clasp your hands on your belly or behind your back. You may also hold the stick horizontally (chest high) with your arms extended straight out in front of you. Keep your upper body still and your chest facing straight ahead while skating in these positions.

Restricting Arms Drill 2

Intermediate to Advanced

Practice skating at top speed while holding the hockey stick with both hands and keeping the stick on the ice. Keep the stick out in front of you (figure 4.27). Practice this without the puck and then with the puck. Push powerfully and rapidly, and try to achieve speed from your legs alone.

Once you can move your legs properly and powerfully without the aid of your arms, skate while holding the hockey stick with just your top hand. Keep the stick on the ice and well out in front of you. Swing your arms diagonally forward and backward, in line with and in rhythm with your legs (see figure 4.9*a* on page 51).

Figure 4.27 Restricting the arms by holding the hockey stick with both hands.

Chapter 5

Backward Stride for Mobility on Defense

The ability to skate straight backward *fast* is essential not just for defenders but for all players. All players are placed in defensive situations from time to time. If backward speed is inadequate, the opposing team has a distinct advantage.

Some players always use backward crossovers when skating backward. They think they can go faster this way than when skating straight backward. However, backward crossovers can be dangerous when used in tight situations. One of the cardinal rules in hockey is that a defender should never make the first move! Crossing over before a forward has committed to a particular direction constitutes as making the first move. The opposing forward knows that the defender has provided an opening, and the forward can take advantage of this mistake by skating quickly in the opposite direction.

Here are two game situations in which using backward crossovers is a definite no-no:

1. A forward with the puck races up the ice. The defender backs up, crossing over one way, then the other. When a player is doing alternating backward crossovers, each crossover step must be followed by a third (neutralizing) step outward in the same direction. This neutralizing step uncrosses the skates and brings them side by side. Only when the skates are side by side can the defender take another stride backward. In close situations, if a defender gets caught with his or her skates crossed over, a shifty forward may recognize this as an opportunity to cut the other way and escape.

2. A forward with the puck races up the ice. The defender backs up, planning to stay in front of the forward and prevent that forward from breaking free. But in backing up, the defender crosses over and puts all his or her weight on the skate that has just crossed over. I call this the pretzel syndrome because the defender's skates and legs are twisted up like a pretzel. The defender has only one option—to use the neutralizing step outward in the same direction. If the defender tries to cross the other skate over and go back in the original direction without taking the neutralizing step, this almost guarantees a fall. I've seen these blunders in critical games—even in Stanley Cup *final* games. These defensive mistakes always create opportunities for the opposing forward to break free and score a goal. Big mistake!

> **COACHING TIP**
>
> Defenders should never make the first move.

Backward crossovers are an excellent way to accelerate backward from a stop or to change gears from slow to fast. But once speed has been built up, players should skate backward using the straight backward stride. In this way, defenders can more readily stay directly in front of onrushing players while keeping their feet in a neutral position. This gives defenders a better chance of staying with, tracking, and moving with opposing players. It helps them follow an opponent's direction and prevent the opponent from escaping.

As in the forward stride, rapid leg turnover alone does not ensure speed. Correct technique applied powerfully, along with rapid leg speed, is the critical combination.

The push of the backward stride is the backward C-cut push, which is done in reverse of the forward C-cut push described in chapter 4. In doing a backward C-cut push, the pushing skate first moves to the front (opposite the direction of travel), then out to the side until the pushing leg reaches full extension. The skate then moves around and then inward to its endpoint beneath the midline of the body. In other words, the push now starts from the top of the C and works down to the bottom of the C.

Just as in the forward stride, the four-part procedure of windup, release, follow-through, and return is important for power and speed on the backward stride. And the elements that are necessary for speed when skating forward—the proper use of edges, knee bend, leg drive, body weight, weight shift, arm swing, and glide—are also necessary for speed when skating backward.

WINDUP

Each backward C-cut push begins with a coiling action. The pushing skate must be under the center of gravity and must dig into the ice with a strong (45-degree) inside edge; the knees must be well bent (90 degrees). The upper body is held in an almost vertical position, with the shoulders held back and the body weight on the front halves of the blades.

To perform the windup for the backward stride, complete these steps (the backward C-cut push is described for pushing with the left skate and leg):

1. Glide backward on the flats of both skates, with the skates directly under your body.
2. Prepare to push with the left skate and leg. Place your weight above the left (pushing) skate and bend your knees deeply (approximately 90 degrees). The knee of the pushing skate should be out ahead of that toe.
3. Pivot the left (pushing) skate outward (heel facing out to the side) so that your skates approximate a right angle, or an upside-down and reversed letter *L* (toes together, heels apart) (figure 5.1, *a-b*). Pivoting the pushing skate is critical to the C-cut push.
4. Dig the inside edge of the left (pushing) skate into the ice by rolling in the ankle and bending the knee. The skate and lower leg should form a

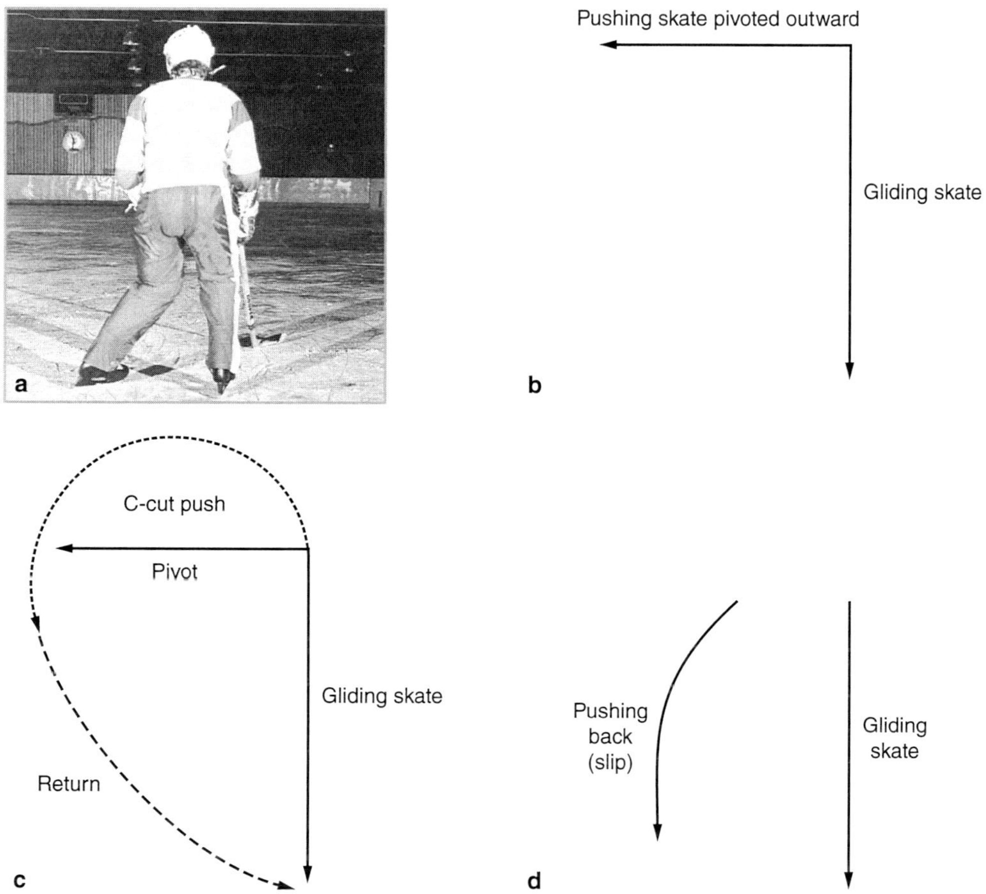

Figure 5.1 Backward C-cut: *(a)* pivot of the backward C-cut; *(b)* pivot; *(c)* push and return; *(d)* incorrect movement.

45-degree angle to the ice. Body weight must be totally concentrated over the pushing skate. You are now coiled to push.

RELEASE

The backward C-cut push is made by cutting an upside-down C into the ice. The push starts from the top of the C. The skate and leg drive first to the front (upward), then out to the side.

1. Push forcefully, using the front half of the blade to execute the push. Start the push with the middle of the inside edge, and finish it with the toe of the inside edge (figures 5.1*c* and 5.2, *a-b*, on page 83). Figure 5.1*d* shows a slip, which results from pushing back rather than upward and outward.
2. At approximately the midpoint of the push, transfer your weight from the left (pushing) skate onto the right (gliding) skate. Because you are skating backward, the body weight is situated over the front half of the gliding skate. However, the *entire* blade length must stay in contact with the ice.

3. Thrust to full extension (figure 5.2*b*). Push forcefully and explosively. Remember that the inside edge must *cut* into the ice in order to deliver an effective push.

FOLLOW-THROUGH

As in the forward stride, the push is completed only when the pushing skate and leg have reached full extension. The final push comes from the front of the inside edge (toe). The locking of the pushing skate and leg coincides with the toe flick of the inside edge. This is a modified toe flick since the heel of the blade does not lift from the ice on the C-cut push. This combination constitutes an effective follow-through (figure 5.2*b*). Trial and error is necessary to help you feel your point of full extension.

1. Finish the push with the front of the inside edge, but keep the entire blade length of the thrusting skate on the ice at the completion of the push.

   Note:

   - If the heel lifts off the ice, the front tip of the blade may catch the ice, and you may fall forward. Even if you don't fall, the recovery phase will be affected because you will be off balance.
   - If you finish the push with the middle of the blade (or even farther back than the middle) rather than with the toe of the inside edge, your weight is likely to be thrown backward, and again, you might fall.
2. Keep the knee of the gliding leg well bent as the pushing skate and leg fully extend and return to the center of gravity.
3. Glide straight backward on the flat of the blade during the push and recovery phases.
4. Keep the entire blade length of the gliding skate in contact with the ice. If the heel lifts off the ice, you may fall forward over the curved toe of the blade.

RETURN

The return of the backward C-cut is exactly opposite from the push. Since the push is a semicircular motion (up and out), the return is also a semicircular motion (around and in), as shown in figure 5.1*c* on page 81. As in the forward stride, the return is an essential part of the backward stride and must not be neglected. Only *complete* leg recovery can set up a powerful next push.

1. After the pushing leg reaches full extension, the pushing skate (now the free skate) must return rapidly to a position under the center of gravity in preparation for the next push. To initiate the return, repivot the left heel inward. The repivot is essential to bringing the free skate back to its starting position under the body (figure 5.2*c*).

2. Draw (pull) the returning skate in under the power pack. A complete return of the free skate completes the C (figure 5.2*d*). Keep the entire blade length on the ice as the skate returns.
3. After the return, make sure the skates are side by side and under your body.

Note: Do not allow the returning skate to move past or behind the gliding skate. This will pull your hips to the side, forcing you to move in a snakelike pattern.

4. The right skate is now prepared to push, and the left skate is prepared to become the new gliding skate. The C is now done in reverse. Put your weight over the inside edge of the right skate, bend your knees, and pivot the right heel outward (figure 5.2*e*). To execute the right C-cut, mirror the procedures for the windup, release, follow-through, and return described for the left C-cut; push to full extension (figure 5.2*f*).

Figure 5.2 Backward stride sequence: *(a)* release, *(b)* follow-through, *(c)* repivot, *(d)* return, *(e)* windup, and *(f)* follow-through.

Points to Remember

Following are some important points to remember when practicing the backward stride.

- The gliding skate travels in a straight line backward, while the pushing skate and leg push and return in a semicircular (C-shaped) motion (figure 5.3 on page 84).

- The gliding skate must be situated directly under the body weight in order to glide straight backward.
- The skate preparing to glide must progress—that is, move slightly ahead of the current gliding skate (when skating backward, this means behind you)—before taking the ice as the new gliding skate. The skate should move approximately three-quarters of a blade length ahead of the current gliding skate.
- Push the C-cut first to the front (forward) and then out to the side. When you are skating backward from a complete stop or traveling very slowly, the angle of the pushing blade to the ice is almost perpendicular to the line of travel, and the push is almost opposite the direction of travel. The angle of the push decreases with speed. At top speeds, the direction of the backward C-cut push is approximately 45 degrees from the line of travel. The precise direction is determined by the direction the blade is facing on the ice (angle of turnout of the blade edge).
- At the full extension of each push, the thrusting skate should be as far away from your body as it will reach, and the entire leg (hip, buttocks, thigh, knee, calf, ankle, and toe) should be locked. The toe of the inside edge provides the finish of the push. The modified toe flick provides the final thrust, similar to the forward stride. Keep the knee of the gliding leg bent strongly during the push and return phases.

Note: As always, full extension is based on a strong knee bend (90 degrees) of the gliding leg.

- Cut the C into the ice only to the point of full extension. The return phase of the C is not a push; it is a glide. If you attempt to cut the ice during the second half of the C (the recovery phase), you will be forced to push in opposition to your motion and will end up going slower.

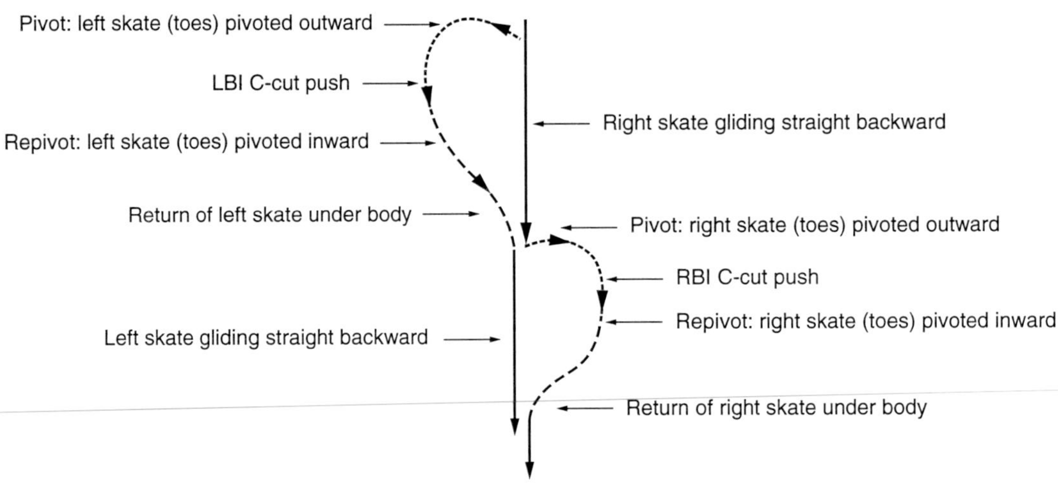

Figure 5.3 Pattern of the backward C-cut.

- Keep the entire blade lengths of both the pushing and gliding skate in full contact with the ice. Lifting one or both heels off the ice causes the body to pitch forward over the curved toes.
- The knee of the pushing leg snaps into the fully extended position at a point corresponding to the middle of the C. However, this knee must be well bent and coiled under your body at the beginning and end points of the C, which correspond to the windup and return points, respectively, of the push.
- Keep your shoulders back, your back straight (almost vertical), your head up, and your eyes ahead. If you have to lean on your stick to prevent yourself from falling, you have either lifted your heels, leaned too far forward, dropped your head, or all of the above.
- Keep your hips square (facing straight ahead) throughout each stride. As in all skating, you travel where your hips face—if you turn them sideways as you cut each C, you will wiggle from side to side.
- Hold the hockey stick with just the top hand and keep the stick on the ice and out in front of you. Move your arms in a diagonal direction forward and backward, in line and in rhythm with your legs (as in the forward stride). As the left leg pushes to the front and side, the left arm drives back; as the right leg pushes to the front and side, the right arm drives back.
- The one-third principle does not apply when skating backward because the push is mainly from the front half of the blade. *If you miss the first half of the push (caused by incomplete leg recovery), you lose 50 percent of the push. If you miss the toe flick, you lose 50 percent. Correct and complete execution is imperative.*

COACHING TIP

The fastest way to travel between two points is in a straight line. Since the gliding skate determines direction, you will go where it travels. If both skates turn during the pivot and C-cut push, you will travel in a snakelike (S) pattern. The push–glide sequence of the backward stride is diagrammed in figure 5.4*a* on page 86. Note that it is not an exact straight line, just as the glide of the forward stride is not an exact straight line.

GLIDE OF THE BACKWARD STRIDE

The glide of the backward stride is the exact reverse of the glide of the forward stride. You don't actually travel in a straight line; you travel in a slightly curved line as in the forward stride (see chapter 4, page 49). Figure 5.4*a* on page 86 diagrams the push–glide pattern of the backward stride. Figure 5.4*b* diagrams an incorrect pattern that results from turning both skates (and hips) the same way during the push.

For learning purposes, practice traveling in a straight line backward on the flat of the blade (along the desired line of travel) while the pushing skate and leg execute the C-cut. You need to develop the coordination required for the pushing and gliding legs to work independently of each other.

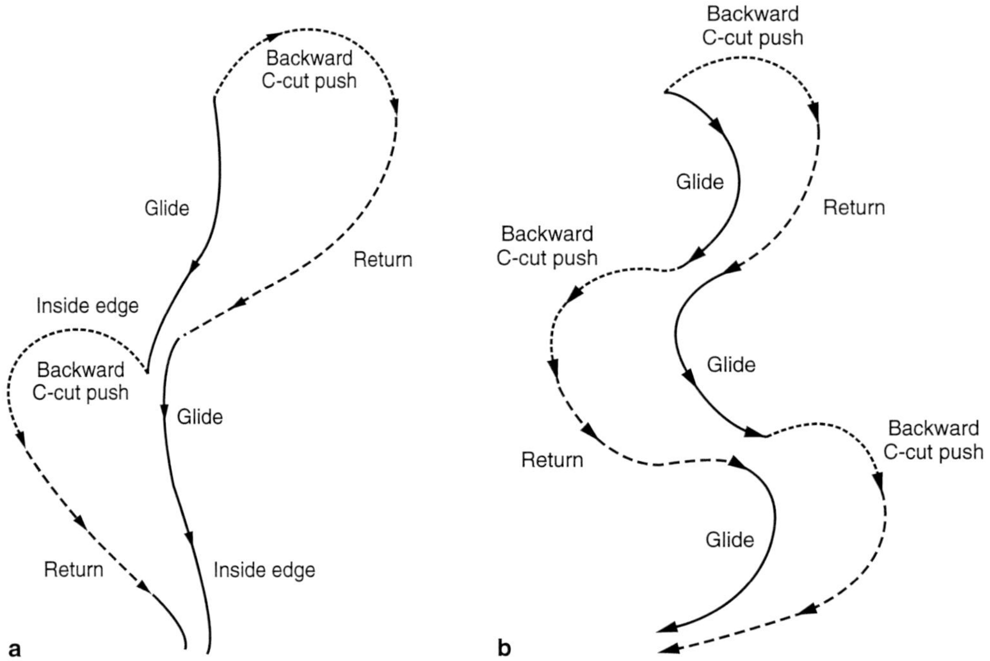

Figure 5.4 Glide of the backward stride: *(a)* correct—traveling straight back; *(b)* incorrect—traveling like a snake.

ARM SWING

The arm swing of the backward stride is similar to the arm swing of the forward stride. The arms swing forward and backward along the same diagonal lines as the legs and in rhythm with the legs. Each arm-swing cycle finishes with one arm extended diagonally forward and the other extended diagonally back; the palms of both hands face upward. The arms match the legs in terms of force, direction of movement, and range of motion. Players should hold the hockey stick with just the top hand and should keep the stick out in front of them so they can poke-check (see figure 3.9*b* on page 40).

STRIDE TEMPO AND LEG RHYTHM

No matter how slowly or rapidly the legs move, all backward strides must be full strides. The difference between a rapid stride and a long stride is leg speed—how quickly the skates and legs change.

The rapidity (tempo) of all strides is determined by how quickly the skates and legs move and change as they push and recover (leg turnover). The faster the skates and legs change, the shorter the time spent gliding. Knee bend, edges, leg extension, and effort expended in pushing should remain the same. The thrusting skate and leg drive to full extension and return fully under the body even when leg motion is very rapid. In addition, the tempo of every stride should be the same. Power is lost if one leg moves rapidly and the other leg moves slowly. The same is true if one pushes fully and the other pushes only partially.

COACHING TIP

All strides must be full strides. Work on increasing the tempo at which you move your legs while still moving them through their full range of motion.

Stride tempos vary with the game situation. You need to develop varying tempos when striding backward (similar to when striding forward). Practice correctly and slowly at first; then practice going faster and faster while still using correct technique. Then practice at speeds that put you out of control (overspeed training). Practice first without a puck, then with a puck. A good way to increase leg speed is by skating to music with fast rhythms.

Remember: Leg tempo should not change the stride length.

DRILLS FOR IMPROVING THE BACKWARD STRIDE

The following drills are designed to help players develop the skill, coordination, and power to become proficient at pushing and skating straight backward. Practice these drills diligently. All pushes used in these drills are backward C-cut pushes.

Backward O Drill

Basic

This drill is an elementary way for novice skaters to learn how to move backward. This drill is performed skating forward in chapter 2 on page 18.

Start with the skates in an inverted V position—toes touching and heels apart—with both skates on inside edges. Bend your knees, keeping your weight on the front halves of the blades. As you glide backward, pull the heels as far apart as possible. As the heels separate, straighten your knees. When both knees are straight, pivot the heels inward and draw them together to form the letter *V*. When the heels touch each other in the V position, you will have completed one full circle, or the letter *O*. Now put the toes of both skates together in the original inverted V position and repeat the maneuver (see figure 2.8, *d-a,* on page 18).

Windup Drills

The Coil

Basic to Intermediate

The coil drill used for the forward stride (see chapter 4, page 54) should also be used to practice the windup of the backward stride. This drill enables players to feel the amount of pressure needed to dig the inside edge into the ice at an angle that allows them to push effectively. Players also experience the strain of maintaining that edge while the other skate is off the ice.

The drill is described for coiling on and preparing to push with the right skate. Remember that the foot, skate, ankle, knee, and body weight must work together to provide a strong cutting edge. Practice the drill equally on each skate.

1. Stand on the right skate. Put all your weight on the right skate, and lift the left skate off the ice.
2. Dig in the inside edge of the right skate, and bend the right knee so that the skate, ankle, lower leg, and knee form a strong (45-degree) angle to the ice. The boot should lean halfway down to the ice.
3. Balance in place on the right inside edge. Apply strong inward pressure on the edge so that the edge angle does not change as you balance on it. The edge must not wobble from edge to flat, and the blade must not move around.
4. Now practice the coil while gliding on the backward inside edge of each skate.

1, 2, 3, 4, Push–Glide–Stop

Advanced

This drill improves a player's ability to coil effectively in preparation for pushing. It demands excellent balance and control. The drill is done in a specific rhythm: 1, 2, 3, 4, push–glide–stop.

1. Stand in place with your weight on the inside edge of the left skate.
2. Roll in the left ankle and bend the left knee, keeping your weight totally on the left skate. While in this position, count to four.
3. After counting to four, push (backward C-cut push) with the left skate and leg, and take one stride backward onto the right skate.
4. Stop.
5. Repeat the sequence on the right skate; balance on the inside edge for a count of four before pushing (backward C-cut push) with the right skate and leg. Take one stride backward onto the left skate.
6. Stop.
7. Repeat several times. Remember to alternate pushing skates equally.

Windup and Release Drills

Flat to Inside Edge Drill

Intermediate

This drill is done skating at a slow to moderate pace; speed is not the goal. The idea is to develop the edging capability needed for an effective backward C-cut push. The action of going from a flat to a strong inside edge simulates that instant of the backward stride when the gliding skate rolls inward onto a strong inside edge in preparation for pushing. Practice the drill on each skate equally.

1. Glide backward on the flat of the left skate; the right skate is off the ice.
2. Keep your weight on the left skate, with the right skate still off the ice. Now quickly roll the left ankle inward and bend the left knee so that the left inside edge cuts deeply (a 45-degree angle) into the ice. The sudden cutting of the left inside edge into the ice will cause the skate to curve to the right (counterclockwise).
3. As the left skate begins to curve, push (backward C-cut push) against the left inside edge and glide backward onto the flat of the right skate.
4. Now quickly roll the right ankle inward and bend the right knee so that the right inside edge cuts deeply into the ice. The sudden cutting of the right inside edge into the ice will cause the skate to curve to the left (clockwise).
5. As the right skate begins to curve, push (backward C-cut push) against the right inside edge and glide backward onto the flat of the left skate.
6. You have finished one cycle. Repeat the drill continuously—pushing with one skate and gliding onto the other skate—for the length of the ice.

Note: If the blade does not roll into a sufficient inside edge, the edge cannot cut into the ice. If this happens, the skate will skid as you attempt to push.

Backward Inside Edge Semicircles

Intermediate to Advanced

This drill helps players improve their skill at backward inside edges. It requires skaters to use deep inside edges with strong knee bend, good body control, and excellent balance.

To perform the drill, start backward from one goal line. Push (backward C-cut push) with the right skate and leg, and glide backward on the inside edge of the left skate. Curve a complete counterclockwise semicircle (shape of the letter *U* or *C*) on the left inside edge. After completing the semicircle, push (backward C-cut push) with the left skate and leg, and glide backward on the inside edge of the right skate. Curve a complete clockwise semicircle on the right skate (see figure 2.15*c* on page 25).

You have finished one cycle. Repeat the drill, pushing with one skate and gliding onto the other skate. Skate continuous alternating semicircles for the entire length of the ice.

Note: You must complete each semicircle before pushing onto the new gliding skate.

Drills for All Elements of the Backward Stride

Backward C-Cuts

All Skaters

Perform a series of backward C-cuts down the ice. Alternate pushing and gliding skates. Concentrate on executing the four parts of the C-cut push—pivot, push, repivot, and return. Dig in with deep inside edges, use powerful leg drive, push to full extension, and return the pushing skate to the center of gravity. The skates should be side by side and on an even plane with each other before you initiate the next push.

Be sure to keep the gliding skate pointed straight back throughout and maintain a deep knee bend on the gliding skate at all times (see "Forward C-Cuts" in chapter 4, page 67).

Note: Do not allow the returning skate to pass the gliding skate. Refer to figure 5.2*d* on page 83.

One-Leg Backward C-Cuts

Basic

Skate backward C-cuts across the ice, but push each time with the right skate and leg. Coming back across the ice, push each time with the left skate and leg. Fully extend each push, and fully recover the pushing skate and leg until the skates are close together (but not touching). Be sure that the gliding skate travels straight backward—don't zigzag.

Variation (Intermediate)

Use only four backward C-cut pushes to get completely across the ice (six for smaller skaters). If you are pushing powerfully, each succeeding push should make you go faster. The gliding skate must travel straight backward—don't zigzag.

Push–Touch

Basic to Intermediate

Perform a series of backward C-cuts across the ice. After each pushing skate returns, it must touch (magnetize with) the gliding skate. The toes and heels of both skates should be lined up with (on the same plane as) each other (refer to figure 5.2*d* on page 83).

Variation—One-Leg Push–Touch (Basic to Intermediate)

Perform a series of backward C-cuts across the ice, pushing with the same skate and leg each time. After the pushing skate returns, it must touch (magnetize with) the gliding skate. The toes and heels of both skates should be lined up with (on the same plane as) each other.

Backward C-Cuts Along the Lines

Basic to Intermediate

Use the blue lines and red line as guides for the gliding skate. Perform backward C-cuts across the ice. The gliding skate must glide straight backward along the line as the pushing skate cuts each C-cut. At the completion of each C-cut push, the pushing skate must return and touch the gliding skate; the skates must line up with and be next to (on the same plane with) each other. See the pattern in figure 5.5.

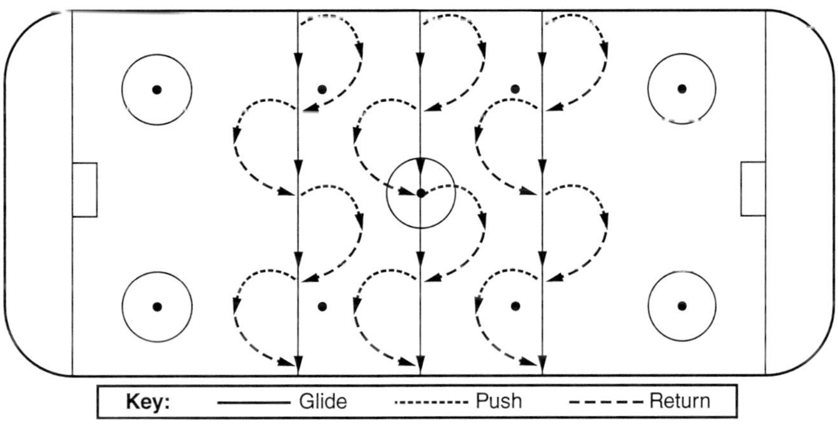

Figure 5.5 Backward C-cuts along the lines.

One-Leg Backward C-Cuts Along the Lines

Basic to Intermediate

Perform the previous drill, but execute each backward C-cut push with the right skate and leg. Coming back across the ice, execute each backward C-cut push with the left skate and leg. See the pattern in figure 5.6. The gliding skate must glide straight backward along the line as the pushing skate cuts each C-cut. At the completion of each recovery, the returning skate must touch the gliding skate as in the previous drill.

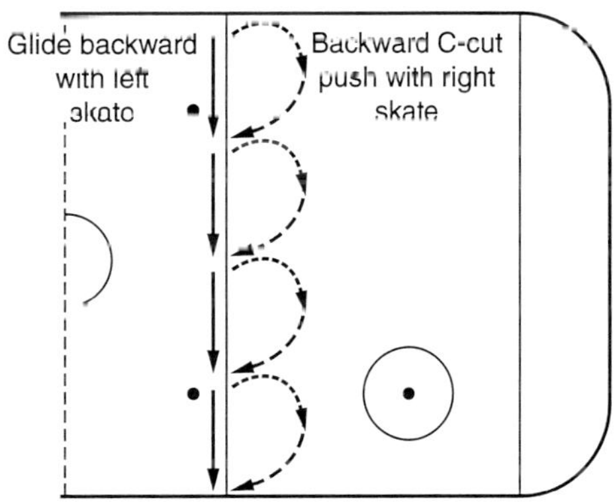

Figure 5.6 One-leg backward C-cuts along the lines.

Backward Shuffle Step

Intermediate to Advanced

The forward shuffle step (described on page 73) can also be done backward. Similar to the forward shuffle step, the backward shuffle step is a preparatory move that is used when players are defending against oncoming opponents. As with the forward shuffle step, the skates are always wide apart. The pushes consist of only the first half of the C-cut; there is no return. The backward shuffle step is done with the front halves of the blades.

To perform the drill, start from the goal line and skate backward using C-cuts to the first blue line. At the first blue line, do a series of backward shuffle steps to the far blue line. At the far blue line, skate backward using C-cuts to the far goal line.

Stride Tempo Drills

The stride tempo drills used for practicing the forward stride can also be used for the backward stride. Refer to chapter 4 for a description of these drills.

Forward Versus Defender

Intermediate to Advanced

Practice with another player by competing as a defender against a forward. The defender stands at the blue line, prepared to skate backward. The forward stands at the goal line directly opposite the defender; the forward is prepared to skate forward. On a whistle signal, both players start racing. The defender skates straight backward (no crossovers) and tries to prevent the forward from catching up, while the forward tries to catch and pass the defender. Alternate so that both players practice equally as forward and defender.

Resistance Drills

Resistance Backward C-Cuts

Intermediate

Resistance drills force skaters to push correctly, powerfully, and completely.

Partner up with another player. Face each other and hold one hockey stick between you. Each player holds onto an end of the stick with *one hand.* The backward skater will pull the forward skater across the ice; the forward skater will resist movement with a two-foot snowplow (see chapter 8, page 171).

Use backward C-cut pushes to pull the resisting skater across the ice (figure 5.7, *a-b*). Make sure that the gliding skate travels straight backward during each push–return cycle and that the skates touch each other at the completion of each return.

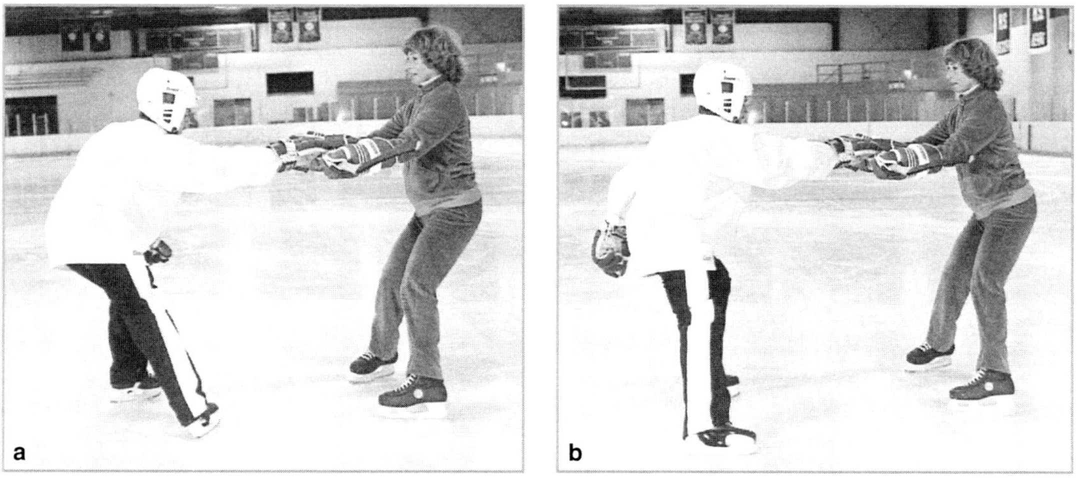

Figure 5.7 Resistance backward C-cuts: *(a)* pivot and push; *(b)* full extension.

Variation—Backward Choo-Choo Resistance Drill (Basic to Intermediate)

Partner up with another player, and face each other. Both players should hold onto one end of each of their hockey sticks. The resisting skater sits on his or her knees, facing forward (facing the backward skater). The backward skater pulls the resisting skater across the ice using a series of alternating backward C-cuts.

The gliding skate must travel straight backward during each push–return cycle. The returning skate must touch the gliding skate at the completion of each return. When you reach the opposite sideboards, switch positions with your partner; the partner now pulls you across the ice. Give equal time to each pushing skate and leg!

Note: Both the pulling skater and the resisting skater must keep their backs straight and their heads up at all times.

Variation—One-Leg Resistance Backward C-Cuts (Basic to Intermediate)

Perform the previous resistance drills, but now use the same skate and leg to push each time. Pull the resisting player across the ice. Be sure to glide straight backward—do not zigzag. When you reach the opposite sideboards, switch positions with your partner; the partner now pulls you across the ice. Repeat this drill several times so that each skate gets the opportunity to be the pushing skate.

Resistance Backward C-Cuts Along the Lines

Basic to Intermediate

This drill is similar to the resistance backward C-cuts drill and the backward choo-choo resistance drill, but in this drill the backward skater must come to a complete stop at the completion of each push.

Pull a resisting player across the ice, staying on one of the hockey lines all the way across. The gliding skate must glide straight backward on the line during each backward C-cut push. The pushing skate must return and touch the gliding skate after each push, and the skates should line up with and be next to (on the same plane with) each other. After the skates touch, come to a complete STOP! Now execute a backward C-cut push with the other skate and leg. Do this until you reach the opposite sideboards. Your partner will then pull you across the ice, doing the same drill.

One-Leg Resistance Backward C-Cuts Along the Lines

Intermediate

Perform the previous drill, but now push each time with the same skate and leg. After each backward C-cut push, the pushing skate must return and touch the gliding skate; the skates should line up with and be next to (on the same plane as) each other. After the skates touch, come to a complete STOP and then do another backward C-cut push with the same leg. Again, stop after the skates touch. Continue this until you reach the opposite boards. Your partner will then pull you across the ice, doing the same drill. Repeat the drill, now pushing with the other skate and leg.

Remember: After the skates touch, come to a complete STOP!

1, 2, 3, 4, C-Cut–Touch–Stop

Advanced

This resistance drill enables players to work on all the elements of the backward stride—the windup, release, follow-through, and return. It demands great balance, power, and control. The movement is done in a specific rhythm: 1, 2, 3, 4, C-cut–touch–stop. Only one stride is performed at a time.

1. Partner up with another player. Stand at the sideboards, prepared to pull the resisting skater.
2. Roll in the ankle and bend the knee of the pushing leg; your weight must be balanced totally over the pushing skate. In this position, count to four.
3. After counting to four, push once (backward C-cut push) and take one stride backward. You should be able to pull the resisting player.
4. At full extension, quickly return the pushing (now free) skate until the skates touch each other.
5. Stop.
6. Repeat with the other skate and leg.
7. Alternate pushing skates as you move backward across the ice until you reach the opposite sideboards.
8. When you reach the opposite sideboards, switch positions with your partner; coming back across the ice, the other player pushes and you resist.

Hockey Stick Drills

These hockey stick drills help players learn how to use their pushing and gliding skates independently of each other. This is very important when skating backward (for perfecting the backward stride).

Hockey Stick Drill

Basic

In this drill, players work on making sure that the gliding skate travels in a straight line backward while the pushing skate executes a backward C-cut push. (The drill is described for pushing with the left skate and leg.)

1. Place a hockey stick on the ice.
2. Stand to the left of the stick (next to the stick).
3. Place the right (gliding) skate close to the stick. The skate is prepared to glide straight backward (parallel with the stick) on the flat of the blade.
4. Pivot the heel of the left (pushing) skate outward and bend the left knee deeply (90 degrees) (figure 5.8*a*).
5. Execute one backward C-cut push. Push to full extension and glide straight backward on the right skate. You should glide straight backward (parallel with the stick) on the right skate during the entire glide (figure 5.8*b*).
6. Continue to glide straight backward as the left skate returns (figure 5.8*c*). At the completion of the return, the skates should be close together and side by side (on the same plane).
7. Stop.

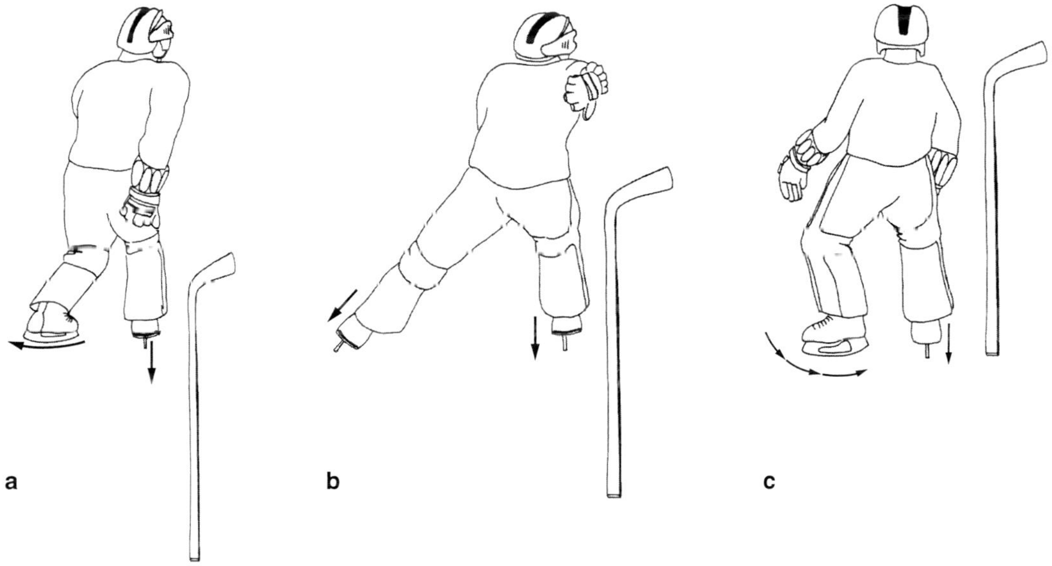

Figure 5.8 Hockey stick drill: *(a)* pivot and push, *(b)* full extension, and *(c)* repivot and return.

8. Repeat the drill; now stand to the right of the stick. Cut one backward C-cut push with the right skate and leg; glide straight backward on the left skate. After the right skate reaches full extension, repivot it and return it under your body until your heels are close together.
9. Stop.

Keep repeating this procedure. Push each time from a complete standstill. Alternate left and right backward C-cut pushes. Keep your head up, your back straight, and your hips square to the line of travel.

Remember: The gliding skate must travel straight backward during the entire push–return sequence.

Variation (Basic)

To ensure that the pushing skate has returned fully, make the skates actually touch each other.

Hockey Stick Drill Using Forward and Backward C-Cuts

Basic to Intermediate

Perform the previous hockey stick drill, but alternate between backward and forward C-cuts.

1. Stand to the left of the stick (next to the stick) for the duration of this drill.
2. Push (backward C-cut push) with the left skate and leg. Glide straight backward on the right skate, staying next to and parallel with the stick.
3. Stop.
4. Push (forward C-cut push) with the left skate and leg. Glide straight forward on the right skate, staying next to and parallel with the stick.
5. Stop.

Do four sets of backward and forward C-cuts on the left side of the stick. Then change sides and do the same drill on the right side of the stick, pushing with the right skate and gliding on the left skate.

Note: At the completion of each return, the skates should be close together and side by side (on the same plane).

Advanced Hockey Stick Drill

Advanced

Do the previous hockey stick drill (forward and backward), but now use two sticks as shown in figure 5.9. The gliding skate must travel straight (forward or backward) between the two sticks; it must not skate sideways or hit either stick at any time during the push–return sequence. At the completion of each return, the skates must be close together and centered under the body.

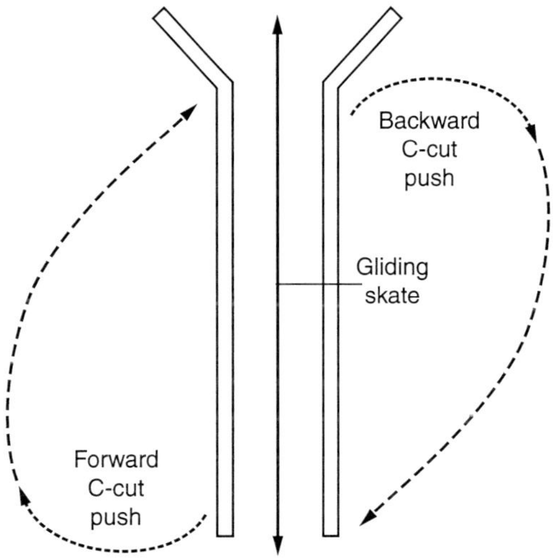

Figure 5.9 Advanced hockey stick drill.

Drills for Backward C-Cuts Around the Ice

You are now prepared to perform and practice backward C-cuts skating entirely around the ice.

Backward C-Cuts Around the Ice

Intermediate

Perform backward C-cuts around the ice in the following manner: Alternate the pushing and gliding skates for the entire length of the straightaway. When skating around the corners, perform four or five consecutive backward C-cut pushes with the *outside* skate. The inside skate creates the curve around the corner by gliding continuously on its outside edge.

When you are skating counterclockwise, the left skate is the pushing skate; it executes each of the backward C-cut pushes while the right skate glides on its outside edge. When you are skating clockwise, the right skate executes each of the backward C-cut pushes while the left skate glides on its outside edge.

Note: This drill can also be used to practice backward crossovers. See chapter 6 for information about executing backward crossovers and the proper body positioning for skating curves.

Advanced Backward C-Cuts Around the Ice

Advanced

Skate straight backward down the ice, performing a series of backward C-cuts. Alternate the pushing and gliding skates. At the far face-off dot, start skating around the corner in a counterclockwise direction. Accelerate around the corner using four or five left-over-right backward crossovers. Continue doing backward crossovers until you reach the face-off circle closest to the corner that you just finished skating around. Then skate straight backward again (using backward C-cut pushes) to the far end of the ice. When you reach the face-off circle at the far end of the ice, use four or five left-over-right backward crossovers to accelerate around the corner. Repeat this pattern four or five times. Then repeat the drill in a clockwise direction.

Note: This drill can also be used for practicing backward crossovers. See chapter 6 for information about executing backward crossovers and the proper body positioning for skating curves.

RESTRICTING THE ARMS

Restricting the use of the arms forces players to concentrate solely on the technique of the backward stride. The following drills restrict arm movement; this trains the legs to work independently of the arms. After you learn to use the legs independently, the arms should be incorporated into the drills, as long as they are used properly (in a forward–backward motion, in line and in rhythm with the legs).

Restricting Arms Drill 1

Intermediate to Advanced

Perform a series of backward C-cuts while holding a hockey stick horizontally behind your back and in the crooks of your elbows (see figure 4.26 on page 73). This eliminates the use of the arms and shoulders and forces the legs to do all the work. Keep the hockey stick still as you skate—it should not move around. Keep your upper body still and your chest facing straight ahead at all times.

Restricting Arms Drill 2

Intermediate to Advanced

Skate backward at top speed. Hold the hockey stick with both hands, keeping the stick on the ice out in front of you. Push powerfully and rapidly, and try to achieve speed from your legs alone. Practice this without the puck and then with the puck.

Once you can move your legs properly and powerfully without the aid of your arms, skate backward holding the hockey stick with just your top hand. Keep the stick on the ice and well out in front of you. Swing your arms in a forward–backward motion, in line and in rhythm with your legs.

Chapter 6

Crossovers for Acceleration on Curves

Crossovers are the moves that players use to travel and accelerate on curves, circles, and corners. These moves allow players to weave in and out of traffic, zigzag, change direction, turn from backward to forward, move laterally (from side to side), and fake (or deke). Powerful, explosive, and quick crossovers are essential for all hockey players. Watch NHL stars such as Scott Niedermayer and Brian Rafalski as they weave down the ice, and you will see excellent examples of crossovers.

As with all other skating maneuvers, practice crossovers slowly at first, then faster, then finally at top speed while controlling a puck. Mastering crossovers takes a lot of practice, but when you do master them, you'll be amazed at how much faster you can skate and accelerate on curves and circles.

CIRCLE PHYSICS AND CROSSOVERS

It is not natural for an isolated body to travel in a circle. A body will travel in a straight line unless forced to do otherwise. Whenever a body is traveling on curves or circles, centripetal and centrifugal forces are at work.

Centripetal force is an inward force that is needed in order to bend the normally straight path of a body into a circular path. This force is the pull on the body that is directed *inwardly*—toward the center of the circle.

Centrifugal force is an apparent *outwardly* directed force that acts on a body rotating around a central point. This force is the pull on the body that is directed away from the center of the circle. It is equal in magnitude, but opposite in direction, to the centripetal force. However, centrifugal force is not a true force. It is actually the effect of inertia, in that a moving object's natural tendency is to move in a straight line.

Think of a ball being twirled in a horizontal circle at the end of a string. Centripetal force acts to pull the string and ball toward the center of the circle.

Centrifugal force acts to keep the string taut and keep the ball at the end of the string. If the string breaks, the ball will not continue to travel in a circle. Centrifugal force will cause the ball to fly away from the center of the circle on a straight line and on a path tangent to the circle.

Skaters need to skate tight curves and circles at great speeds. The edges and knee bend must be deep—strongly leaning toward the center of the curve or circle. The skates must ride on the periphery of the circle, while the body must ride slightly inside the circle. When skating these tight curves and circles, skaters must be able to counteract the powerful circular forces acting on the body to remain upright and stable.

To balance these tight curves and circles, the lower body (hips, knees, and skates) leans strongly inward (toward the center of the arc) to create the curve. To offset the inward lean of the lower body, the upper body (head, shoulders, chest, and torso) counterleans slightly outward (away from the center of the circle). The purpose of this counterlean is to keep the upper body vertical (necessary for balance) and to allow the skater to apply maximum body weight to the legs and edges.

Note: Tilting the upper body into the center of the curve or circle, especially at fast speeds, often results in a fall.

CHARACTERISTICS OF ALL CROSSOVERS

The term *crossover* refers to the passing of the outside skate (the one closer to the outside of the curve) in front of the toe of the inside skate (figure 6.1). Forward and backward crossovers are similar in the following ways:

1. Every crossover sequence includes two steps (and two corresponding pushes).
    - First step: The inside skate glides on its outside edge.
    - Second step: The outside skate crosses over in front of the toe of the inside skate to take the ice and glide on its inside edge.

Figure 6.1 Crossovers: The outside skate crosses over in front of the toe of the inside skate.

2. Because the skater glides on the edges, the line of travel is *always* a curve or circle. The inside skate always glides on its outside edge, and the outside skate always glides on its inside edge.
3. When measured between thigh and shin, the knee bend of the pushing *and* gliding legs should approximate a 90-degree angle.
4. All crossovers require simultaneous edging with both skates

(pushing and gliding skates). Strong edges are required for the pushing skate to grip the ice and for the gliding skate to skate a sharp curve. Deeper edges and high speeds produce sharper curves. The angle of the engaged skate blade (edge) to the ice at high speed and on sharp curves is approximately 45 degrees (figure 6.2). The manner in which the skates and body coordinate to produce edges for crossovers is discussed in chapter 1.

Figure 6.2 The skates and body coordinate to produce edges for crossovers.

5. Since the crossover sequence includes two steps, it also includes two pushes. Power is achieved by employing the principles of windup, release, follow-through, and return on each push. Review the principles of edges, knee bend, body weight, weight shift, and glide. Apply these principles to crossovers as described in the following list:
   - Each push begins with the pushing skate directly under the center of gravity and finishes with the pushing skate and leg fully extended away from the body. The knees are bent deeply (approximately 90 degrees), and the body weight is concentrated over the pushing skate.
   - You must push first and change feet second. In other words, the push must begin before you step onto the new gliding skate. The transfer of body weight from pushing skate to gliding skate takes place at the midpoint of each push.
   - The edge of each gliding skate is placed directly underneath (and glides directly underneath) the outside hip. Therefore, the body weight must be concentrated over the outside skate on both steps of the crossover.
   - The body weight does not shift from front to back or from side to side.
   - The knee of the gliding leg stays bent throughout the push–return cycle.
   - Pushes are outward and inward, not forward and backward.
   - The toe of the pushing skate *never* points straight downward.
   - After reaching full extension, the pushing skate and leg return quickly to a position directly under the center of gravity to prepare for the next push.
   - The skate stays within an inch (2.5 cm) of the ice throughout the push–return cycle.
   - The shoulders are held still—they do not swing or move around.

- The upper body does not tilt (lean) into the circle. The shoulders are usually held level to the ice. But at fast speeds, the inside shoulder is sometimes held higher than the outside shoulder. This enhances the counterlean of the upper body, which in turn enhances the skater's balance on a tight curve or circle.

6. The combination of powerful, complete leg drive and rapid leg tempo yields speed. One without the other is insufficient.

FORWARD CROSSOVERS

These instructions are for skating on a counterclockwise circle. The left skate is the inside skate. The right skate is the outside skate. Forward crossovers in the counterclockwise direction are referred to as right-over-left crossovers.

First Push: Stride-Push

I call the first push of forward crossovers the *stride-push* because it is essentially identical to the push of the forward stride. This push is always against the inside edge and is executed with the outside skate and leg. It is executed to full extension (including the toe flick).

1. Prepare to glide forward on the LFO of the inside skate and to push against the inside edge of the right (outside) skate.

Windup

2. Place your weight over the right skate, bend your knees deeply, and dig the right inside edge into the ice so that the skate and lower leg form a 45-degree angle to the ice.

Release

3. Push directly back and out against the entire length of the inside edge (figure 6.3, *a-b*). Do not push the leg straight back in a walking or running motion—this will cause a slip against the flat of the blade rather than a push against the edge.

Follow-Through

4. Start the push with the heel of the inside edge; during the push, shift your weight forward on the blade and push to full extension. Complete the push with the toe flick (front of the inside edge), as on the thrust of the forward stride (figure 6.3*c*).
5. At the midpoint of the push, transfer your weight from the RFI onto the LFO and glide on the LFO (figure 6.3*b*). The LFO takes the ice approximately three-quarters of a blade length forward of where the RFI had been gliding on the ice before the first push.

Note: On all skating strides, the skate preparing to take the ice moves slightly ahead of the skate that is already on the ice in a progression of movement before taking the ice.

6. Keep the left knee well bent throughout the glide. The knee of the left (gliding) leg maintains a strong 90-degree knee bend throughout the push.
7. Complete the push with the toe flick. At the finish of the push, the knee of the right (pushing) leg (now the free leg) locks; the toe of the skate should be about 1 inch (2.5 cm) from the ice. At the completion of the toe flick, the toe is slightly closer to the ice than the heel (figure 6.3*c*).

Figure 6.3 Forward crossover sequence: *(a-c)* stride-push, *(d)* return of the outside skate, and *(e-f)* X-push.

Note: The tendon guard must press into the back of the leg in order to achieve the toe flick.
Note: The new gliding skate takes the ice ahead of the previous gliding skate—forward if skating forward, or backward if skating backward—by approximately three-quarters of a blade length.

Return

8. Immediately after the right (pushing) leg locks, return it quickly and move it forward in preparation for crossing it over in front of the toe of the left (gliding) skate (figure 6.3*d*).
9. Keep the right skate close and almost parallel to the ice as it returns, moves forward, and crosses over in front of the left skate.

Note: Since the stride-push of forward crossovers is a straight-out motion, the return is a straight-in motion, reversing the outward path of the push.

10. At the midpoint of the second push, transfer your weight to the RFI, which now becomes the gliding skate. The RFI takes the ice slightly forward of where the LFO had been gliding (figure 6.3*e*). Maintain a deep knee bend on the right knee as the RFI takes the ice.
11. While crossing over, leave at least an inch (2.5 cm) of space between the heel of the right skate and the toe of the left skate. This will prevent your feet from hitting each other or getting tangled up during the crossover.

Second Push: X-Push

I call the second push of forward crossovers the *X-push* or *scissor push* because of the X or scissorlike motion created by one skate crossing under the body to push while the other skate crosses over to take the ice and glide. The X-push is always executed against the outside edge of the inside skate. The X-push is sometimes called a *crossunder push* because the skate actually crosses (drives) under the body to generate power.

Beginning skaters might find it helpful to use their arms to learn how to create the X. To create an X, one arm moves one way (let's say to the right) to cross over the other, while the other arm moves the other way (in this case, to the left) to cross under the other arm. *Both arms* must actively move in opposite directions to accomplish this X-like motion. Think of it as an over–under motion.

Now create the letter *X* with your legs to learn how to execute the second push of forward crossovers.

1. Before the right skate takes the ice to glide on the RFI, begin to push with the left skate and leg. Until now you have been gliding on the LFO.

Windup

2. Deepen the LFO by increasing the pressure against the outside of the skate and by bending your knees. Keep your weight over the LFO (figure 6.3*d*).

Release

3. Drive the left skate and leg straight underneath your body—directly back and out against the entire length of the left outside edge (figure 6.3*e*).

Follow-Through

4. Push to full extension. Start the push with the heel of the outside edge. During the push, shift your weight forward on the blade, and complete the push with the toe flick of the outside edge (figure 6.3*f*). The toe flick requires that the pushing skate and leg be fully locked with the tendon guard pressed into the back of the leg.
5. Push straight out (underneath your body). At the finish of the push, the blade should be almost parallel with the ice, although the toe will be slightly closer to the ice than the heel. Do not push the leg straight back in a walking or running motion—this causes a slip against the flat of the blade rather than a push against the edge.

Note: Avoid pointing the toe down because this will cause the front tip of the skate to catch the ice. As a result, your skate will slip backward, disengaging the outside edge, eliminating the thrust, and possibly causing a fall (figure 6.4).

6. At the midpoint of the X-push, transfer your weight from the LFO onto the RFI, which now becomes the gliding skate.
7. Thrust until the left skate and leg reach full extension outside the circle (figure 6.3*f*). Keep the knee of the gliding leg deeply bent throughout the push.
8. At the finish of the push, the knee of the pushing leg—now the free leg—is locked; the toe is about 1 inch (2.5 cm) from the ice. The toe will be slightly closer to the ice than the heel.

Note: The one-third principle of the forward stride applies to both the stride-push and the X-push of forward crossovers.

Figure 6.4 Incorrect X-push: The skate slips back.

Return

9. Immediately after locking the left (pushing) skate and leg, bring the skate quickly back to center under your body in a side-by-side position with the gliding skate. The X-push of forward crossovers is a straight-out motion; therefore, the return is a straight-in motion, reversing the outward path of the push.

Figure 6.5 Return.

10. Keep the left (returning) skate almost parallel with the ice as it returns (figure 6.5). Do not point the toe straight down. Pointing the toe straight down as the skate returns may cause the toe to catch the ice, leading to a loss of balance and a possible fall.
11. Keep the left (returning) skate close to the ice as it returns. Lifting it high off the ice raises the center of gravity and delays the return process.

You have completed one sequence of the forward crossover. Repeat the crossover sequence by once again pushing against the RFI and gliding onto the LFO.

Skating Clockwise

Mirror the previous procedure to skate in a clockwise direction (left-over-right forward crossovers). The right skate is now the inside skate and will glide on the RFO. The left skate is now the outside skate. After pushing (stride-push), the left skate will cross over in front of the right skate and glide on the LFI.

Points to Remember for Forward Crossovers

Gliding:

- When you are gliding on the outside edge, your body weight must be on the back half of the blade. If your body weight is too far forward, the outside edge will not retain its grip against the ice; the skate will fishtail into a skid, causing a loss of balance. Even a deep outside edge will skid if your body weight is too far forward. The tighter the curve and the greater the speed, the more important it is to concentrate your body weight over the back half of the outside edge.
- When you are gliding on either the outside or inside edge, keep the entire blade length of the gliding skate in complete contact with the ice. It is very difficult to balance if part of the blade loses contact with the ice.

Pushing:

- The one-third principle applies to both pushes of forward crossovers. Use powerful and full leg drive. Remember that the push and return for both the stride-push and the X-push are straight-line motions.

Crossing Over:

- The process of crossing the inside skate under the body to push is more pronounced than the process of crossing the outside skate over in front of the inside skate to glide.

Accelerating:

- Skaters often run the first one or two crossover steps on the toes (front of the edges) to accelerate explosively. While you are running the crossovers, your body weight must stay low and project outward in the desired direction of travel. Small hopping steps take you nowhere fast; jumping upward destroys forward momentum.

Note: On all skating strides, the directional skate must move ahead of the previous skate in the desired direction of travel—forward if skating forward, or backward if skating backward—by approximately three-quarters of a blade length.

BACKWARD CROSSOVERS

Backward crossovers are important for all players but are especially critical in defensive situations. Defenders use backward crossovers to track opponents and to take them out of the play (for example, a defender may use this move when turning from backward to forward to cut off an attacking player at the boards).

Defenders must always face the action and the opposition. This means they must be able to start out explosively from a backward position. Players who can't do this are forced to start out forward, take a couple of strides, and then turn around backward. In doing this, they are unaware of the action behind them. Thus, they are breaking one of the cardinal rules in hockey: Never turn your back to the play.

I teach players to start from a complete stop using one or two backward crossovers. In general, backward crossovers are the fastest and most effective way of accelerating backward while still being able to see the action. But players must know when it's appropriate to use backward crossovers and when it isn't. A good rule is that backward crossovers can be used when there is plenty of distance between the attacker and the defender. But when the attacker is bearing down on a defender, the defender should *not* cross over because this creates an opportunity for the attacker to cut the other way and escape.

When backward crossovers are skated on counterclockwise curves or circles, the inside skate (closer to the center of the curve) is the right skate, and the outside skate (closer to the outside of the curve) is the left skate. As in forward crossovers, the outside skate always crosses over in front of the toe of the inside skate (figure 6.6) as the inside skate crosses (drives) under the body to push.

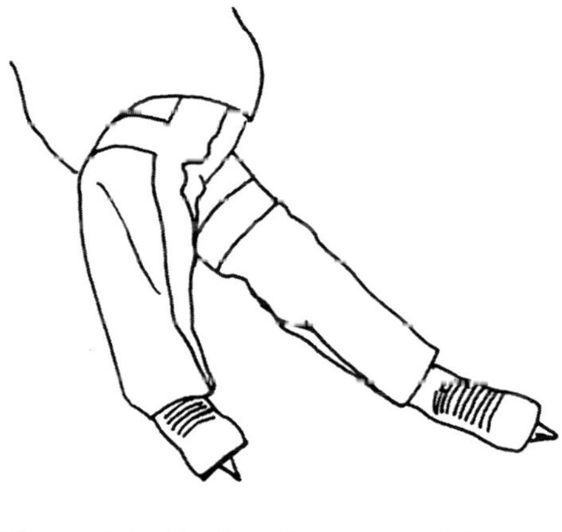

Figure 6.6 Backward crossover: left over right.

The instructions given here are for skating on a counterclockwise circle (left-over-right backward crossovers).

First Push: Stride-Push

The first push of a backward crossover is the stride-push. Since the stride-push of the backward stride is the backward C-cut push, the first push of a backward crossover is the backward C-cut push. This push is always executed with the outside skate and leg. However, instead of gliding in and centering under the body as it does with the backward stride, the returning C-cut skate crosses over in front of the toe of the gliding skate. It then takes the ice on its inside edge and becomes the new gliding skate.

1. Prepare to glide backward on the RBO and to push (backward C-cut push) with the left (outside) skate and leg.

Windup

2. Place your weight over the left (outside) skate, bend your knees deeply, and dig the inside edge of the left skate into the ice so that the skate and lower leg form a 45-degree angle to the ice.

Release

3. Pivot the left heel outward (toward the outside of the circle), and execute a backward C-cut push against the inside edge of the left skate (figure 6.7*a*). Thrust the left skate and leg to the front and side, pushing directly against the entire blade length of the inside edge.
4. At the midpoint of the push, transfer your weight from the inside edge of the left (pushing) skate to the outside edge of the right skate (RBO). Keep the knee of the right (gliding) leg well bent during the glide (figure 6.7*b*).

Follow-Through

5. Push to full extension, finishing the push with the toe (front of the inside edge). At the completion of the push, the pushing leg (now the free leg) should be locked, with the free skate close to or on the ice.

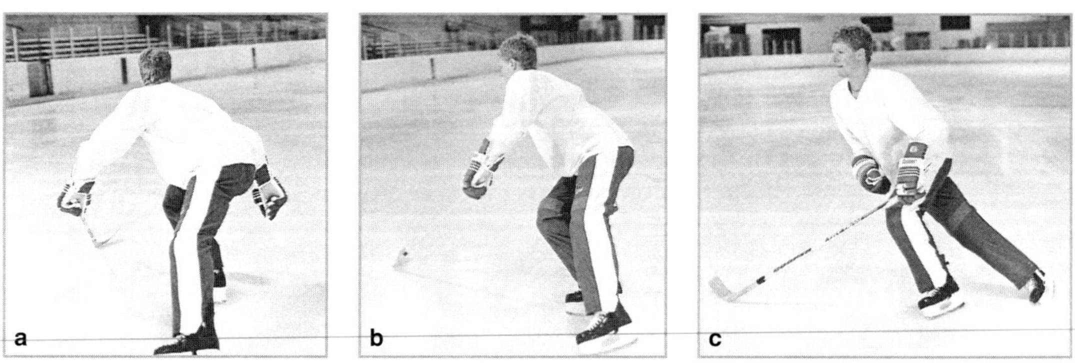

Figure 6.7 Backward crossover sequence (counterclockwise).

6. Immediately after locking the left (pushing) leg, return it quickly and begin to cross it over in front of the toe of the right skate. Keep the left skate close to (or on) the ice as it moves to cross over (figure 6.7*b*).
7. While crossing over, leave at least an inch (2.5 cm) of space between the heel of the left skate and the toe of the right skate. This will prevent your feet from getting tangled.

Note: The C-cut push of backward crossovers is a semicircular motion outward. Thus, the return is also a semicircular motion, reversing the outward path of the push.

Second Push: X-Push

The X-push of backward crossovers is identical to the X-push of forward crossovers. The push is against the outside edge, and it is executed to full extension by the inside skate and leg. Before the left skate takes the ice to glide on its inside edge, the right (inside) skate, which has been gliding on its outside edge, must be activated to provide the second push (X-push).

Windup

1. Deepen the RBO by increasing the pressure against the outside of the boot, bending your knees, and placing your weight over the RBO.

Release

2. Push against the outside edge of the right skate (RBO); push sideways underneath your body, directly forward and outward against the outside edge (figure 6.7*c*).

Follow-Through

3. Start the push with the middle of the outside edge; shift your weight forward on the blade during the push, and complete the push with the toe flick of the *outside* edge. The toe flick requires that the pushing leg be fully locked with the tendon guard pressed into the back of the leg.
4. Push straight out (underneath the body). Do not push straight back in a walking or running motion. Avoid pointing the toe straight down and the heel up because this will cause the front tip of the skate to catch the ice. If this occurs, it will create a slip against the flat of the blade rather than a push against the edge. The skate will slide backward, disengaging the outside edge, eliminating the push, and possibly causing a fall.
5. At the midpoint of the X-push, transfer your weight from the RBO onto the LBI, which now takes the ice as the gliding skate. Keep the knee of the left leg well bent throughout the glide.
6. Continue to push with the right skate until the right leg reaches full extension outside the circle. At the completion of the push, the knee of the right (pushing) leg—now the free leg—should be locked; the free skate

should be close to and almost parallel with the ice, although the toe will be slightly closer to the ice than the heel (figure 6.7*c*).

7. Keep the knee of the left (gliding) leg deeply bent during the entire X-push.

Return

8. Immediately after the right (now free) leg reaches full extension, return the skate quickly to center under the body in a side-by-side position with the left (gliding) skate. The X-push of backward crossovers is a straight-out motion; therefore, the return is a straight-in motion, reversing the path of the push.
9. Keep the right skate almost parallel with the ice as it returns. Do not point the toe straight down. Pointing the toe straight down as the skate returns may cause the toe to catch the ice, leading to a loss of balance and a possible fall.
10. Keep the right skate close to the ice as it returns. Lifting it high off the ice raises the center of gravity and delays the return process.

You have completed one sequence of the backward crossover. Repeat the procedure by pivoting the left skate outward and executing a backward C-cut push against the inside edge of the left skate; glide backward on the RBO.

Skating Clockwise

To skate clockwise, mirror the previous procedure. The left skate is now the inside skate, and the right skate is now the outside skate (figure 6.8, *a-c*). You will now do right-over-left backward crossovers.

Remember: On all skating strides, the directional skate must move ahead of the previous skate in the desired direction of travel—forward if skating forward, or backward if skating backward—by approximately three-quarters of a blade length. Be sure to place each gliding skate slightly ahead (when skating backward, this means behind you) of where the previous skate was gliding before it pushed.

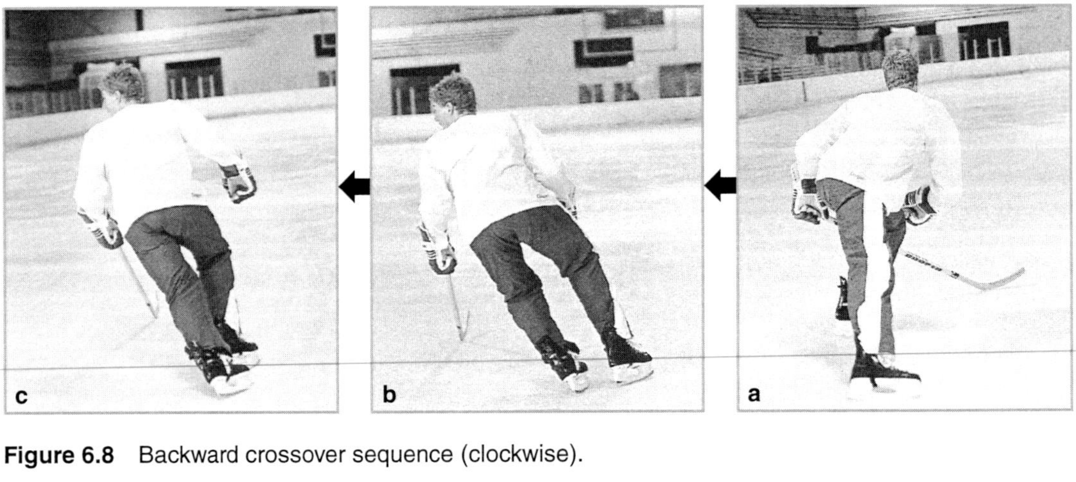

Figure 6.8 Backward crossover sequence (clockwise).

Points to Remember for Backward Crossovers

Gliding (on either the outside or inside edge):

- The body weight must be over the front half of the blades, but the entire blade lengths of both skates must be in full contact with the ice.
- The upper body should be almost vertical (almost perpendicular) to the ice. If the skater leans too far forward, the body weight will pitch over the toes. A skater should not have to lean on the hockey stick for balance.

> **COACHING TIP**
>
> At this point, we have discussed most of the pushes used in hockey skating: forward stride-push, forward C-cut push, backward stride-push (backward C-cut push), forward X-push, and backward X-push. See page 40 in chapter 3 for more details on these pushes. When a coach tells a skater to push, the skater has to choose from one of these pushes. Skaters must know which push to use for each maneuver, and they must know how to apply each push properly and powerfully.

Pushing:

- To achieve a more complete C-cut push, do the following: Simultaneously with the C-cut push (and while the inside skate is still off the ice), reach the inside skate and leg sideways into the circle. When the inside skate takes the ice, the feet should be somewhat wider apart than the shoulders (figure 6.9*a*).
- The backward X-push is executed as if the inside skate and leg were pulling (scooping) the ice underneath the body (figure 6.9*b*).

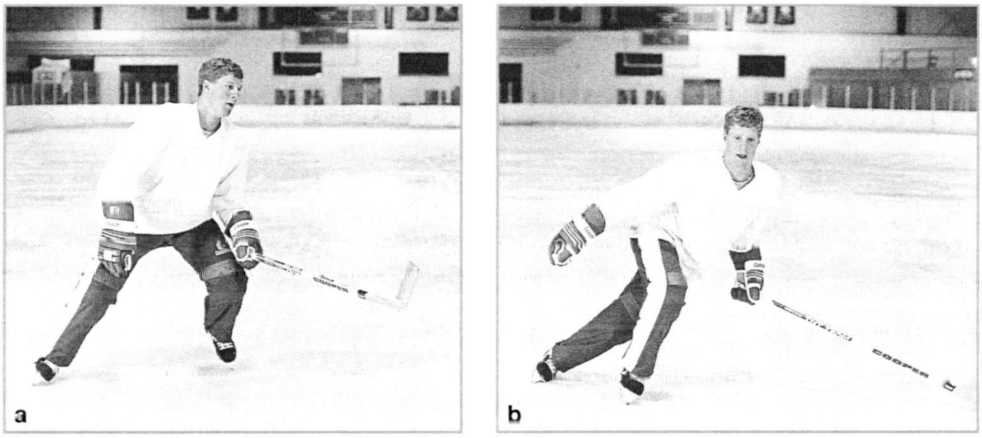

Figure 6.9 *(a)* The inside skate reaches into the circle; *(b)* the inside skate and leg scoop the ice under the body.

Crossing Over:

- The X-push skate must be well underneath the body before the outside skate crosses over. Drive the inside leg underneath your body *before* attempting to cross the outside skate over. If you don't follow this sequence, the inside skate will still be where the outside skate needs to go, and the skates might get tangled up as you attempt to cross over.
- The process of crossing the inside skate under the body to push is more pronounced than the process of crossing the outside skate over the inside skate to glide.
- Keep the hips and skates facing the curved line of travel. Many skaters have a tendency to turn the hips sideways during the C-cut push; this will force the skater to skate sideways instead of backward.

Backward Versus Forward Crossovers:

Backward crossovers differ from forward crossovers in the following ways:

- As in all backward skating, body weight is over the front half of the blades.
- When you execute right-over-left backward crossovers, the curve is clockwise. The left skate is the inside skate, and the right skate is the outside skate. Left-over-right backward crossovers are just the opposite.
- The push from the inside edge is the backward C-cut push (as in straight backward skating), and the thrust is to the front and side.
- After executing the C-cut push, the returning (free) skate may stay in (slight) contact with the ice during the return and as it crosses over. Even if it stays on the ice, it is unweighted. In forward crossovers, the returning skate is *not* on the ice after the stride-push.

BODY POSITION AND CONTROL IN CROSSOVERS

The ability to skate fast on a curve or circle is greatly affected by the positioning and control of the upper body.

- The hips and skates always face the direction of travel.
- The upper body remains still. Excessive movement of the upper body affects balance, agility, and maneuverability (BAM), as well as the ability to control the puck.
- The shoulders stay level with the ice. *Do not drop the inside shoulder.*
- The upper body (from waist to shoulders) rotates (twists) approximately one-quarter turn in opposition to the hips, which always face the direction of travel. This is called torque. Torque is essential for proper body positioning for forward and backward crossovers.
- Two upper body positions may be used for forward crossovers. Since the position used may depend on the game situation, both positions must be mastered:

1. The upper body faces toward the center of the curve or circle (figure 6.10*a*).
2. The upper body faces toward the outside (away from the center) of the curve or circle (figure 6.10*b*).

- Only one upper body position is used for backward crossovers—the upper body faces toward the center of the curve or circle.
- Although the upper body torques, the head and eyes face straight ahead so that you can see the entire ice. Do not look into or out of the circle because this may limit your ability to see what's going on around you.

Note: *Leaning* into the circle refers to leaning the lower body (skates, knees, and hips) into the circle. The upper body does not lean into the circle, and the shoulders do not tilt inward—the shoulders stay level with the ice. Sometimes the inside shoulder is actually held higher than the outside shoulder. This is true for both upper body positions and for both forward and backward crossovers.

Practice forward and backward crossovers while holding the hockey stick with both hands. Keep the stick on the ice in its correct position for controlling a puck. Practice this on both the forehand and backhand sides. Practice both body positions for forward crossovers (see figure 6.10). Also practice crossovers while holding the hockey stick with just the top hand—first without a puck, then with a puck.

Note: Keep your arms, chest, and shoulders still! Excessive upper body movement will cause you to lose the puck.

COACHING TIP

Balance is lost when a skater leans or tilts the upper body into the curve or circle.

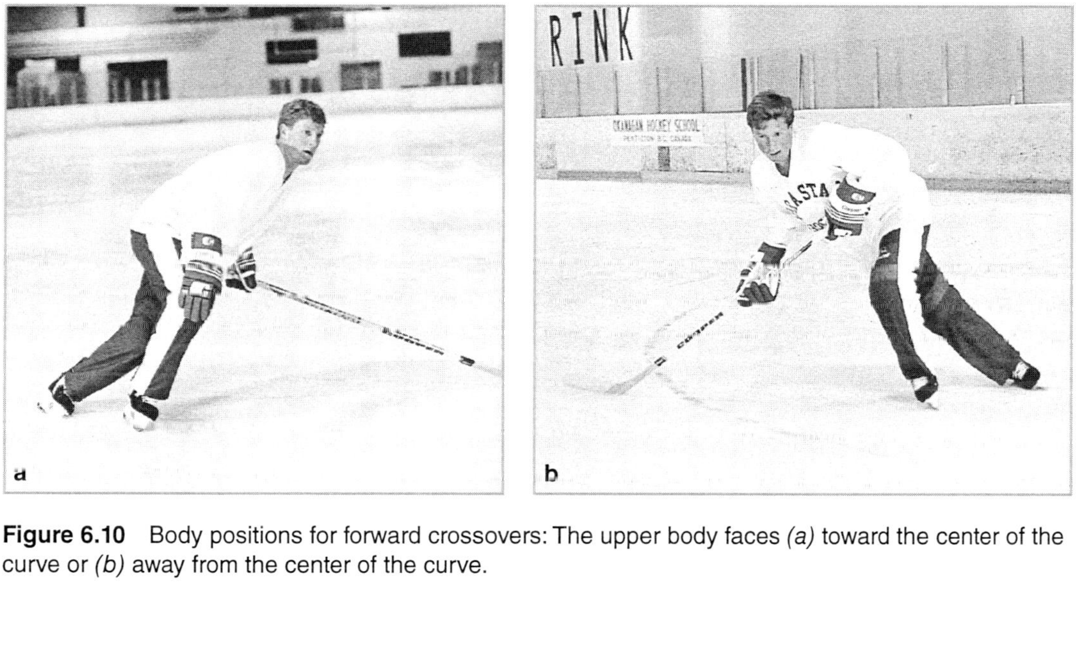

Figure 6.10 Body positions for forward crossovers: The upper body faces *(a)* toward the center of the curve or *(b)* away from the center of the curve.

STRIDE TEMPOS

As in straight forward and backward skating, the stride lengths and stride tempos of each crossover sequence must be equal. A crossover in which one leg pushes fully and the other pushes only partially is insufficient. The same is true of a crossover in which one leg moves rapidly and the other moves slowly.

Try to develop varying tempos for forward and backward crossovers. Remember that all strides must be full strides and that stride tempos depend on how quickly the free skate returns so that you can change feet. Practice crossovers slowly and correctly at first, then faster and faster (but still correctly), and finally at speeds that put you out of control (overspeed training). First practice without a puck and then with a puck.

Points to Remember for Forward and Backward Crossovers

- Every crossover sequence includes two pushes—the first from the inside edge of the outside skate, and the second from the outside edge of the inside skate. If one is eliminated, half of the potential power is lost.
- Body weight is always situated above the outside skate. The body weight doesn't change when the skater changes feet; rather, the skates change underneath the body. There is no change of weight from forward to backward or from side to side.
- The outside skate is always the one that crosses over—it crosses over in front of the toe of the inside skate.
- The quality of the X-push affects the quality of the crossover maneuver. If this push is only partially used, power is lost and the crossover itself is incomplete. When the scissoring action is executed properly, the legs cross at the top of the thighs, not just at the knees.
- The depth of the edges applied to the ice is directly related to speed and to the sharpness of the curve. Use shallower edges when traveling slowly on a large curve (compared to when traveling fast on a sharp curve). Develop the ability to adjust the depth of the edges based on the situation at hand: Sharper curves and greater speed require a greater lean of the edges and knees—and a greater counterlean of the upper body.
- The manner in which the skates and body coordinate to produce curves (as explained in chapter 1) should be carefully reviewed.
- The process of crossing the inside leg under the body to push is more pronounced than the process of crossing the outside leg over in front of the inside skate.
- The free skate stays close to and almost parallel with the ice during each push and during each return. Kicking up the heels (caused by pointing the toe straight down) or lifting the skate high off the ice (caused by excessively flexing the knee of the free leg) delays the return process and raises the center of gravity.
- The hips and skates face the line of travel at all times. If the hips turn sideways, the skater is forced to go sideways (i.e., like a snake). If either skate

takes the ice facing a different direction (i.e., sideways), the skater is forced to go that way. This is impossible, and the skater is likely to fall.

- In forward or backward crossovers, the skates stay parallel to each other and facing along the line of travel. If either skate turns at an angle different from the line of travel, the line of travel will change. You might end up with your skates sliding sideways into a skid.
- The ability of goalies to perform forward and backward crossovers depends on a complete scissoring action. When the X-push drives fully under the body, there is more space for the outside leg to cross over beyond the bulky pads.

DRILLS FOR IMPROVING FORWARD AND BACKWARD CROSSOVERS

The drills in this section help players develop the following aspects of crossovers:

- Proper use of the edges
- Power on both pushes
- Correct body position and control

Practice all drills equally in the clockwise and counterclockwise directions.

Edge Drills

The following edge drills can help players improve their use of the blade edges. These drills require skaters to use deep edges with strong knee bend. They also require players to have good balance and body control. In addition to the following drills, the coil drill and the flat to inside edge drill can be used to improve crossovers. These two drills were described for the forward stride in chapter 4 (see pages 54 and 55) and for the backward stride in chapter 5 (see pages 88 and 89).

Forward Inside Edge Semicircles

Intermediate

Note: Each push in this drill is the forward stride-push.

Skate forward from one goal line. Push off with the right skate and leg, and glide forward onto the LFI. Curve a *complete* semicircle (shape of the letter *U* or *C*) on the LFI. After completing the semicircle, push off with the left skate and leg, and glide forward onto the RFI. Curve a complete semicircle on the RFI. After completing the semicircle, once again push off with the right skate and leg, and glide forward onto the LFI. Skate continuous alternating semicircles for the entire length of the ice (figure 6.11). Be sure to complete each semicircle before gliding onto the new skate.

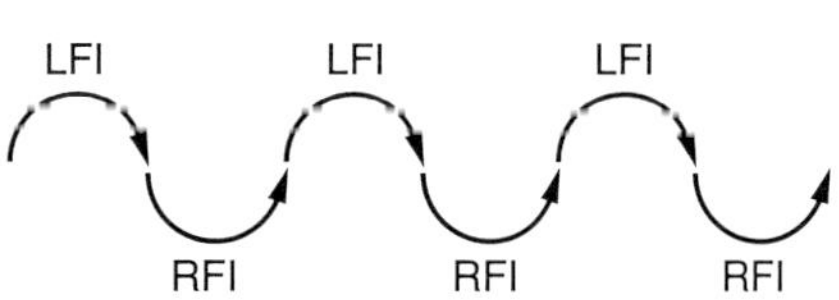

Figure 6.11 Forward inside edge semicircles.

Backward Inside Edge Semicircles

Intermediate

Note: Each push in this drill is the backward stride-push (backward C-cut push).

Skate backward from one goal line. Push off with the right skate and leg (backward C-cut push), and glide backward onto the LBI. Curve a *complete* semicircle (shape of the letter *U* or *C*) on the LBI. After completing the semicircle, push off with the left skate and leg (backward C-cut push), and glide backward onto the RBI. Curve a complete semicircle on the RBI. After completing the semicircle, once again push off with the right skate and leg, and glide backward onto the LBI. Skate continuous alternating semicircles for the entire length of the ice (figure 6.12). Be sure to complete each semicircle before gliding onto the new skate.

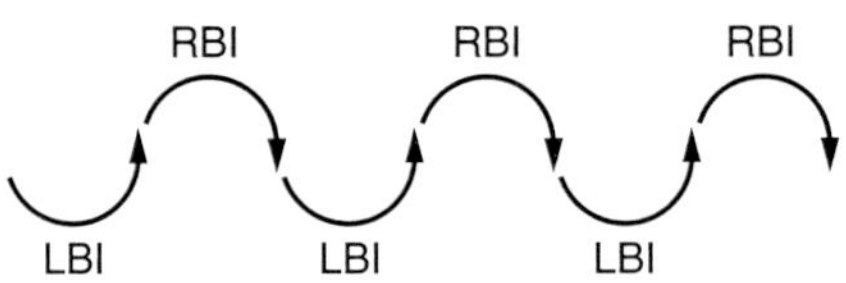

Figure 6.12 Backward inside edge semicircles.

Forward Outside Edge Semicircles

Intermediate

Note: Each push in this drill is the forward stride-push.

Skate forward from one goal line. Push off with the right skate and leg, and glide forward onto the LFO. Curve a *complete* semicircle (shape of the letter *U* or *C*) on the LFO. After completing the semicircle, push off with the left skate and leg, and glide forward onto the RFO. Curve a complete semicircle on the RFO. After completing the semicircle, once again push off with the right skate and leg, and glide forward onto the LFO. Skate continuous alternating semicircles for the entire length of the ice (figure 6.13). Be sure to complete each semicircle before gliding onto the new skate.

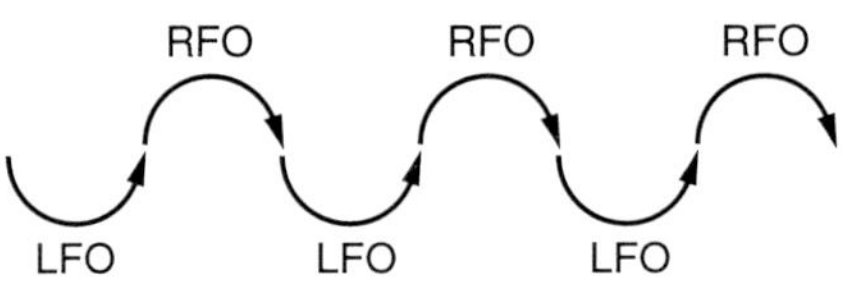

Figure 6.13 Forward outside edge semicircles.

Backward Outside Edge Semicircles

Intermediate to Advanced

Note: Each push in this drill is the backward stride-push (backward C-cut push).

Skate backward from one goal line. Push off with the right skate and leg (backward C-cut push), and glide backward onto the LBO. Curve a *complete* semicircle (shape of the letter *U* or *C*) on the LBO. After completing the semicircle, push off with the left skate and leg (backward C-cut push), and glide backward onto the RBO. Curve a complete semicircle on the RBO. After completing the semicircle, once again push off with the right skate and glide backward onto the LBO. Skate continuous alternating semicircles for the entire length of the ice (figure 6.14). Be sure to complete each semicircle before gliding onto the new skate.

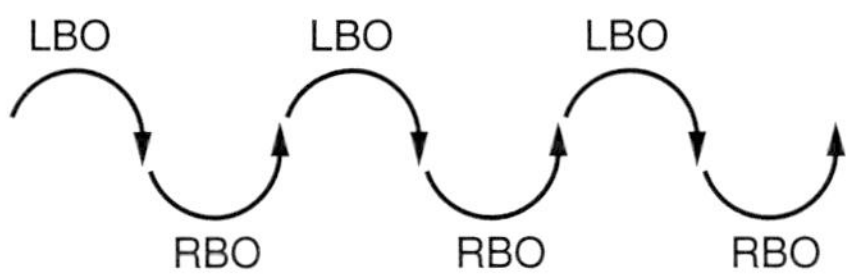

Figure 6.14 Backward outside edge semicircles.

Forward S-Cuts

Advanced

This drill involves executing a series of S-cuts into the ice. It is performed on one skate at a time—the other skate is off the ice throughout. The drill is a difficult but excellent drill for helping players master inside and outside edges, both of which are essential for skating curves and circles. This drill is also excellent for developing balance, knee bend, and strong quadriceps.

S-cuts are created by cutting a small semicircle into the ice with the edge (i.e., outside edge) of one skate, followed by cutting another small semicircle into the ice with the other edge (i.e., inside edge) of the same skate—and repeating the sequence continuously. When you cut with the RFO, the curve is clockwise; when you cut with the RFI, the curve is counterclockwise (figure 6.15 on page 118). For you to successfully execute forward S-cuts, your body weight must be on the back half of the cutting edge at all times.

1. Glide forward on a deep RFO (45 degrees) with the right knee well bent. Keep the left skate off the ice, next to the right skate.
2. While still on the RFO, slightly straighten the right knee to release your weight. As you release your weight, flip the right ankle inward and

simultaneously rebend the right knee deeply, shifting your weight over the inside edge; this changes the skate from leaning on an outside edge to leaning on an inside edge. You will now be skating on the RFI (45 degrees).

3. While on the RFI, slightly straighten the right knee to release your weight. As you release your weight, flip the right ankle outward and simultaneously rebend the right knee deeply, shifting your weight over the outside edge; this changes the skate from leaning on an inside edge to leaning on an outside edge. You will now be skating on the RFO (45 degrees).
4. Each edge must *cut* a semicircle into the ice. By applying a deep knee bend after each edge change and by keeping the body weight on the back half of the edge, you will be able to accelerate forward on each S-cut.
5. See how many S-cuts you can execute before having to put the left skate down.
6. Try to skate the entire length of the ice on the right skate, accelerating on each edge.
7. Repeat the drill on the left skate.

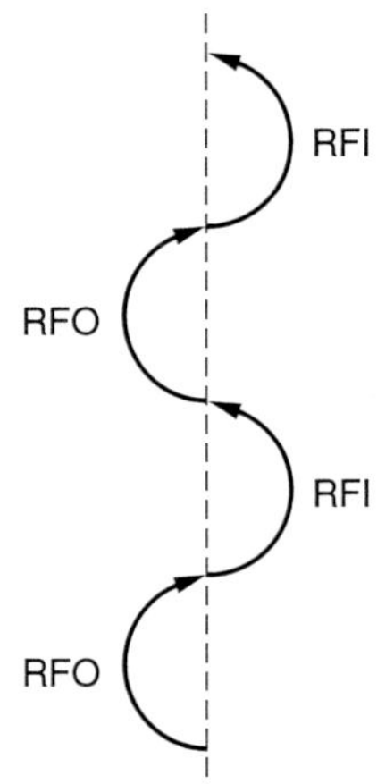

Figure 6.15 Forward S-cuts on the right skate: An imaginary axis divides the outside edge curve from the inside edge curve.

Backward S-Cuts

Advanced

Repeat the S-cuts drill, now skating backward. Only one skate is on the ice for each set of S-cuts. When skating backward, your body weight is on the *front* half of the edge. When you perform S-cuts on the RBO, the direction of the curve is counterclockwise. When you perform them on the RBI, the direction of the curve is clockwise. Try to skate the entire length of the ice on the same skate, accelerating on each edge.

Note: Your body weight must be on the back half of the edge when performing forward S-cuts. Your body weight must be on the front half when performing backward S-cuts.

Remember: Strong edge angles and a strong rise and fall of the skating knee are needed to perform this drill. A long-term goal is to perform one set of S-cuts on each skate (forward and backward) for an entire *lap* of the rink.

Jumping S-Cuts

Advanced

Repeat the S-cuts drill, but when changing each edge, jump off the ice. Land each jump on the other edge. For instance, when jumping from the inside edge, land on the outside edge, and vice versa. Perform this drill forward and backward.

COACHING TIP

Cutting with the inside edge is easier than cutting with the outside edge. Try to develop the ability to cut equally with outside and inside edges so that the depth of each cut (curve) is the same.

Crossover Drills

Over–Under Drill

Basic

To learn how to execute the X-push properly, skaters must learn how to accomplish the scissoring action of the legs. This drill uses the arms to teach the legs how to scissor.

Stand in place with your arms fully extended straight out in front of you. Cross the right arm over in front of the left arm, and simultaneously cross the left arm under the right arm in a scissoring action that forms the letter *X*. Cross from above the elbows to make the X as large as possible. It is impossible to make a big letter *X* if you only move one arm; both arms must actively move—equally and in opposite directions.

Now do this with the legs. Cross one leg over in front of the other while crossing the other leg underneath. Alternate the leg that crosses over and the leg that crosses under. Be sure to activate both legs; move them equally and in opposite directions. If only one leg moves to cross over the other, or if one leg moves fully while the other moves only partially, it is impossible to make a big letter *X*.

Walking Crossovers

Basic

This is an effective drill for learning the basic steps of the forward and backward crossover sequence.

Stand at one of the sideboards and face the goal line. Keep both skates pointed at this goal line as you perform walking crossovers across the ice. Walk to the left, performing right-over-left crossovers. The right (outside or trailing) skate pushes against its inside edge (forward stride-push) as the left (inside or leading) skate steps down onto its outside edge. After pushing, the right skate crosses over in front of the left skate; at the same time, the left skate crosses (pushes) straight under the body (X-push). Do not let the pushing leg slip back! Land the crossover on the right inside edge. Perform these walking crossovers until you reach the opposite sideboards.

Facing the same goal line, walk back across the ice. The crossovers are now left-over-right crossovers.

Variation (Basic)

Do the same drill, but now push to full extension on each push. This helps develop the ability to feel both the direction (sideways) and extension of the legs on the stride-push and the X-push.

C-Cuts on a Circle

Basic

This drill trains skaters to execute continuous C-cut pushes with the outside skate and leg while gliding on the outside edge of the inside skate. The drill should be performed forward and backward.

Forward C-cuts on a circle: Skate forward on a face-off circle in a clockwise direction. The left (outside) skate executes continuous C-cut pushes against its inside edge while the right (inside) skate continuously glides on its outside edge (figure 6.16). Be sure to bring the pushing skate and leg completely back to center on the return phase of each C-cut push. Keep the knee of the gliding leg well bent at all times—no bobbing up and down. Repeat the drill skating forward C-cuts in a counterclockwise direction.

Backward C-cuts on a circle: Perform the same drill skating backward and doing backward C-cut pushes on a face-off circle (both directions).

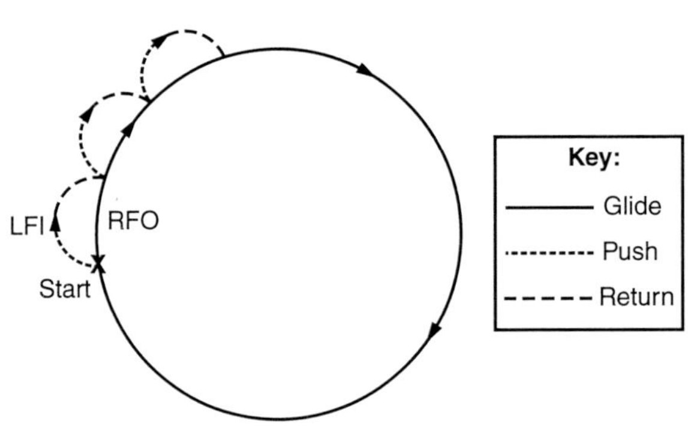

Figure 6.16 Forward C-cuts on a circle (clockwise).

Resistance Crossovers

Intermediate

This drill helps players develop correct and powerful leg drive on forward and backward crossovers. The drill involves pushing a resisting player while executing crossovers.

Partner up with another player. Stand sideways to the other player, holding a hockey stick horizontally at chest height between you. The backward skater faces you and prepares to resist by braking with a backward snowplow stop (see chapter 8, page 176).

Push the resisting player across the ice by executing a series of crossovers. These are actually walking crossovers except that both legs must drive powerfully and fully. If you were doing crossovers, the leading skate would correspond to the inside skate; it steps onto and pushes against its outside edge. The trailing skate corresponds to the outside skate; it thrusts against its inside edge, crosses over in front of the toe of the inside skate, and steps down onto its inside edge.

Drive to full extension on every push. Push the player across the ice doing right-over-left crossovers (figure 6.17, *a-d*). Coming back, use left-over-right crossovers. Keep your head up and your shoulders back throughout the drill. As always, practice both sides equally.

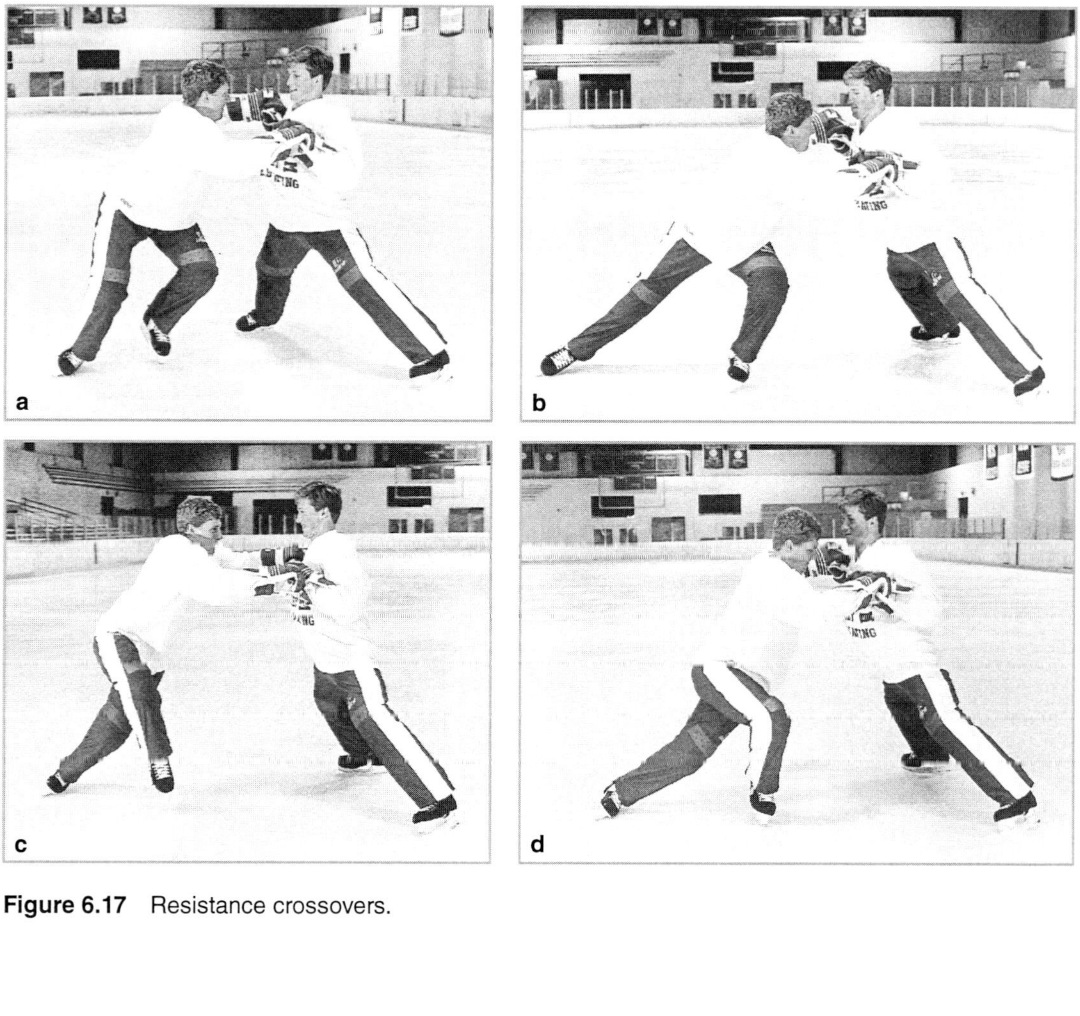

Figure 6.17 Resistance crossovers.

Outside Edge X-Cuts (Scissor Cuts)

Intermediate to Advanced

Outside edge pushes are more difficult to master than inside edge pushes. This drill helps players to practice outside edge pushes. Both the gliding skate and pushing skate are on *outside* edges at all times. Note the scissoring action of the legs as one skate crosses under the body to push and the other crosses over to glide.

1. Skate forward on the LFO, with the right skate off the ice. The LFO glides a counterclockwise curve (figure 6.18*a*).
2. Begin to cross the right skate over in front of the left.
3. Drive the left skate against its outside edge (X-push) as the right skate crosses over. Push sideways and to full extension (underneath your body). After crossing over, the right skate takes the ice on its RFO and glides a clockwise curve (figure 6.18*b*).
4. After the left skate reaches full extension, lift it off the ice and uncross it. Bring it forward and alongside the right skate in preparation for crossing it in front of the right skate (figure 6.18*c*). As the left skate uncrosses and moves forward, keep it close to and parallel with the ice.

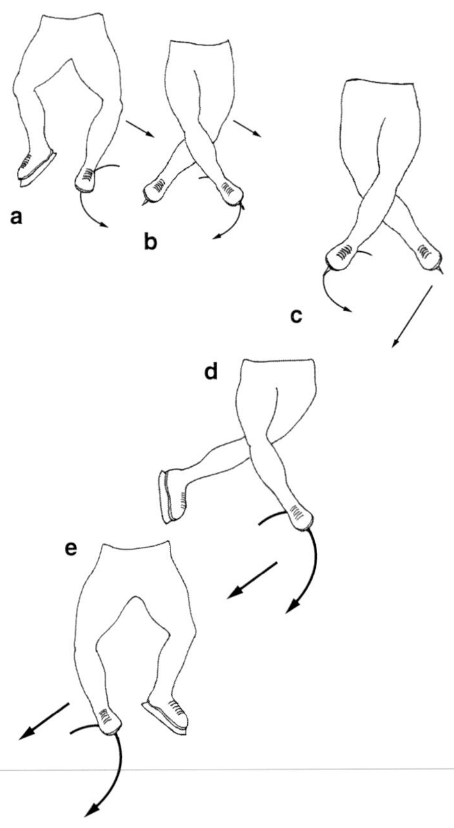

Figure 6.18 Outside edge X-cuts (scissor cuts), alternating feet.

5. As the left skate moves forward, prepare to push with the right skate and leg (X-push).
6. Drive the right skate against its outside edge as the left skate crosses over. Push sideways and to full extension (underneath your body). After crossing over, the left skate takes the ice on its LFO and glides a counterclockwise curve (figure 6.18, *d-e*).
7. You have completed one sequence. Keep repeating the sequence, continuously crossing over and pushing under.
8. Now perform outside edge X-cuts skating backward (figure 6.18, *e-a*).

Start this drill slowly and try to build speed with each push. Merely maintaining speed with each push is not sufficient. Pushing involves *gaining* speed.

Points to Remember

- Glide on and push from the outside edges.
- Glide on and push against the entire blade lengths.
- Push to full extension.

Drills for Crossovers on a Circle

When first learning to execute crossovers on a circle, hold the hockey stick with both hands and keep the stick on the ice in a position that will allow you to maintain control of a puck. With forward crossovers, you can use either of the two upper body positions—chest facing into or out of the circle. Keep your upper body quiet; shoulders and arms should be still. You can't control a puck if your chest, shoulders, and arms move around; every movement of the upper body causes a corresponding movement of the hockey stick.

As you gain upper body control, practice holding the hockey stick with just the top hand. Again, keep the upper body quiet and unmoving. Now perform crossovers with a puck—first holding the hockey stick with two hands, then with one hand.

Perform the following drills skating backward as well as forward crossovers. For backward crossovers, make sure you use the appropriate upper body position—chest and shoulders facing into the center of the circle. Hold the hockey stick with just the top hand.

Consecutive Crossovers

All Skaters

Skate consecutive crossovers on a face-off circle. Basic-level skaters should focus on learning to use the edges properly. More advanced skaters should focus on learning to use deep edges and knee bend; these skaters should work on making the circle as tight as possible while skating correctly as fast as possible.

Avoid leaning (tilting) the inside shoulder into the circle; this will cause the upper body to fall into the circle, which results in a loss of balance, especially at high speeds.

Note: When skating in the direction that requires you to hold the hockey stick on the backhand side (bottom hand across your body), it is difficult to eliminate all lean of the shoulders into the circle; in this case, try to minimize it.

Variation (All Skaters)

Skate the circle three times using forward crossovers, then turn backward and skate the circle three times using backward crossovers.

Parallel Blade Drill

Intermediate to Advanced

This drill teaches skaters how to achieve the proper X-push; this requires that the blade of the pushing skate be almost parallel to the ice at the completion of the push.

1. Stand in place with the skates side by side. Reach one skate and leg forward and place the heel of the blade into the ice; the toe of the blade should be pointed up (to the ceiling).
2. Keeping the same blade position, cross the skate and leg under your body until they are fully extended; keep the blade off the ice. If the toe remains pointed up while the heel remains pointed down (toward the ice) while the skate and leg are fully extended, the blade will be parallel to the ice (figure 6.19*a*).

If the toe points straight down (toward the ice), the blade will be perpendicular to the ice. It is impossible to push if the blade is in this walking or running position. This is a common mistake that results in inadequate acceleration (incomplete pushing) when executing crossovers.

3. Perform forward and backward crossovers skating slowly at first so that you can *feel* whether the blade is parallel to the ice at the finish of each X-push.

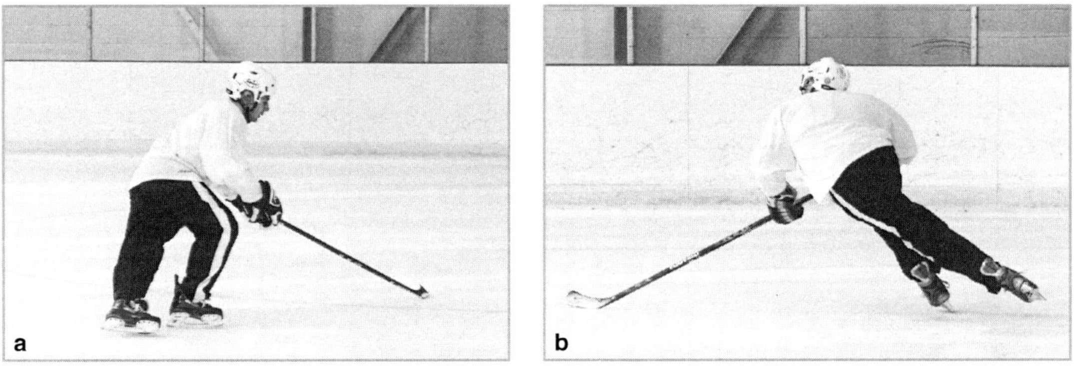

Figure 6.19 Parallel blade drill: *(a)* X-push parallel to the ice; *(b)* full extension on X-push with toe flick.

4. After mastering this parallel blade position, complete the X-push with the toe flick. The finish of this push involves driving outward against the front (toe) of the outside edge; the blade is almost parallel to the ice, although the toe is slightly closer to the ice than the heel (figure 6.19*b*).

Freeze Drill

Intermediate to Advanced

Perform consecutive forward crossovers on a face-off circle, skating at high speed. On a whistle signal, freeze! Stop skating and balance on whichever edge you happen to be gliding on when the whistle blows; keep the other skate off the ice. See how long you can balance (freeze your weight) on that edge without putting the other skate down. Be sure to freeze on both outside and inside edges and in both directions. Now do this while performing backward crossovers. This is an excellent test of balance on each edge and at any given instant.

Hold Drill

Advanced

This drill must be performed slowly. Its purpose is to train skaters to *feel* the difference between correct and incorrect execution on both the stride-push and the X-push. Perform this drill with both forward and backward crossovers and in both directions. For details on correct execution, see figures 6.3*c* and 6.3*f* (on page 103) for forward crossovers and figures 6.7*b* and 6.7*c* (on page 108) for backward crossovers.

Skate SLOW crossovers on a circle. Hold each glide for a count of four. During the hold phase, try to feel exactly what your skates and legs are doing. Try to feel any mistakes, and try to correct them as you skate. For example, consider the following questions:

- Have you achieved a complete stride-push?
- Is the pushing skate fully extended on the stride-push (with toe flick)?
- Are the pushing skate and leg fully extended on the X-push (with toe flick)?
- Is the blade parallel to the ice at the finish of the X-push, or is the toe pointed down?
- Do the pushing (now free) skate and leg return fully?
- Is the blade parallel to the ice during the return phase, or is the toe pointed down?

Forward X-Push

Intermediate to Advanced

Skate forward from the goal line to the first blue line. At the first blue line, glide straight ahead on your right skate—with the left skate and leg in the X-push position—until you reach the far blue line. When you reach the far blue line, skate forward to the opposite goal line. Coming back down the ice, glide forward on your left skate, with your right skate and leg in the X-push position. Be sure that the pushing (X-push) leg is fully extended, with the skate blade parallel to the ice, during the entire glide.

Backward X-Push

Intermediate to Advanced

Skate backward from the goal line to the first blue line. At the first blue line, glide straight backward on your right skate—with the left skate and leg in the X-push position—until you reach the far blue line. When you reach the far blue line, skate backward to the opposite goal line. Coming back down the ice, glide backward on your left skate, with your right skate and leg in the X-push position. Be sure that the pushing (X-push) leg is fully extended, with the skate blade parallel to the ice, during the entire glide.

Counterlean Drill

Intermediate to Advanced

This drill is used to practice the counterlean position.

Skate a series of consecutive forward crossovers on a counterclockwise circle. Keep the inside shoulder raised so that it almost touches your chin; simultaneously, keep the outside shoulder as low as possible. The shoulders will lean (tilt) strongly toward the outside of the circle. Repeat on a clockwise circle. Then repeat the drill doing backward crossovers.

Variations (Intermediate to Advanced)

1. To exaggerate this feeling even more, have the inside shoulder actually touch your chin as you skate the circles.

Note: These positions are exaggerations of the actual upper body position. Exaggerating the position allows you to more readily feel the difference between leaning the upper body outward (correct) and leaning it inward (incorrect). Once you are able to feel the correct position, modify it so that the inside shoulder is held only slightly higher than the outside shoulder so that your upper body leans only slightly outward.

2. Combine the previous counterlean drills with the freeze drill (page 125): Skate a series of consecutive forward crossovers on a counterclockwise circle. Keep the inside shoulder raised so that it almost touches your

chin; simultaneously, keep the outside shoulder as low as possible. On a whistle signal, freeze (stop skating) and glide on whichever edge you are on when the whistle blows. Try to feel the exaggerated upper body position as you glide and balance on each edge. Maintain this upper body position as you resume skating the circle. Be sure to freeze on both inside and outside edges. Repeat on a clockwise circle. Then repeat the drill doing backward crossovers.

Five-Circle Crossovers

All Skaters

Start skating from one corner of the rink. Skate one complete circle of crossovers (either forward or backward) on the nearest face-off circle. Then skate to the next face-off circle, and skate one complete circle of crossovers on it in the other direction. Then skate to the next circle, and skate one complete circle of crossovers on it in the original direction. Continue until you have skated one complete circle of crossovers around all five face-off circles. Finish in the opposite corner (figure 6.20).

Go slowly at first, making sure you use proper technique; think about and feel what you're doing, and try to correct errors. As technique improves, accelerate the pace until you can perform correct technique at increasingly faster speeds. Then practice this drill with a puck.

Practice both upper body positions when skating forward crossovers. When skating backward crossovers, make sure the upper body always faces toward the center of the circle. Hold the hockey stick with both hands and then with just the top hand. When skating (forward or backward) from circle to circle, hold the stick with just the top hand and stride properly. Use a proper and full arm swing.

Note: Spend additional time working on the more difficult direction.

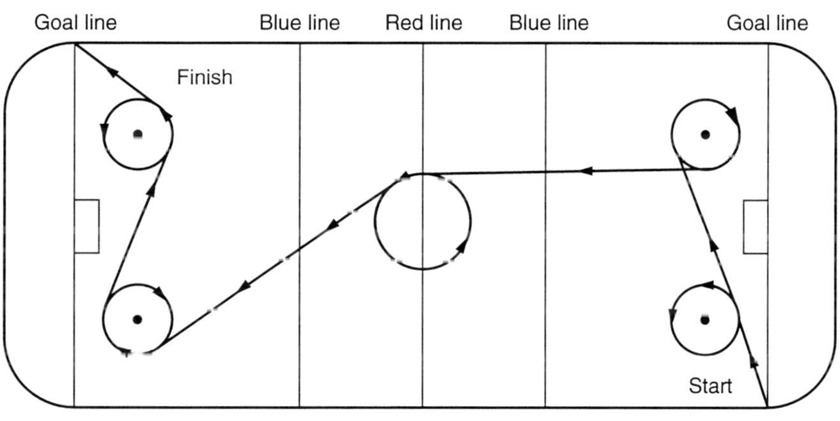

Figure 6.20 Five-circle crossovers.

Variations on Crossover Drills

Numerous variations on crossover drills can be used for training. The following variations are just a sampling and may be expanded on or changed.

Crossovers in Figure-Eight Patterns

Intermediate to Advanced

1. Skate consecutive forward crossovers around a circle two full times. Then skate to a second, tangential circle and skate around it two full times in the opposite direction. Now skate back to the original circle and skate crossovers around it two full times in the original direction. Keep repeating this sequence. Do the same skating backward crossovers.
2. Skate forward crossovers around a circle two full times, then skate to a second circle and skate backward crossovers around it two full times. Return to the original circle and skate forward crossovers around it two full times. Keep repeating this sequence.
3. Repeat the drill as outlined in steps 1 and 2, but now with the puck.

Note: Use both upper body positions for forward crossovers. When skating backward crossovers, make sure the upper body always faces toward the center of the circle. Refer to figure 6.10 on page 113.

Crossovers on the Same Circle

Intermediate to Advanced

1. Skate forward crossovers two times around a face-off circle clockwise. On a whistle signal, stop, change direction, and skate crossovers around the same circle counterclockwise. Now do this using backward crossovers.
2. Skate forward crossovers two times around a face-off circle, then turn and skate backward crossovers two times around the same circle. Practice both directions equally.
3. Incorporate the puck and practice forward and backward crossovers with the puck, using the appropriate upper body positions.

Crossovers Around Pylons

Intermediate to Advanced

Place six to eight pylons in a straight line on the ice, approximately 15 feet (4.5 m) apart. Start from one goal line and skate straight forward (or backward) to the first pylon. Skate forward (or backward) crossovers one full time around the pylon before proceeding to the next pylon. Do this around all of the pylons, alternating the direction of crossovers at each pylon. After skating around all the pylons, skate straight forward (or backward) to the far goal line.

Note: Crossovers can be all forward or all backward, or they can alternate (one forward then one backward, and so on).

Forward C-Cut Crossovers

Advanced

This drill involves skating forward crossovers around a circle. However, all pushes are forward C-cut pushes, so the heels of both skates *stay on the ice* at all times.

Forward C-cut crossovers help develop many of the skills needed for effective forward crossovers:

- Maintaining a strong knee bend on the gliding leg during the crossover
- Keeping the body weight on the pushing skate and leg for an effective push
- Using the back half of the blade to initiate each push
- Developing powerful leg drive
- Developing full extension
- Training the returning skate to stay close to and parallel with the ice during the return phase

The edges used for gliding and pushing are the same as in regular crossovers, but the pushes (from the outside skate and from the inside skate) are executed solely with the back half of the blades. *The toes are not used.* The instructions given are for skating around a counterclockwise circle.

First Push

This is a forward C-cut push against the inside edge.

1. Use the inside edge of the right (outside) skate to execute a forward C-cut push.
2. Push with the back half of the blade. Keep the heel of the skate on the ice as the skate and leg push and reach full extension (figure 6.21*a*).
3. During the push, shift your weight onto the LFO and glide on the LFO.
4. Keep the right heel on the ice as you bring the right skate forward to cross it over in front of the toe of the left skate.

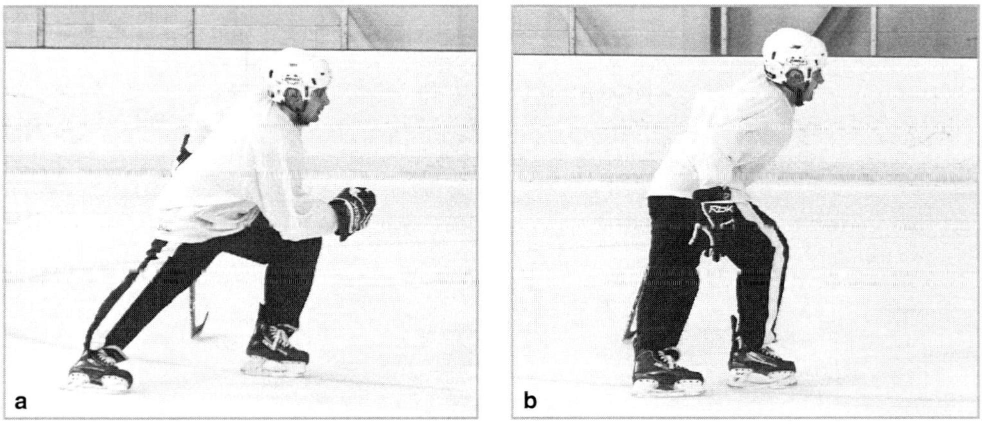

Figure 6.21 Forward C-cut crossovers: *(a)* C-cut push and *(b)* X-push.

Second Push

This is a C-cut push against the outside edge.

1. Drive the left (inside) skate against its outside edge and cross it under your body. The push forms a reverse C-cut (figure 6.21*b* on page 129).
2. Push with the back half of the blade. Keep the heel of the skate on the ice as the leg pushes and reaches full extension under your body. The push simulates the X-push.
3. During the push, shift your weight onto the RFI and glide on the RFI.
4. After the left leg reaches full extension under your body, glide the left skate back to a position alongside the right skate. Keep the heel of the left skate on the ice during the return. You have completed one sequence.
5. Keep repeating the sequence.
6. Mirror these instructions to practice the drill on a clockwise circle.

Backward C-Cut Crossovers

Advanced

The previous forward C-cut crossover drill can also be used for backward crossovers; however, because of the difficulty of this version, it is recommended mainly for advanced skaters.

To perform the backward C-cut crossover drill, you will use backward C-cut pushes instead of forward C-cut pushes. Use the front halves of the blades to push. If you push with your heels, your weight may be forced back over the pushing blade, and you may fall.

Body Control Drills

The following drills stress upper body positioning and control. You must learn to position the upper body properly and to avoid excessive upper body movement. You will be a better balanced and stronger skater as a result. Some pro hockey players who are not exceptionally fast compensate by having superb balance and control.

Crossovers: Chest Facing Into the Circle

Basic to Intermediate

Skate these drills with the chest facing toward the center of the circle. The object is to train the upper body to remain still while you perform forward and backward crossovers.

1. Skate forward crossovers around a circle. Hold the hockey stick with both hands, keeping the stick blade on the ice. If the chest and shoulders

are positioned properly, the stick will ride inside the circle, and the tip of the stick blade will point toward the face-off dot at the center of the circle. This is the case on both the forehand and backhand sides.

Do not let the stick move around. If you can keep the stick in the same position while you skate, this indicates that your upper body is under control. If your arms, chest, and shoulders move around, it's because your upper body is not under control. You will be forced to move the hockey stick, which will cause you to lose the puck. Skaters must learn to skate with the upper body unmoving and under control.

2. Skate forward and backward crossovers around a circle while holding a hockey stick in the air with both hands, at chest height and parallel with the ice. Do not let the stick tilt inward (toward the center of the circle). If anything, it should tilt outward (toward the outside of the circle), indicating that the inside shoulder is higher than the outside shoulder.

Intermediate to Advanced

1. Skate forward and backward crossovers with a hockey glove balanced on top of each outstretched hand. This requires you to keep the arms, chest, and shoulders still; if you move them, the gloves will fall.
2. Skate forward and backward crossovers while holding a full cup of water in each hand. Do not spill the water. This requires you to keep the upper body, arms, and hands extremely still and under control.
3. Skate forward and backward crossovers with your hands clasped behind your back (or with hands on hips). This minimizes arm, chest, and shoulder movement.
4. Skate forward and backward crossovers in the following manner: A group of six to eight players form a circle. They are linked together by their hockey sticks. Extend the right arm in front of you while holding the butt end of your hockey stick, and at the same time extend the left arm behind you and grasp the stick blade of the player behind you. Each player's chest faces the center of the circle. Linking up in this manner locks the shoulders and chest in the desired upper body position, and it trains players to feel and maintain the correct upper body position.
5. Now practice the crossovers by yourself, maintaining this upper body position. Hold the hockey stick with just the top hand, and keep the stick in its proper place on the ice for carrying a puck. Also practice this while carrying a puck on the stick.

Note: In the previous drill, you will skate in a counterclockwise circle when skating forward crossovers, and you will skate in a clockwise circle when skating backward crossovers.

Now do this drill in the opposite direction; for step 4, extend left arms in front and right arms behind.

Crossovers: Chest Facing Outside the Circle

Intermediate to Advanced

This body position is used for forward crossovers only. This position is used when an attacking player needs to protect the puck from a defender. The attacker protects the puck by putting his or her back to the defender; the attacker wards off the defender with his or her inside arm and shoulder. To accomplish this, the attacker's chest must face out of the curve. See figure 9.25 (bulling) on page 221. In these game situations, attackers often hold the hockey stick with just the top hand, which gives them more reach for protecting the puck.

Skate the following drills (forward crossovers only) with your back facing the center of the circle (chest facing away from the center of the circle). The hockey stick will ride outside the circle. The idea is to train the upper body to remain unmoving and correctly positioned in order to protect the puck.

1. Skate forward crossovers on a circle with your back facing the center of the circle. Your chest will face away from the center of the circle, and the hockey stick will ride outside the circle. Keep the hockey stick on the ice and in the same position as you skate the circles. Do not allow the stick to move around.
2. Perform steps 1, 2, 3, and 4 from the previous drill—crossovers: chest facing into the circle (intermediate to advanced level)—but now with chest and shoulders facing *outside* the circle.
3. A group of six to eight players form a circle. They are joined together by their hockey sticks (as in step 4 of the previous drill). Players now hold the sticks so that their chests face outside the circle (backs facing the center). For forward crossovers around a counterclockwise circle, the left hand extends in front to hold the stick of the player in front, and the right hand extends behind to hold the stick of the player in back. Again, the goal is to position the shoulders and chest correctly, to feel this upper body position, and to eliminate excessive arm, chest, and shoulder movement.
4. Practice forward crossovers by yourself using this upper body position. Hold the hockey stick with just the top hand. Keep the hockey stick in its proper place on the ice (outside the circle) as you skate; do not move it around. Now practice this while controlling a puck.

Running Crossovers

Intermediate to Advanced

Players often run or leap the first few forward crossover strides in order to accelerate quickly. When performed correctly, these running or leaping crossover strides are very effective.

Practice running forward crossovers by sprinting on the edges. Use the full thrusting action of the legs even when running. Leap outward, not upward (figure 6.22). When you are running, the body weight should be on the toes (fronts of the edges), similar to when starting (see chapter 7 for information on starts). The *toe* is the area from the ball of the foot to the toe.

Skate forward crossovers on a circle at a very slow pace. On a whistle signal, run a few steps of the crossovers. Accelerate with powerful, rapid, and fully extended pushes. On the next whistle, slow down. Use slow crossovers; do not run. On the next whistle, run a few steps of the crossovers again.

Perform the drill without a puck and then with a puck.

Figure 6.22 Running forward crossovers.

WEAVING CROSSOVERS FOR LATERAL MOBILITY

Today's hockey is notable for its lateral mobility. Players weave in and out, zigzag, and crisscross from one side to another. Not only does this make the game exciting, but it is also the basis for faking (deking). Faking is accomplished by moving one way and then suddenly moving the other way. Crossovers are often used to enhance an attacking player's ability to fake. The attacking player may move and cross over one way (e.g., right over left), then fake (as if to continue crossing over or skating in the same direction), and then quickly move the other way (if crossing over, left over right).

Defenders often use weaving crossovers to accelerate backward. Although defenders don't need lateral mobility for faking, they must be able to move with, follow, and stay in front of attacking players.

All weaving crossovers require that a third step be added to the two-step crossover sequence. The purpose of the third step is to neutralize the feet, the body weight, and the original direction of curve, as well as to prepare the skater to move in a new direction. The neutralizing step involves uncrossing the skates and stepping out wide so that the skates and legs are wide apart and in a neutral position. Only after the third (neutralizing) step is it possible for the player to skate in a new direction (or to fake and move back in the original direction) Watch Alexander Ovechkin and you will see a master of lateral mobility.

In this chapter, you have learned how to execute the first two steps and the first two pushes of forward and backward crossovers. We will now discuss how to execute the all-important third step and the accompanying third push of weaving crossovers.

A weaving crossover is a three-step sequence instead of a two-step sequence. Since players need to gain speed on the third step (as well as on the first two steps), they must use a third push that enables them to do so. Many players neglect the third push and thus limit their ability to move from side to side with power and speed.

The third push is always against the inside edge of the blade, and it is always done with the skate that did the first push. The third push is in fact identical to the first push, which is the stride-push! When you are skating forward, the third push is the forward stride-push. When you are skating backward, the third push is the backward C-cut push.

The third step lands on the skate that would be the inside skate if you were doing a regular crossover. This is the skate that would ordinarily glide on the outside edge. However, in this move, the skate (i.e., the inside skate) lands on its *inside edge* instead of on its outside edge!

In addition, the third step is a wide step (as wide as possible). It is planted on a strong inside edge, and the body weight is totally committed over it (the skate that is stepping wide). Planting a strong inside edge on the third (wide) step allows the player to change direction instantaneously on the following step. *This is the key to lateral mobility!*

Note: Contrary to straight forward or backward striding, the ability to move sideways requires a wide base. To shift weight from side to side, a player's skates should be somewhat wider apart than the shoulders.

Figure 6.23 shows the sequence for weaving forward crossovers. Figure 6.24 shows the sequence for weaving backward crossovers. Figure 6.25 diagrams the pattern for weaving backward crossovers.

Figure 6.23 Weaving forward crossovers.

Figurc 6.24 Woaving backward crossovers.

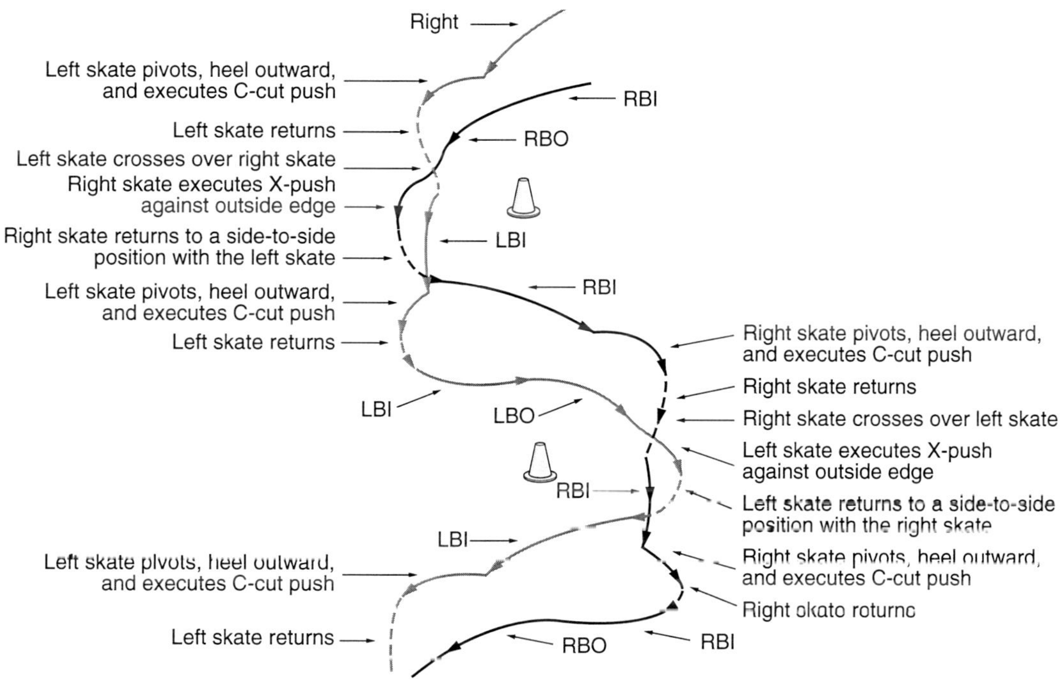

Figure 6.25 Pattern for weaving backward crossovers.

DRILLS FOR WEAVING CROSSOVERS (LATERAL MOBILITY)

Weaving Crossovers Around Pylons

Intermediate

1. Practice weaving crossovers (forward and backward) around pylons. Try to skate a tight S-curve pattern (figure 6.26*a*).
2. Vary the pylon setup. Skate forward crossovers in an S-like pattern around two pylons. Then turn around and do the same thing skating backward crossovers. Figure 6.26*b* shows a slightly different, more difficult course.

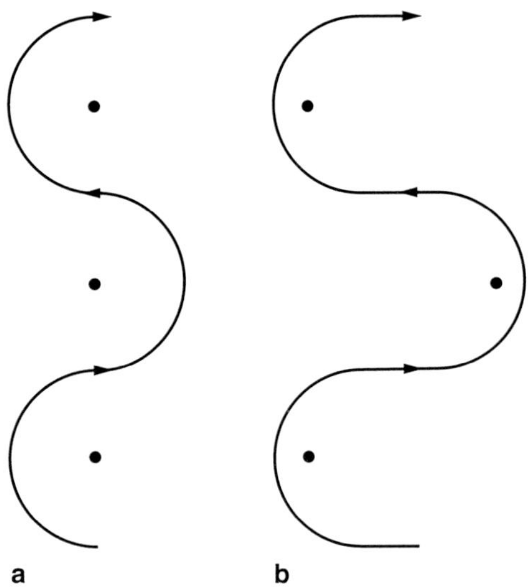

Figure 6.26 Two patterns of weaving crossovers around pylons.

Side-to-Side Jumps

Intermediate to Advanced

This drill is for the third step of weaving crossovers. It trains players to leap wide (laterally) and to land on inside edges.

Place a hockey stick on the ice. Stand facing the stick; you should be positioned at about the middle of the stick. Prepare to jump from side to side. Start with small side-to-side jumps. Gradually increase the distance of each jump until you can jump from one end of the stick to the other (figure 6.27). Land each jump on the inside edge of the landing skate, and land with a deep knee bend of the landing leg. Immediately after landing each jump, bring your skates together and quickly jump toward the opposite end of the stick. Do a series of side-to-side jumps. The idea is to reach the other end of the stick. To accomplish this, you will have to push very powerfully on each jump (stride-push).

Note: Jump outward, not upward (like a line drive, not a fly ball). Upward motion is useless!

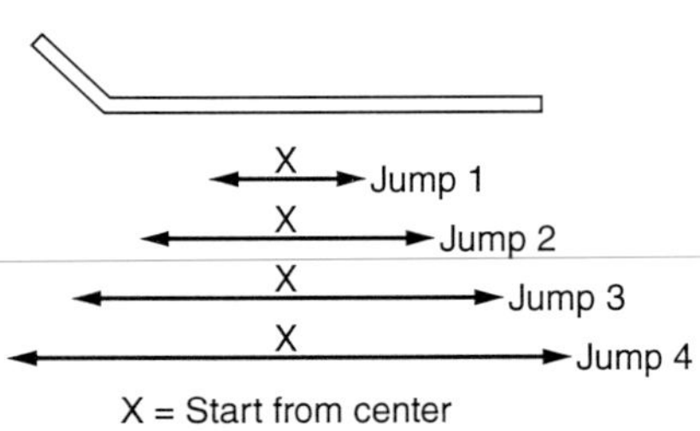

Figure 6.27 Side-to-side jumps.

Weaving Crossovers Down the Ice

Intermediate to Advanced

Practice forward and backward weaving crossovers for the length of the ice. Use one crossover in each direction (with a wide neutralizing step in each direction). Alternate the side of each wide step. Be sure to plant a strong inside edge on each wide step.

Variations (Intermediate to Advanced)

- Practice forward and backward weaving crossovers for the length of the ice. However, do two or three crossovers in the same direction (i.e., right over left) followed by one wide (neutralizing) step in that direction. Then do two or three crossovers in the other direction (i.e., left over right) followed by one wide (neutralizing) step in that direction.
- Practice forward and backward lateral mobility for the length of the ice without using any crossovers before the wide steps. Start from the goal line and skate straight forward or straight backward to the first blue line. Between the blue lines, do a continuous set of wide steps in each direction (out to the left, then out to the right, and so on). When you reach the far blue line, skate straight forward or straight backward to the far goal line.

Note: Step onto a deep inside edge on the wide (neutralizing) step of each sequence.

- Work with another player. One player skates as a forward and the other as a defender. The forward (with a puck) starts at the goal line and skates forward, using weaving crossovers to fake and get away from the defender. The defender starts at the first blue line and skates a similar pattern of backward crossovers. The defender tracks the forward and tries to prevent the forward from passing or escaping.

Forward Lateral Mobility With Toe Drags

Advanced

This drill requires the skater to use a toe drag on the outside edge of the toe on each X-push. The skater must also use a toe drag on the inside edge of the toe on each stride-push.

Start from the goal line and perform the previous drill (forward weaving crossovers down the ice) with the following difference: At the finish of each push, drag the toe of the pushing skate. The toe drag simulates the toe flick that is necessary at the finish of each push.

Note: Both the first push and the third push are the forward stride-push. The second push is the X-push.

Backward Lateral Mobility With Toe Drags

Advanced

Very advanced skaters can practice the previous drill skating backward; this is quite difficult at first. Both the first push and the third push are the backward stride-push (backward C-cuts). The second push is the X-push.

Forward and Backward Lateral Mobility With C-Cuts

Advanced

This drill is a variation of the C-cut crossover drills (pages 129 and 130). It is done skating down the ice instead of on a circle.

Start from the goal line and skate the previous weaving crossover drill with the following difference: Each push is a C-cut push. Both the first push and the third push are the C-cut push against the inside edge. The second push is a C-cut push against the outside edge.

Note: The C-cut push does not include a toe drag.

Lateral Leap to Change Direction on Circles

Advanced

High-level hockey players will need to skate tight circles at high speeds. In this drill, players must skate tight figure-eight circles at high speeds. They must transition from circle to circle quickly and suddenly—with a minimum amount of time spent gliding as they change from one circle to the other. Because they are skating so fast, they sometimes run out of space. In attempting to avoid hitting the boards, players are forced to glide momentarily; the result is that they slow down.

Most players find it very difficult to do the following:

1. Keep the circles tight as speed increases, especially after changing from one circle to another.
2. Minimize gliding during and after the transition from one circle to another.

This drill teaches players to make quick transitions from circle to circle while keeping the legs moving at the same tempo (which is necessary for maintaining speed)—without running out of space.

At the apex of each figure eight, step out very wide and onto a deep inside edge (figure 6.28). This step is a variation of the third step of weaving forward crossovers. Using this wide step between the circles accomplishes two things:

1. Stepping out wide takes you in the other direction momentarily. This provides more space for skating the new circle, and it allows you to keep the next circle tight.
2. Landing on a deep inside edge allows you to push instantaneously into the new set of crossovers and eliminates the need to glide.

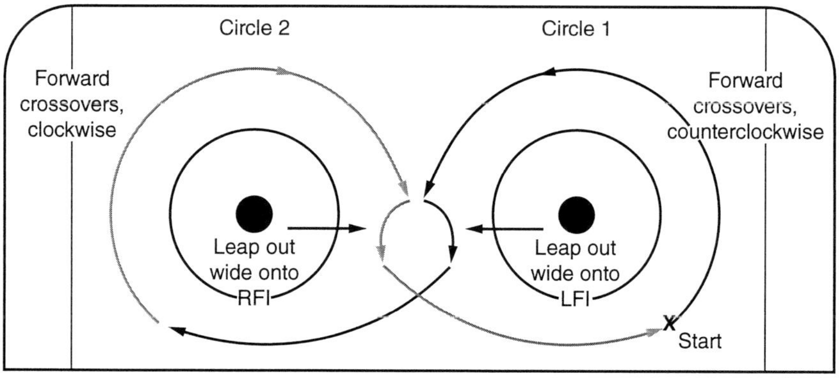

Figure 6.28 Lateral leap to change direction on circles.

Note: Because the speeds are so fast, you must take the upper body position for the new circle (inside shoulder high) on the wide step. If you wait to take the new upper body position until you are already skating the new circle, balance will be impaired. You may have to glide (slow down) to avoid falling—or you may fall!

Chapter 7

Explosive Starts for Gaining the Advantage

Goals can be scored and hockey games can be won or lost in fractions of a second. Players who start out the fastest are often the ones who get to the puck first and get the advantage for their team. Those who don't start out fast may end up hopelessly behind the play. Players *must* develop the ability to accelerate quickly and explosively from a complete stop. They must also be able to shift instantly from low to high gear. Great hockey skaters can take off instantly from any position.

Hockey players starting on skates are comparable to sprint runners starting out of the blocks. To get going quickly and explosively, runners lean forward strongly and take the first few steps on the balls of their feet. Hockey players need to do the same thing—they should run the first few strides on the toes of the skates (the front 2 to 3 inches [5.1 to 7.6 cm] of the inside edges).

These running strides are choppy because the skates do not glide. The strides are extremely rapid, but contrary to their appearance, they are not short. They are accompanied by a forward lean along with extremely powerful and complete leg drive. Explosive acceleration means you need to get somewhere—fast.

When should players start on their toes? I call toe starts the escape valve. Anytime players need to get away quickly, they should start on their toes! Instant acceleration is crucial on a face-off, when changing gears (i.e., from slow to fast), when racing for the puck, when trying for a breakaway, when chasing an opponent, or in any situation when players want to create an advantage. Starting on the toes is the key to this. Players who start on the full blades tend to glide on the initial strides. This makes leg speed slower, and players often feel as though they are stuck in the mud.

At my power skating clinics, I often see players executing great toe starts. However, in games, I often see these same players starting on the full blades. This may be from lack of concentration or from lack of practice. There's no point in learning how to do toe starts (or any other maneuver) if you don't practice them all the time and then use them in game situations.

When working on toe starts, follow the same process as in all other skating maneuvers—first learn to execute them correctly; then correctly and powerfully; then correctly, powerfully, and quickly. Then do *thousands* of them, in all kinds of situations! When a coach blows the whistle to GO, always take the first few accelerating steps on the toes, regardless of whether you need to start from a complete stop or whether you need to accelerate from slow to fast. You may fall and mess up in the process of mastering toe starts; however, you will eventually master them, and they will become an automatic response.

Three components are necessary for achieving explosive acceleration on the ice:

1. **Quickness—quick feet, or rapid leg turnover.** To achieve quickness, a skater runs the first few strides on the toes (fronts of the inside edges) of the skates. The skates play touch and go with the ice—they do not glide. If the entire blade length contacts the ice, the skate is forced to glide. Gliding takes time and delays the next stride.

2. **Power.** Power is derived from the force exerted by the legs and body weight driving directly against the gripping edge. Full leg drive and total leg recovery are as imperative when starting as when striding. Nothing can propel the skater forward unless the legs drive fully in the opposite direction.

3. **Distance—outward motion.** To achieve distance, a skater must project the body weight outward in the desired direction of travel. The distance covered in the starting strides depends largely on the forward angle of the upper body (a strong forward angle of the upper body produces greater distance). Because the skating (contact) foot must take the ice under the center of gravity (midsection), the farther forward the upper body is projected, the farther forward the foot must reach in order to step down under the center of gravity and maintain balance. In other words, while the skater runs the first few strides, the body weight is thrown outward. This is similar to what a sprinter does when taking off from the starting block.

Three basic starts are used in hockey skating: forward (front), crossover (side), and backward. As in every aspect of skating, the ingredients for explosive starts include

- proper use of edges to provide grip into the ice,
- proper distribution of body weight,
- optimum leg drive, and
- rapid leg motion.

By developing the three starts, you will be able to perform an explosive takeoff regardless of which way you are facing when you stop or which direction you want to go when you start.

Players must keep the puck well out ahead of them in order to accelerate explosively with the puck. If the puck is too close to the body, it blocks the player's progress. The general rule for accelerating with the puck is that the puck goes first and the player follows it.

The principles of windup, release, follow-through, and return apply to starts as well as to all other hockey skating maneuvers.

Note: All toe starts require that the muscles of the feet be used in the same way that they are for the toe flick of the forward stride. The feet must be arched and the toes scrunched up (figure 7.1), and the tendon guard of the boot must press into the back of the leg.

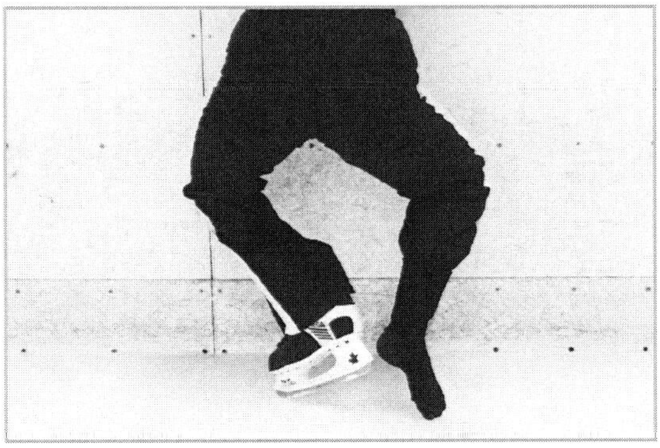

Figure 7.1 Foot position for toe starts: toes scrunched up.

FORWARD (FRONT) STARTS

A forward start is used when players are facing straight ahead in the direction that they intend to go—for example, if they have skated backward, stopped, and need to skate forward in the direction they came from. Another example is after a face-off—if the puck ends up straight ahead of the starting player, the player should use the forward start to get to the puck. The forward start relies on the V-diamond position of the skates and legs. In the following instructions, the initial push is done with the right skate and leg.

First Stride

Preparation

1. Pivot both skates and knees outward in an exaggerated V-diamond position (heels together, toes apart). Each skate should be turned outward approximately 80 to 85 degrees to the forward line of travel (figures 7.2 and 7.3*a* on page 145). The pushing edge must dig into the ice to prevent the skate from slipping. When starting from a complete stop, the turn-out angle of the gripping edge must be sideways to the line of travel.

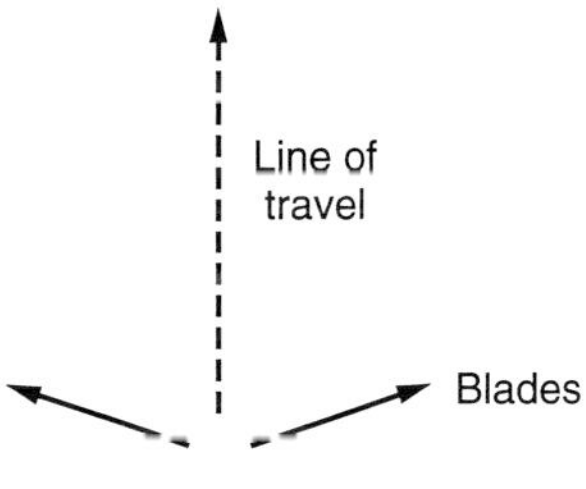

Figure 7.2 Forward start: skates pivoted outward about 80 to 85 degrees from the line of travel.

2. Place your entire body weight over the right (pushing) skate (figure 7.3*b*).

Windup

3. Bend your knees deeply (90 degrees) and dig the inside edge of the pushing skate into the ice so that the skate and lower leg form a strong (approximately 45-degree) angle to the ice. The stronger the pressure into the ice (created by the edge, knee bend, and body weight), the more power available for the thrust.

Release, Follow-Through, and Return

4. As you begin to push, shift your body weight strongly forward in the desired direction of travel. Body weight must be low and angled well forward, ready to be propelled powerfully by the thrusting skate and leg, which push directly against the cutting edge (figure 7.3*c*). Because the body weight is angled well forward, the primary thrust is executed with the front portion of the inside edge. As you shift your weight outward (forward), reach forward with the left (front) knee and skate. Keep moving the left skate forward until it makes contact with the ice under your center of gravity (figure 7.3, *d-e*). Powerful leg drive, the lean of the upper body, and the reach of the left knee and skate combine to produce forward motion.
5. The left (front) skate must contact the ice on the first 2 inches (5.1 cm) (toe) of the inside edge (45-degree edge angle) with the skate turned outward approximately 70 to 75 degrees from the forward line of travel. The heel of the blade should *not* touch the ice. When the left skate touches down properly—gripping the ice strongly with the inside edge, with your body weight over it—it is immediately prepared to push (figure 7.3*e*). If the skate does not touch down on a strong edge or if your weight is on the heel of the blade, the skate will be forced to glide. Gliding breaks the acceleration process because it delays the next stride.
6. After pushing, immediately return the pushing skate (now the free skate) to the center of gravity. This skate should immediately pass by the contact skate in the V-diamond position and reach forward in preparation for becoming the new contact skate. Keep the returning skate turned outward as it returns, passes the contact skate, and moves forward to take the ice (figure 7.3*f*).

Second Stride

1. When the left skate takes the ice, make sure it does so on the toe of the inside edge, with the body weight centered over it and the knee well bent. If the left skate contacts the ice properly, the skate is already in the windup position and is immediately prepared to become the new pushing skate.

Note: Landing on the toe of the skate, on a deep inside edge, and with a deep knee bend is critical to pushing instantaneously.

Figure 7.3 Forward start sequence.

Release, Follow-Through, and Return

2. Push powerfully, directly against the inside edge. Keep your body weight low and angled well forward. Push to full extension. As you push, continue to shift your weight and reach the right knee and skate forward, moving the skate forward until it makes contact with the ice under your center of gravity (figure 7.3*g* on page 145).
3. When the right skate takes the ice, it must touch down only on the toe of the inside edge; the skate is still turned outward, the knee is well bent, and the body weight is totally over the edge. On the second stride, the landing skate must be turned outward about 60 to 65 degrees from the forward line of travel. Your weight must be only on the front 2 to 3 inches (5.1 to 7.6 cm) (toe) of the inside edge. If your weight is on the heel of the blade, the skate will be forced to glide, causing slower leg speed and a delay of the next stride.
4. After pushing, immediately return the left skate (now the free skate) to the center of gravity. This skate must immediately pass by the contact skate in the V-diamond position and reach forward to become the new contact skate. Keep the returning skate turned outward as it returns, passes the contact skate, and moves forward to take the ice under your center of gravity.

Subsequent Strides

You have completed the first two running steps of the forward start. Some skaters like to take three or four running steps. The number of running steps is usually determined by the specific game situation. If there is a lot of open ice ahead, you can take up to three or four running steps to escape. If the opponent is pressing, one or two running steps may be all that are possible.

After the initial running steps, transfer to a sprinting forward stride. Do not continue to run—you need to take advantage of the glide of the skate. Continue to move the legs in a rapid sprinting motion. The angle of the upper body to the ice gradually becomes more upright. By the fifth or sixth stride, the upper body should be in the forward stride position, inclined at approximately 45 degrees to the ice. If the upper body becomes upright too suddenly, forward motion is broken. Many of the players who accelerate fast maintain a strongly inclined body angle for a longer period (longer than skaters who start less explosively).

Points to Remember

- It takes several running strides to accelerate.
- Push powerfully to full extension on every stride, using a quick, sprinting tempo. Remember that each sprinting stride must use the same tempo (leg rhythm).
- Recover each returning skate completely. The skates must return and pass each other in the V-diamond position before taking the ice on the next step.

- Each running stride takes you farther than the preceding one. On the first step, you are limited in the distance you can travel because your body is not yet in motion (you are overcoming inertia).
- Keep your body weight inclined well forward.
- Leap *outward*—do not jump upward! Height off the ice is not the objective and should be minimal.
- The function of the edges is to form a solid wedge in the ice against which you can vault yourself forward.
- Drive the arms in a forward–backward diagonal motion, in rhythm with the legs and on the same line of force as the legs.
- Keep the hockey stick on the ice in a position that allows you to keep the puck well ahead of you as you accelerate. If the puck jams your body, you are forced to slow down.
- An explosive start is a process of falling. It is actually a controlled fall. After a lot of practice, you will learn to control the fall, but while learning you may fall many times. For balance and stability, keep your shoulders back and your chest upright. Look straight ahead and keep your head and chin up.
- If toe starts are done correctly, the cuts that the edges make in the ice are short, well turned out, and deep. The cuts indicate that force has been successfully concentrated over a very short distance (preferably 2 to 3 inches [5.1 to 7.6 cm], but definitely not longer than the length of the blade). This allows for explosive motion. Long marks in the ice indicate gliding strides rather than running strides. Gliding dissipates force and is a process of deceleration. Figure 7.4 diagrams the initial strides of an explosive forward start.

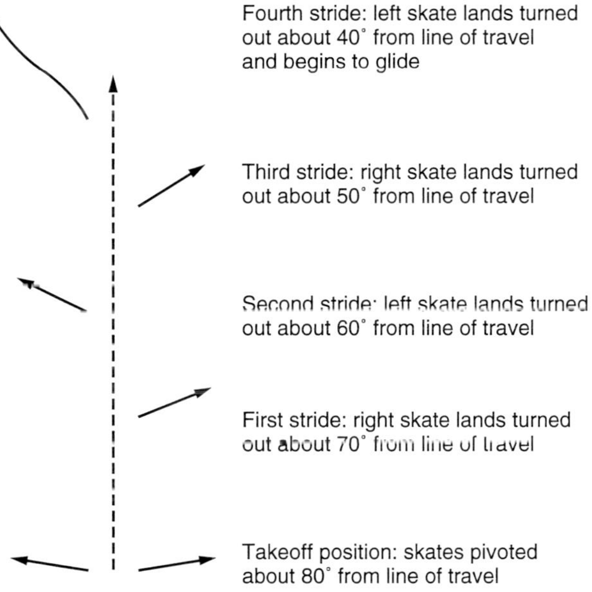

Figure 7.4 Forward start (showing cuts in the ice).

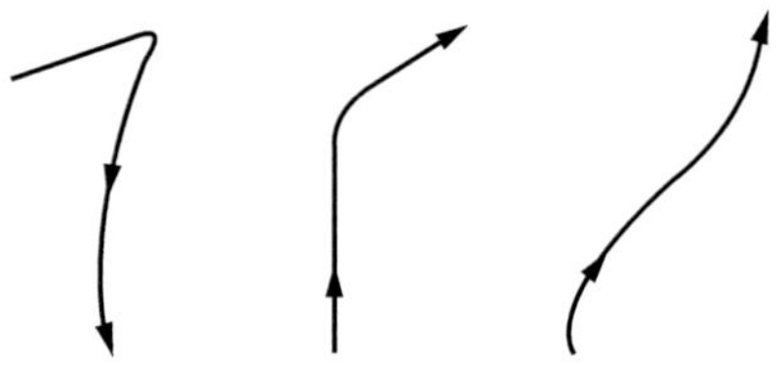

Figure 7.5 Marks on the ice indicate different errors on the initial strides of the forward start: *(a)* toe turned straight down; *(b)* blade contacted ice facing straight forward; *(c)* heel of blade contacted ice.

Figure 7.5 shows incorrect marks traced in the ice during the forward start. Learn to identify these incorrect marks and to understand the mistakes that may cause them. Practice starts on clean ice so you can study the marks. The marks shown in figure 7.5*a* indicate a short, well-turned-out blade. However, at some point during the push, the pushing toe turned to point straight down, causing the skate and leg to slip back on the flat of the blade. This results in no push, plus a loss of balance.

The marks shown in figure 7.5*b* indicate that the skate blade made contact with the ice facing straight ahead instead of outward. This caused a glide. To push, the skater needed to first pivot the skate outward. The result of this mistake is a loss of quickness.

The marks shown in figure 7.5*c* indicate that the heel of the blade made contact with the ice. This caused the skate to glide, resulting in slower leg speed.

Gliding may result from a variety of errors, including the following:

- Insufficient inside edge on the toe of the contact skate
- Weight too far back (on the heel) of the blade
- Heel of the blade contacting the ice
- Insufficient knee bend
- Body weight not inclined far enough forward
- Insufficient turnout angle of the contact skate (skate faces forward on touchdown rather than being turned well outward)
- Slow or incomplete leg recovery

Accelerating From Slow to Fast When Skating Forward

Many situations arise in which players must accelerate instantly from a coasting or gliding mode. In these situations, players must be able to gun the engine to get going FAST. This is an explosive maneuver that is extremely thrilling to observe.

- **Accelerating from slow to fast using toe starts:** Accelerating from slow to fast on a straightaway is similar to starting. In these situations, the player needs to break out quickly and explosively. Therefore, the initial steps must be QUICK! To accomplish this, take the first two steps on the toes, as in a forward start. The same can be done when accelerating from slow to fast on a curve or circle; this is similar to a crossover start.

- **Accelerating from slow to fast using the double pump:** Another method of accelerating from slow to fast is what I call the double pump. In this maneuver, the player pushes twice in succession with the toe of the pushing skate. The pushes must be powerful and quick. The double pump can be used to accelerate from slow to fast on a straightaway. It can also be used to accelerate on a curve or circle. When used on a curve or circle, the double pump is followed by a series of forward crossovers.

CROSSOVER (SIDE) STARTS

The crossover (side) start is an effective method of starting after a hockey stop (see the section on hockey stops in chapter 8, page 174). A hockey stop often leaves players facing sideways to the new direction of travel, which positions them perfectly for using a crossover start (figure 7.6). The crossover start can be used either to launch off in the opposite direction or to continue in the same direction.

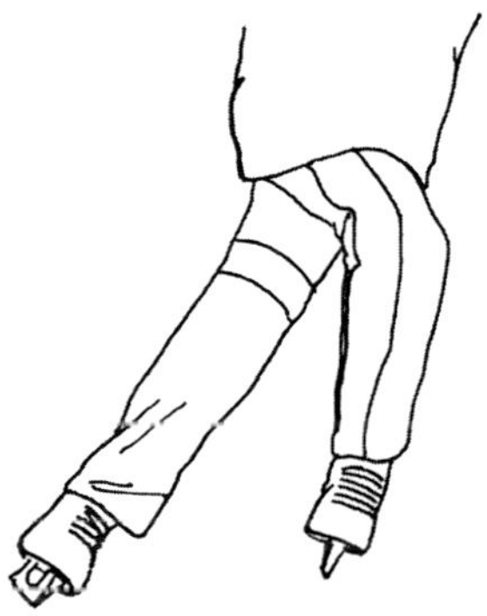

Figure 7.6 Crossover (side) start, right over left.

This start is a crossover move—the outside skate pushes first (stride-push against the inside edge), and the inside skate pushes second (X-push against the outside edge). The inside skate drives under the body as the outside (trailing) skate crosses over in front of the inside skate and lands on the toe (front 2 to 3 inches [5.1 to 7.6 cm]) of its inside edge. As in the forward start, the body weight must be projected low and outward (outward is now to the side).

To perform an explosive crossover start, shift your weight as if you were pushing a heavy weight (e.g., a car) with your shoulder. As in the forward start, the initial steps should be rapid, powerful running steps. The combination of quickness (rapid leg speed), powerful leg drive, and distance covered yields an explosive start.

The crossover itself is done as if you were leaping sideways along a line, crossing over as you move, and keeping your skates and body sideways (perpendicular) to the intended line of travel (figure 7.7). This is critical—if either or both skates turn forward to face the line of travel during the crossover itself, the edges will not grip the ice and the skates will glide forward, making a crossover start impossible.

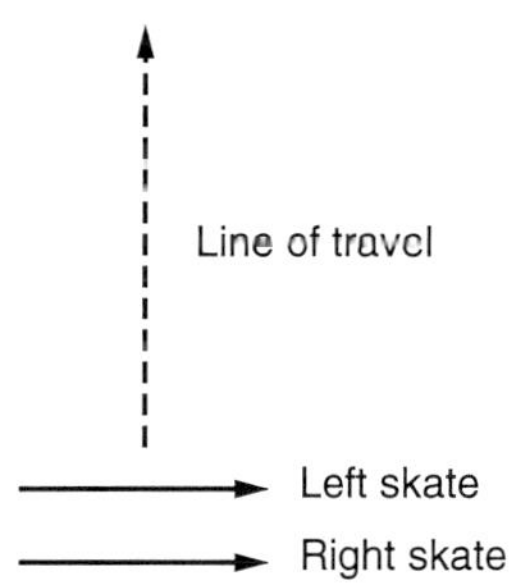

Figure 7.7 Crossover (side) start: The skates are perpendicular to the line of travel.

The following instructions are for a crossover start moving to the left (right-over-left crossover). To start to the right, reverse the instructions.

First Stride

Preparation

1. The left skate is the inside (leading) skate, and the right skate is the outside (trailing) skate. Stand on the outside edge of the left skate and on the inside edge of the right skate; the skates should be shoulder-width apart and perpendicular (sideways) to the intended line of travel. Bend your knees deeply (figure 7.8*a*).

Windup

2. Place your weight over the inside edge of the right (outside) skate. Bend your knees even more deeply, and dig the inside edge into the ice.

First Push—Stride-Push

3. Push the right (outside) skate against its inside edge. During the push, shift your weight sideways (to the left) over the left outside edge, and simultaneously drive your body weight to the left (figure 7.8*b*).

Second Push—X-Push

4. Leap out to the side (to the left) while doing a right-over-left crossover. Drive the left (inside) skate against its outside edge as the right (outside) skate begins to cross over in front of the left skate. Drive the X-push to full extension under your body (figure 7.8, *c-d*).
5. The right skate must land on the front 2 to 3 inches (5.1 to 7.6 cm) of its inside edge. On landing, the skate must still be facing sideways—at approximately 70 to 75 degrees from the forward line of travel—and your body weight must be concentrated over the inside edge (figure 7.8*e*). The heel of the blade must not touch the ice. As you start, drive your body weight and right (crossing) knee as far out to the left as possible. Leap outward! Jumping upward breaks the outward motion. Strive for distance, not height.
6. After pushing, immediately return the left skate (now the free skate). This skate must immediately pass by the right (contact) skate in the V-diamond position and reach forward in preparation for becoming the new contact skate (figure 7.8*f*).

Second Stride

1. Do only one crossover. The second stride is taken in the frontal position.
2. As the right skate contacts the ice, it immediately becomes the new pushing skate. As you land on the right inside edge after the crossover, the right skate and your hips must still be sideways to the line of travel. Just before pushing with the right skate and leg, pivot your hips to face forward (figure 7.8*f*). The next and all subsequent steps are the powerful sprinting steps of the forward start. All subsequent pushes are the pushes of the forward stride (figure 7.8*g*).

Figure 7.8 Crossover start sequence.

3. When the left skate contacts the ice (in a frontal position), make sure it lands on the toe and that your body weight is concentrated over the edge; the heel must be off the ice. This is the same as the second step of the forward start.
4. After the forward stride-push, immediately return the right skate (now the free skate). This skate must immediately pass the left skate (skates and legs in the V-diamond position) and reach forward to become the new contact skate.

Subsequent Strides

On the third or fourth stride, the skates must begin to glide, and the angle of the upper body to the ice must gradually become more upright. After five or six strides, the upper body will achieve the body angle of the forward stride (approximately 45 degrees to the ice).

Points to Remember

- On the crossover, the contact skate must touch down sideways (approximately 70 to 75 degrees from the line of travel), or the edge won't dig in properly. Figure 7.9 diagrams the cuts made in the ice when the crossover start sequence is correctly performed.

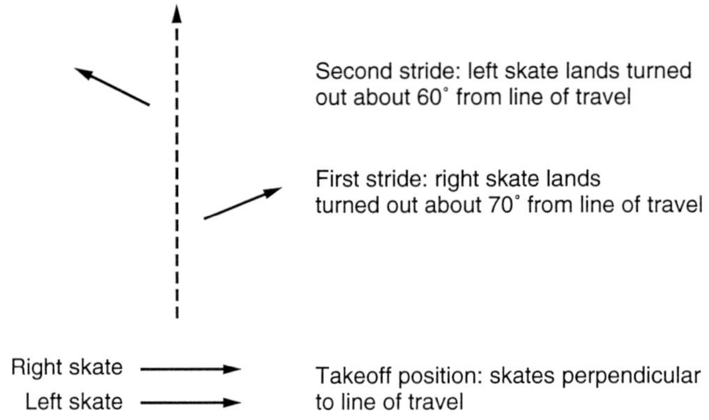

Figure 7.9 Right-over-left crossover start (showing cuts in the ice).

- The first push (from the outside skate) shifts the body weight out to the side. The second push (from the outside edge of the inside skate) drives the body weight even farther out to the side.
- The edges must grip the ice strongly.
- Drive each pushing skate directly against the gripping edge. Do not let the pushing skate slip back.
- For balance and stability, keep your shoulders back and your chest upright. Look straight ahead and keep your head and chin up.

BACKWARD STARTS

One of the cardinal rules in hockey is that players must always face the play. Therefore, in game situations, players often have to start out facing backward. Defenders must be able to accelerate backward explosively to stay ahead of (and face) the opposition. Defenders who have not mastered backward starts have to start forward and then wheel around backward. This is a major no-no because by turning their backs to the action, they can't see what's happening—as a result, they risk being taken advantage of by the opposition.

When starting backward, you are limited in how much you can shift weight or angle the upper body backward (in the direction of travel), because you are at risk of falling over backward. Therefore, when starting backward, it is not possible to accelerate as quickly as when starting forward.

Two types of backward starts are used in hockey. One is the straight backward start, and the other is the backward crossover start. In games, players should use the one that is more advantageous to the specific situation. For example, a defender must not commit to a direction prematurely because the attacker might cut the other way. The advantage of the straight backward start is that the defender's feet are in a neutral position. In addition, the direction of travel is a straight line that keeps the defender straight ahead of the attacker. If the attacker makes a move to one side, the defender can move or turn quickly to that side to cut off the attacker. However, the straight backward start is not quite as quick as the backward crossover start. If an attacker is not pressing closely, the backward crossover start might be preferable.

The backward crossover start has a distinct disadvantage—in crossing over, the defender is committed to that side. This may create an opportunity for the attacker to fake and break away in the opposite direction. A cagey forward knows to wait for the defender to cross over prematurely and immediately sees the opportunity to take off the other way. When using a backward crossover start, make sure that there is a lot of space between you and the attacker—otherwise, you stand a good chance of "getting burned."

Note: In situations where the opposing forward is very closely pressing the defender, the defender might have no other option but to start forward, build speed, and then turn backward. However, this method is risky. Whenever possible, start backward so that you face the play.

Straight Backward Start

The straight backward start is used primarily in situations when players need to keep their skates neutral to the opposition. As in all starts, the first few strides are critical for building explosive speed.

To perform the straight backward start, execute a sequence of powerful and quick backward C-cut pushes while aiming the gliding skate straight backward. The difference between the straight backward start and the straight backward stride is leg speed—the legs move much more rapidly on the initial steps of the start. The contact skate should glide as little as possible. However, each pushing skate must still move through its full range of motion. See chapter 5 for details on the backward C-cut push.

> **COACHING TIP**
>
> Although the start requires a very rapid leg tempo, you must ensure that you get full leg drive and full leg recovery.

Windup

1. Just as in the C-cut pushes of straight backward skating, the push is against the inside edge. Pivot the heel of the pushing skate outward, bend both knees deeply, place your body weight over the pushing skate, and dig the inside edge into the ice in preparation for pushing (figure 7.10*a*).

Release, Follow-Through, and Return

2. Execute each backward C-cut push against a strong inside edge. Use the front half of the blade length to push; finish each push with the toe. Push powerfully and rapidly to full extension (figure 7.10*b*).
3. Recover the pushing (now free) skate rapidly so the other skate can immediately push (figure 7.10, *c-e*).
4. After several pushes, you should approach top speed.
5. Swing your arms in rhythm and in the same (diagonal) line with your legs. The right arm goes back and outward as the right leg drives forward and outward (and vice versa).

Points to Remember

- Explosive acceleration depends on powerful leg drive along with rapid leg motion. The objective is to cover distance quickly. Small, hopping steps may be rapid, but they provide little thrust, and you will end up going nowhere fast.
- Keep your hips square to the line of travel. If they turn sideways with each push, you will waddle from side to side rather than skate straight backward.
- Keep the contact (gliding) skate pointing straight backward.

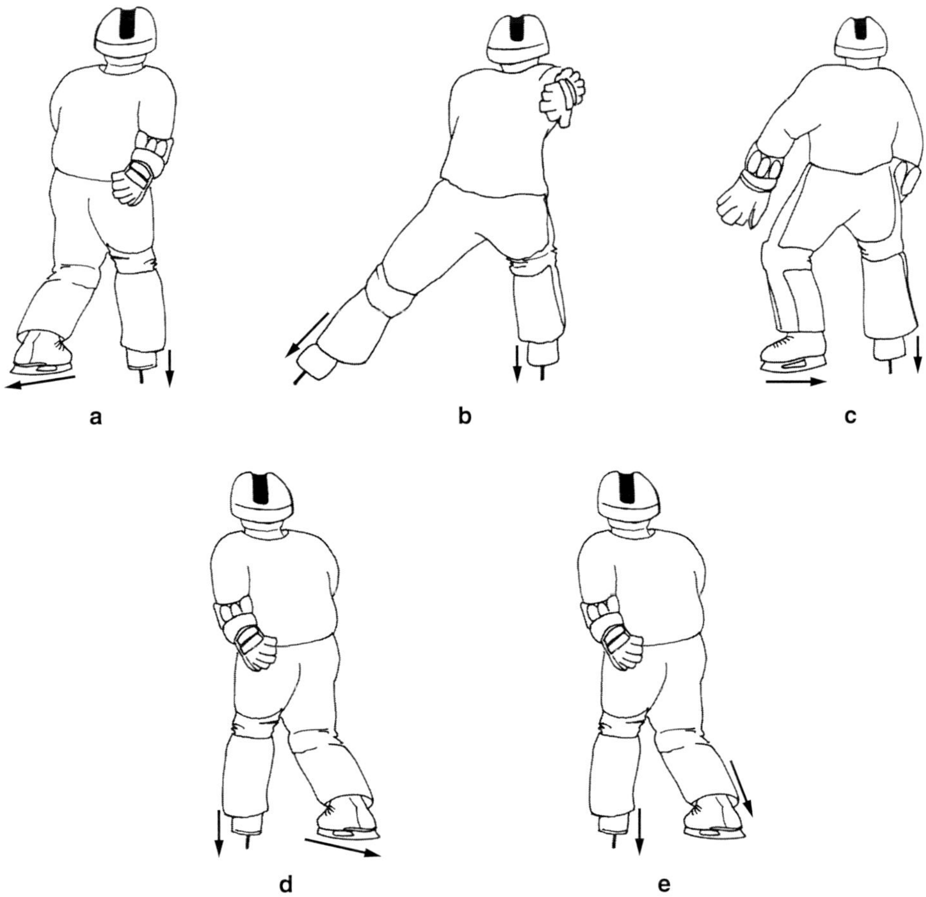

Figure 7.10 Straight backward start sequence.

- Keep the entire blade length of the pushing skate in contact with the ice. If the heel lifts off the ice, you will not be able to complete the push or return the skate properly.
- Keep the entire blade length of the gliding skate in contact with the ice. If the heel lifts off the ice, you may fall forward over the curved toes.
- Keep your shoulders and your back upright. As always, your chin, eyes, and head should be up.

Backward Crossover Start

Many defenders believe they can start out faster with a backward crossover start than with the straight backward start. But before doing the backward crossover start, be sure that the crossover will not create an opportunity for the opposition to escape.

As with the straight backward start, the backward crossover start begins with the powerful C-cut push. Execute the C-cut push powerfully and quickly to full extension before crossing it over (figure 7.11, *a-b*). Then drive the inside skate under your body (X-push) as the outside skate (now the free skate) crosses over (figure 7.11, *c-d*). (See the information on weaving crossovers in chapter 6 for details of the procedure.) Figure 7.12 diagrams the backward crossover start.

Figure 7.11 Backward crossover start sequence.

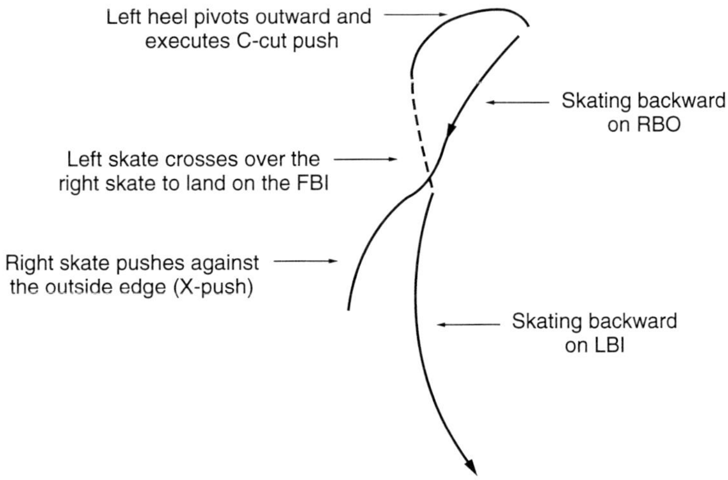

Figure 7.12 Pattern of the backward crossover start.

DRILLS FOR IMPROVING STARTS

The following drills are specifically designed to help players improve their forward, crossover, and backward starts. Also practice the combination drills (drills for improving stops and starts) described in chapter 8.

Drills for Forward Starts

The following drills help players develop the coordination, edge control, and body angles necessary for explosive forward starts.

Toe Steps Against the Boards

Basic

1. Stand facing the boards at approximately arm's length from the boards. Hold onto the boards with both hands.
2. Turn the skates and knees into an exaggerated V-diamond position—heels facing in, knees and toes facing out. With the skates and knees in this position, stand on the inside edges of the toes of both skates (figure 7.13*a* on page 158).
3. While holding onto the boards for balance, step from one skate to the other. On each step, the contact skate should touch down with your weight on the front 2 to 3 inches (5.1 to 7.6 cm) of the inside edge; the skate should be turned outward about 80 to 85 degrees from the line of travel, and the heel should be about 3 inches off the ice (figure 7.13*b*).

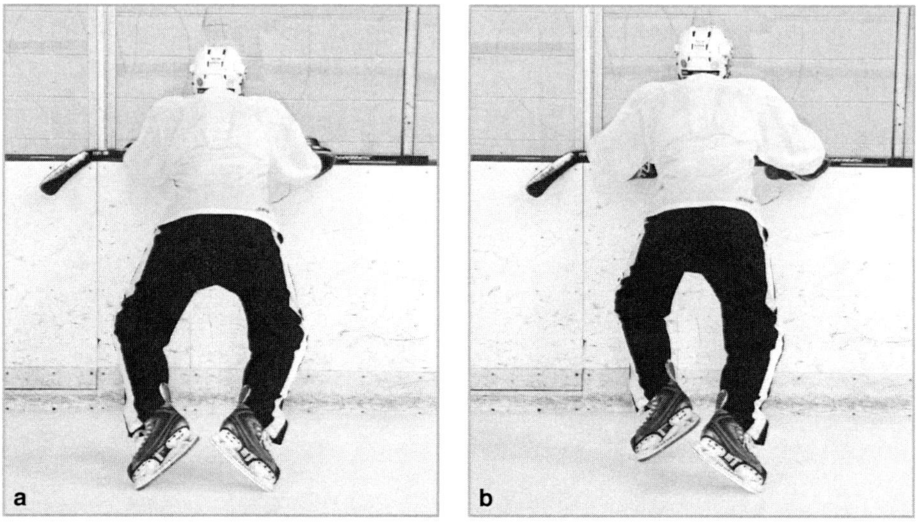

Figure 7.13 Toe steps against the boards.

Toe Starts Against the Boards

Intermediate

This drill trains players to do the following:

- Get on and use the toes properly for starts
- Reach the knee of the contact skate forward for distance rather than upward for height
- Angle the upper body forward
- Fully extend the pushing skate and leg while reaching the front knee forward
- Maintain the turned-out (V-diamond) position of the skates and knees through the push and return

To perform toe starts against the boards, complete these steps:

1. Stand facing the boards at approximately arm's length from the boards. Hold onto the boards with both hands.
2. Turn both skates and knees into an exaggerated V-diamond position—heels facing in, knees and toes facing out—and stand on the toes of both skates (figure 7.14*a*).
3. Angle your body forward so that your chest lines up above the front knee. Keep your back straight and your head up; do not slouch.
4. Move the contact skate forward so that it passes the pushing skate in the V-diamond position; keep the heels facing in and the toes facing out as each skate passes the other.
5. Reach the knee of the contact skate forward until it touches the boards. The contact skate should touch down with your weight on the toe, the skate turned outward about 80 to 85 degrees from the line of travel, and the heel about 3 inches (7.6 cm) off the ice.

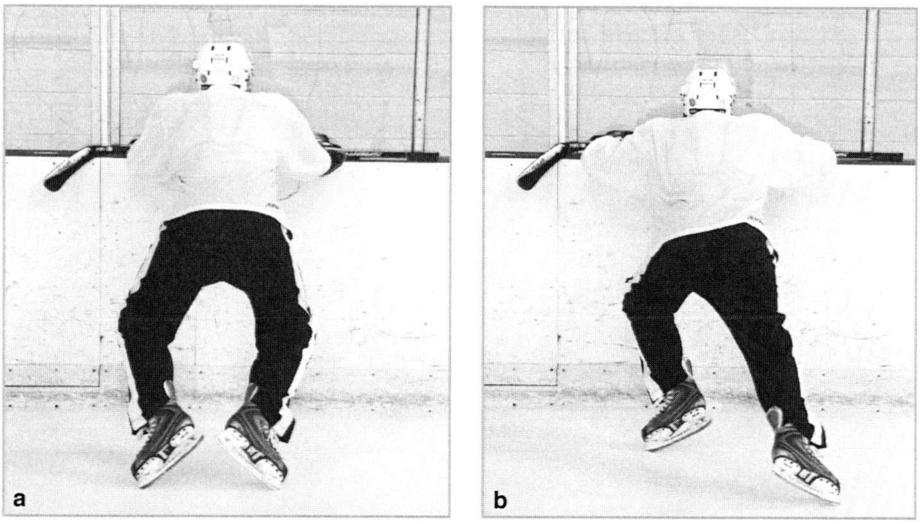

Figure 7.14 Toe starts against the boards.

6. As the knee of the contact skate reaches forward toward the boards, drive the pushing skate and leg to full extension. At full extension, only the toe of the inside edge should be on the ice (in the toe flick position). The heel should be about 3 inches (7.6 cm) off the ice (figure 7.14*b*).
7. Repeat on the other skate.
8. Repeat the drill, increasing the speed at which you change feet and push.

Note: Land on the toe only. The heel of the contact skate should never touch the ice.

Penguin Walk

Intermediate

In this drill, you walk across the ice on the toes of the skates in a penguinlike or ducklike manner. The knees and toes remain in the V-diamond position throughout the drill.

1. Place the skates and knees in the exaggerated V-diamond position heels together, knees and toes apart. The skates should be turned out about 80 to 85 degrees from the line of travel.
2. Bend your knees deeply.
3. Keeping your knees bent, roll in your ankles so that the lower leg and the inside edge of each skate form a strong angle with the ice; keep the heels together and the toes apart.
4. Place your weight over the front 2 to 3 inches (5.1 to 7.6 cm) of both inside edges, and lift your heels so that the toes (fronts of the inside edges) are in contact with the ice and the heels are 3 inches off the ice. Maintain the same edge angle and knee bend while standing and balancing in this position (figure 7.15*a* on page 160).

5. When you can balance on the toes in the V-diamond position, walk across the ice like a penguin. On each step, touch down on only the toes of the engaged inside edge (45-degree angle); the heel is elevated, the knee is bent, the knee and skate are turned out, and the body weight is pressing downward over the engaged edge (figure 7.15*b*). Do not let the heel of either skate touch the ice at any time during the penguin walk. To maintain this penguinlike position, the heels must face each other. The knees and toes must face outward (V-diamond position) as each skate passes the other.
6. The marks in the ice from each step should be sideways to the direction of travel and should be no more than 2 to 3 inches (5.1 to 7.6 cm) long.

Note: If the marks are as long as the length of the blade, this indicates that the heel has touched the ice, which will cause a glide. If either toe touches the ice facing forward, you will be forced to place the entire blade on the ice; this also causes a glide.

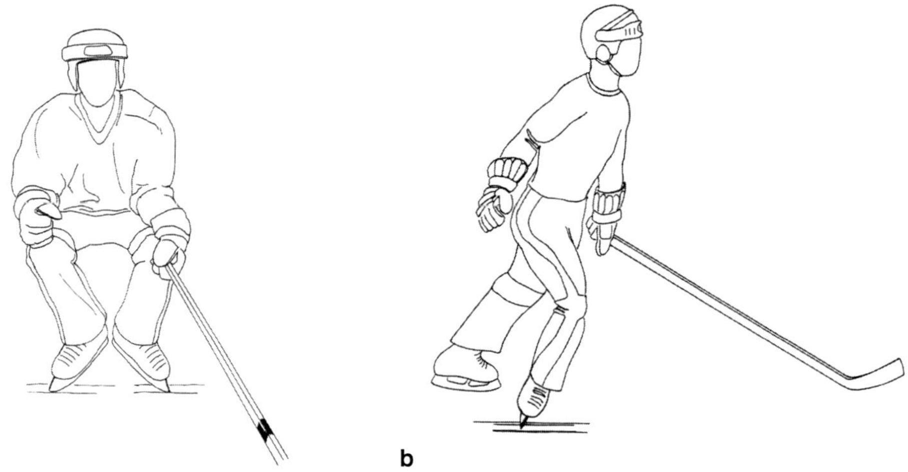

a b

Figure 7.15 Penguin walk.

Penguin Run

Advanced

1. Run in place on the toes (inside edges) in the penguinlike (V-diamond) position—heels facing in, knees and toes facing out. Keep your weight on the toes as you run in place; do not allow the heels to touch the ice.
2. Run between the blue lines in this penguinlike position. Do not glide! If the heel of the contact skate touches the ice, it will force the skate to glide.
3. Run between the blue lines as in step 2, but now push to full extension on each step as you run between the blue lines.
4. See how far you can run down the ice before the full blade touches the ice and the skates begin to glide.

Resistance Forward Starts

Advanced

Resistance starts help players learn how to do the following:

- Get on and stay on the toes
- Use the contact skate properly to touch down on and push against the toes of the inside edges
- Feel the upper body angle required for explosive starts
- Push powerfully and to full extension

Push a resisting player across the ice while stepping down only on the toes (of the inside edges). The player moving backward resists with a backward two-foot snowplow stop (see chapter 8, page 176). Keep the skates and knees in the V-diamond position (heels together, knees and toes apart) with the heels off the ice throughout (figure 7.16, *a-b*). Note the strong forward angle of the upper body of the pushing player in figure 7.16*b*.

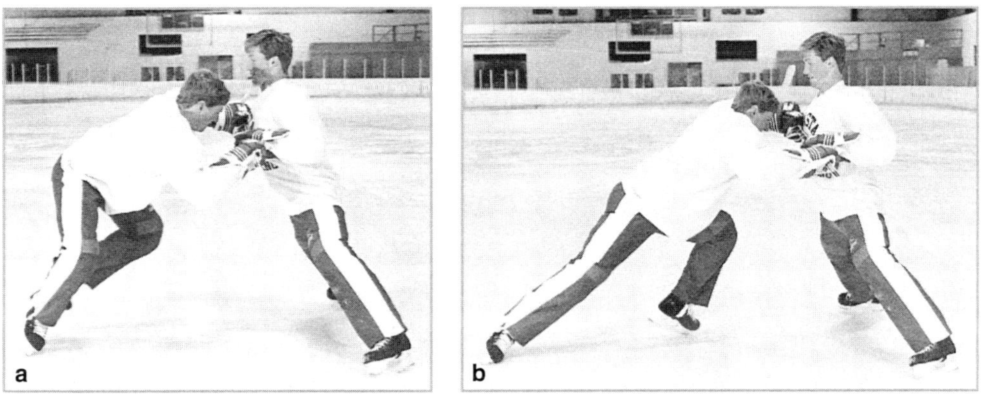

Figure 7.16 Resistance forward starts.

Forward Starts Over Hockey Sticks

Advanced

Starts over hockey sticks help train the legs to drive harder and the upper body to shift out farther in order to achieve more distance on each starting step. Drive your body weight outward for distance, not upward for height. The instructions are for pushing first with the right skate and leg.

Team up with three other players of similar heights and abilities. One skater performs the drill while the others observe, but the players take turns so that everyone gets to do the drill.

1. Place four hockey sticks on the ice as diagrammed in figure 7.17 on page 163. The distance between the sticks gets progressively greater. The

sticks are spaced so that on each of the initial (three or four) steps of the forward start, the skaters have to project their weight well forward and cover more distance than on the previous step. Distances between the sticks must be modified to accommodate each skater's size and ability. The distances should be challenging but not impossible to achieve. If the sticks are placed too close together, players merely jump up to get over them rather than leap forward (outward) to get beyond them. In all of the stick drills, the area between the first two sticks is called the no-zone. Do *not* step into the no-zone.

2. Face the hockey sticks and stand in the exaggerated V-diamond position with the toes almost touching the first stick. Prepare to push with your right skate and leg (figure 7.18*a*).
3. Place your weight over the right (pushing) skate, bend both knees, and dig the inside edge of the right skate into the ice (45 degrees). Shift your body weight well forward.
4. Push hard and leap beyond the second stick. Land on the toe of the LFI. The left skate must land facing outward (sideways to the direction of travel), with the body weight over it and with the heel off the ice (figure 7.18*b*). The cut in the ice should be short and facing outward (sideways), indicating that the skate did not glide.
5. Repeat, now pushing with the left skate and landing beyond the third stick. Land on the toe of the RFI; the body weight should be over the right skate, and the skate should face outward, with the heel off the ice (figure 7.18*c*). Again, the cut in the ice should be short and facing outward (sideways), indicating that the skate did not glide.
6. Push again with the right skate; land beyond the fourth stick. Land on the toe of the LFI, with the left skate facing outward (sideways) and with the heel off the ice (this step is not shown in figure 7.18). After passing the fourth stick, sprint until you reach top speed. Your body angle must rise gradually—at top speed, your body angle should be approximately 45 degrees to the ice.
7. As this drill becomes easier, move the sticks farther apart. Force your legs to drive hard and your weight to shift farther out to clear the sticks, but don't make it impossible. Leap out to get beyond the sticks, not high to get over them.
8. Repeat the drill, now pushing first with the left skate and leg. Remember that the legs must be equally capable of making the all-important first push.
9. Take the sticks away and see if you can go as far as or farther than you did with the sticks. Move your legs as rapidly as possible. Do not sacrifice leg speed in trying to go farther.

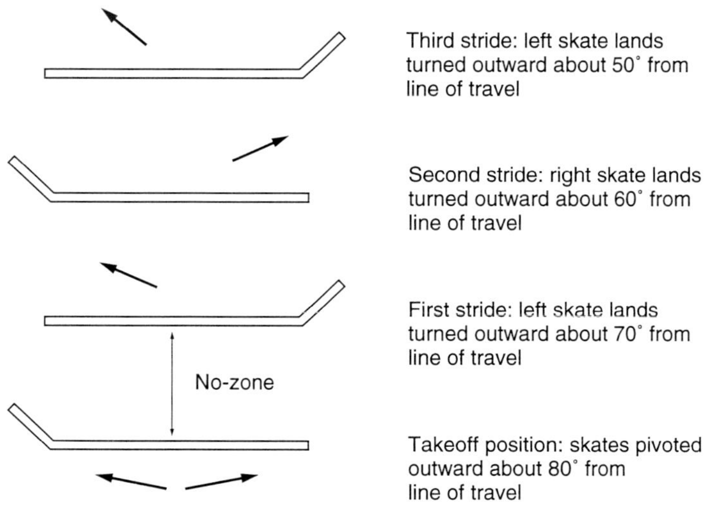

Figure 7.17 Forward starts over hockey sticks (note the angle of the skates to the line of travel).

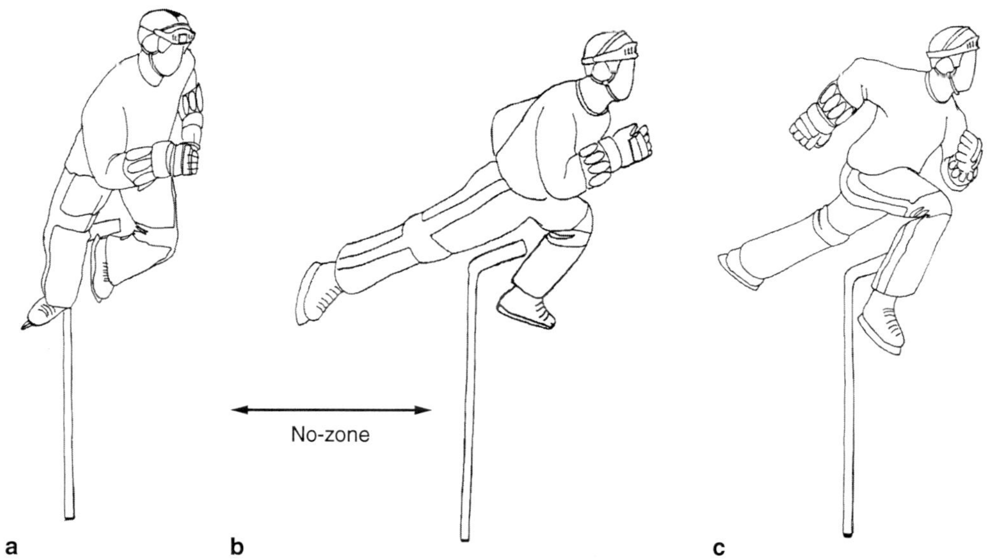

Figure 7.18 Forward starts over hockey sticks.

Sprint Starts

Advanced

Start from the goal line. Take two or three running strides and then sprint forward to the first blue line. Combine power, quickness, and distance on the starting strides. Time yourself; try to improve your time.

Note: The more adept you become with these starts, the better your times should become.

Drills for Crossover Starts

Drills for crossover starts help players develop the coordination, edge control, and body-weight projection necessary for explosive crossover starts. Practice these drills on both sides so that you develop the ability to use the left and right legs equally on the initial push.

The following drills for crossover starts require you to perform a series of walking or running crossovers. To perform the drills, you will walk or run laterally (sideways).

Lateral Walking Crossover Starts

Basic to Intermediate

The instructions given are for right-over-left crossovers.

Stand facing sideways (perpendicular) to the intended direction of travel. Walk to the left, crossing the right (outside) skate over in front of the left skate as you walk sideways. The left (leading or inside) skate always steps onto its outside edge, then crosses under the body to push (X-push). The right (trailing or outside) skate, after pushing (forward stride-push), crosses over in front of the left skate and steps onto its inside edge.

Start from one sideboard and walk across the rink doing crossovers the entire way. Be sure to keep both skates sideways to the line of travel as you walk.

Lateral Running Crossover Starts

Intermediate to Advanced

Repeat the previous drill, but instead of walking, run sideways across the ice. Stay on the toes and use both pushes (stride-push and X-push) on every running stride. Keep the heels off the ice! Strive for distance on each stride; run outward, not upward.

Lateral Leaping Crossover Starts

Advanced

Repeat the previous drills, but now do lateral leaping crossovers. Try to get as much sideways distance as possible on each step of each crossover sequence. Use the stride-push from the outside skate and leg to shift your weight out to the side. Use the X-push from the inside skate and leg to drive your weight even farther out to the side. Push to full extension on all pushes, and keep the heel of each contact skate off the ice.

Zigzag Lateral Leaping Crossover Starts

Advanced

Start from the goal line and skate forward along the boards (figure 7.19). Stop at the near blue line. Do lateral leaping crossovers (left over right) along

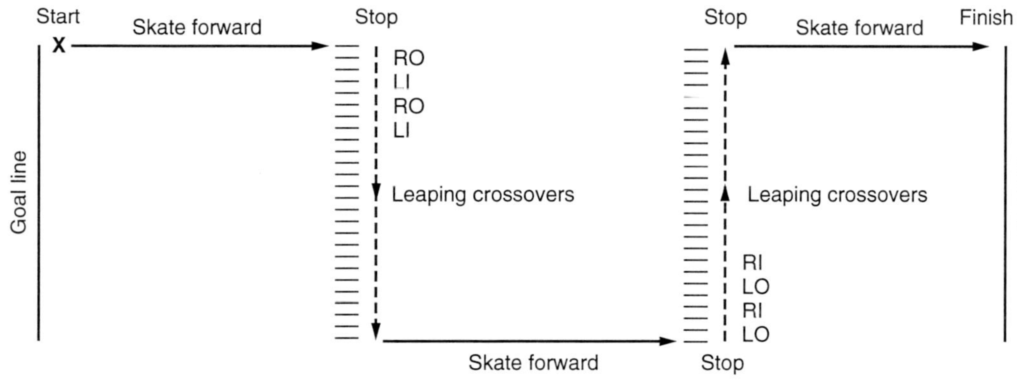

Figure 7.19 Zigzag lateral leaping crossover starts.

the blue line across to the opposite sideboards. Stop. Skate forward to the far blue line, stop, and do lateral leaping crossovers (right over left) along the blue line back to the original sideboards. Stop, skate forward along the boards to the goal line, and stop again.

Remember: Leap outward on all pushes. Stay on the toes during each leaping crossover (the heels should not touch the ice). As always, strive for distance, not height.

Lateral Leaping Crossover Starts on Whistles

Advanced

On a whistle signal, use right-over-left crossovers to leap out sideways to the left as rapidly as possible. Get as much lateral distance as you can, and move your legs as quickly as possible. On the next whistle, stop and change direction; leap out sideways to the right (left-over-right crossovers). Alternate directions on each whistle signal. Keep the heels off the ice during the leaping crossovers.

Note: Keep the skates and body facing sideways (at right angles) to the line of travel on all of the previous lateral crossover drills.

Crossover Starts Over Hockey Sticks

Advanced

This drill trains the legs to drive harder and the upper body to shift out farther to the side in order to achieve greater distance on the first three or four steps of the crossover start. Concentrate on driving the body weight outward for distance, not upward for height.

The sticks must be spaced to challenge each player's ability. The idea is to train players to use their legs and body weight to project themselves outward. Each starting step must cover more distance than the previous one. The following instructions are for a right-over-left crossover start.

Team up with three other players of similar height and ability. Place four hockey sticks on the ice (figure 7.20). Follow the guidelines given for the forward starts over hockey sticks drill.

1. Stand to the right of the sticks, with both skates parallel to each other and to the sticks (sideways to the intended direction of travel). Place the left skate next to and still parallel to the first stick. Your skates must be slightly wider than shoulder-width apart. Your knees must be well bent, and your body weight must be over the right (outside, back, or trailing) skate.
2. Do one right-over-left crossover and land beyond the second stick (not in the "no-zone"). Land on the toe of the right inside edge with the right skate almost sideways (70 to 75 degrees) to the line of travel (figure 7.21, *a-b*). The pushes for this crossover are done as follows:
    - The first push—which is from the right skate and leg—is to full extension (stride-push). This push shifts the body weight outward to the left (figure 7.21*a*).
    - The second push—which is from the left skate and leg—drives under the body (X-push) as you do a leaping right-over-left crossover and land on the toe of the right inside edge (figure 7.21*b*).

Note: Keep the heel of the right skate off the ice on the landing. If the heel touches the ice, you will glide.

3. While still on the toe of the right skate, pivot your hips, chest, and shoulders 90 degrees until you face fully forward in the forward start position. Now drive the right skate against the right inside edge as in a forward start. Leap forward and land beyond the third stick. Land on the toe of the left inside edge, with your weight over it and with the heel off the ice (figure 7.21*c*). The left skate should touch down facing outward (sideways) as in the forward start, enabling the inside edge to grip the ice.
4. Push again with the left skate and leg and leap forward as in the forward start. Leap beyond the fourth stick. Land on the toe of the right inside edge (RFI), with the right skate facing outward (sideways). This step is not shown in figure 7.21. Now sprint until you reach full speed. Your body angle must rise gradually until it reaches the skating angle of the forward stride (approximately 45 degrees).
5. Concentrate on leaping out beyond (farther than) the sticks rather than over (higher than) them.

Remember: Leap for distance, not height.

To execute the drill in the opposite direction, face the other way. The right skate is now next to the first stick. Leap to the right, crossing left over right.

Take the sticks away and see if you can get more distance in the same (or less) time. Measure how far outward you travel on the first three steps of the start (one crossover, two forward steps), and time how fast you execute these steps. Keep trying to increase the distance and shorten the time. Remember, more distance covered in the same or less time means a faster start!

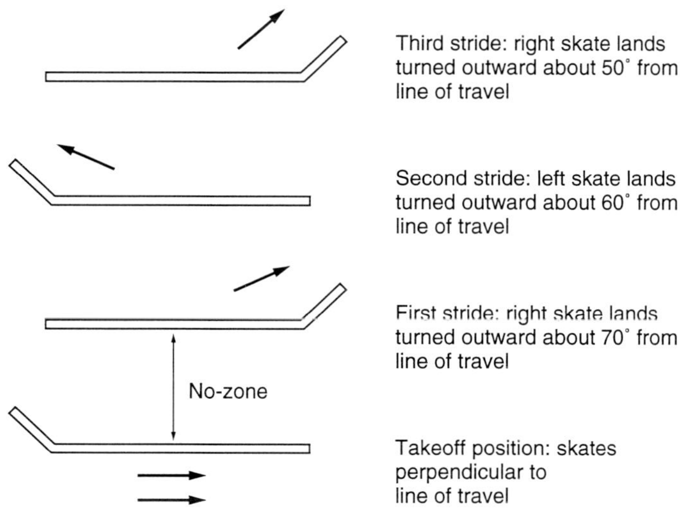

Figure 7.20 Crossover starts over hockey sticks (note the position of the skates to the line of travel).

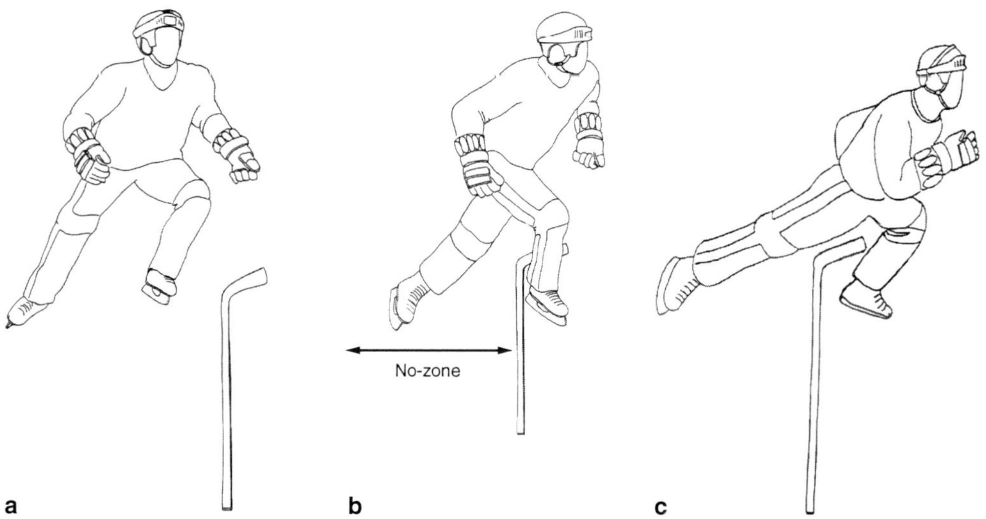

Figure 7.21 Crossover starts over hockey sticks.

Sprint Crossover Starts

Intermediate to Advanced

Start from the goal line. Using a crossover start, take two or three running steps (only one crossover) and then sprint to the blue line. Stop. Start again (only one crossover) and sprint to the far blue line. Stop. Start again and sprint to the goal line at the far end of the rink. Stop. Alternate the side on which you start, and try to better the starts in both directions.

Remember: The crossover start should include only one crossover. All other starting steps are in the frontal position.

Sprint Stops and Starts

Intermediate to Advanced

Practice stops and starts, alternating the direction of the stops and starts. On each start, concentrate on leaping out as far and as quickly as possible. Time yourself. Try to improve your starting times in both directions. (See chapter 8 for a detailed description of hockey stops and some of the drills that should be used to practice starts as well as stops.)

Crossover Starts Over the Goal Crease

Advanced

The purpose of this drill is to train the legs to push harder and the body weight to shift farther out to the side. More weight projection helps achieve greater distance on the starting steps. This drill is similar to crossover starts over hockey sticks; the outer line of the goal crease is the target that the first contact skate must reach.

Note: This drill is recommended for more advanced skaters. Young skaters cannot achieve (nor is it advantageous for them to achieve) this distance.

1. Stand with your feet parallel to the goal line (sideways to the intended line of travel). Prepare to do a right-over-left crossover start and to sprint to the first blue line. Place the left (leading or inside) skate on the goal line. The right skate must be parallel to the left, and the skates must be slightly wider than shoulder-width apart. The knees must be well bent, and the body weight must be over the outside (right) skate.
2. Do one leaping crossover, right over left, and land on or close to the outer crease line. Land on the toe of the right inside edge (RFI), with the right skate almost parallel to the outer line of the crease (about 70 to 75 degrees from the line of travel). Now pivot forward and sprint to the blue line.
3. Repeat with a left-over-right crossover start.

Drills for Straight Backward Starts

Three-Push Drill

Intermediate

Stand close to and facing the boards. With your weight over the left (pushing) skate, bend the left knee deeply and dig the left inside edge into the ice. Execute a backward C-cut push against the left inside edge. Use powerful leg drive and aim the right (gliding) skate straight back. After completing the push, return the pushing skate and leg back under your body as rapidly as possible. Now push with the right skate and leg. Cut a total of three C-cut pushes. Move your legs as rapidly as possible and travel straight back. Come to a stop after the third C-cut push and see how far you have traveled after three pushes. Repeat the sequence, trying to increase the distance and shorten the time. Then repeat the drill using the right skate and leg to perform the initial push.

Straight Backward Starts With Resistance

Intermediate to Advanced

Working against resistance forces players to push correctly and powerfully, which improves straight backward starts.

Perform the previous drill, but now pull a resisting player as you practice the straight backward start. The resisting player holds one end of a hockey stick, and you hold the other end. (The resisting player resists using a forward snowplow.) Keep the stick at chest height and horizontal to the ice. Refer to the partner resistance drills in chapter 5 (page 92) for more information on the procedure.

Backward Sprint Starts

Intermediate to Advanced

Start from the goal line using the straight backward start, and then skate straight backward to the first blue line. Time yourself. Alternate the initial pushing skate and leg—each leg must develop the power and coordination to make the initial push. With practice, you should be able to significantly improve your times.

Drills for Backward Crossover Starts

Three-Push Backward Crossover Starts

Intermediate to Advanced

Perform the three-push straight backward start drill, but do the three steps and pushes of the backward crossover start. The first push (backward C-cut push) is done with the outside skate. Push to full extension before crossing the outside skate over in front of the inside skate. As the outside skate crosses over, drive the inside skate and leg under your body (X-push). The third step is the wide step (neutralizing step) onto the inside edge—this step is necessary before continuing to skate backward. A corresponding third push is also necessary; this is another backward C-cut push, and it is done with the same skate that did the first C-cut push. Concentrate on maximizing all three pushes.

Backward Crossover Starts With Resistance

Advanced

Working against resistance forces players to push correctly and powerfully, which improves backward crossover starts.

This drill is performed the same as the straight backward starts with resistance drill. You will pull a player who creates resistance (by doing a forward snowplow) as you execute the backward crossover start. The resisting player holds one end of a hockey stick as you hold the other end. Keep the stick at chest height and horizontal to the ice.

Backward Crossover Sprint Starts

Advanced

Using a backward crossover start, time yourself from the goal line to the first blue line. Then time yourself from the goal line to the center red line. Next, time yourself from the goal line to the far blue line. Use only one backward crossover to start out; skate straight backward the rest of the way. Be sure to alternate the initial pushing skate of the backward crossover starts.

Note: With practice, you should be able to significantly improve your times.

Variation (Advanced)

Perform the previous drill, but after the backward crossover start, do weaving backward crossovers to the first blue line. See chapter 6 (page 133) for details on performing weaving crossovers.

Forward Versus Defender

Advanced

Team up with another skater. One player competes as a forward, and the other as a defender. The defender stands at the blue line, prepared to start and skate backward. The forward stands at or slightly inside the goal line directly opposite the defender; the forward is prepared to start and skate forward. On a whistle signal, both players start out and race down the ice. The forward tries to catch and pass the defender. The defender skates backward and tries to prevent the forward from catching up. Switch with your partner so that both players practice equally as forward and defender.

Note: With such a big lead, the defender should not be caught!

Chapter 8

Stops for Halting on a Dime

In hockey, explosive stops are just as essential as explosive starts. Coaches spend a lot of time training their players to stop on a dime. Mastering all the stops enables players to use the stop that is most appropriate for the situation at hand. In games, players often need to jam on the brakes or to stop and change direction instantaneously. Games also include instances when it is better to slow down or stop gradually.

FORWARD STOPS

The forward stops covered in this chapter progress from the most basic to the most difficult.

Forward Two-Foot Snowplow Stop

The two-foot snowplow stop—which is similar to the skier's snowplow—is the easiest stop to learn and therefore the first stop taught to beginning skaters. In game situations, this stop is used mainly for slowing down or stopping very gradually. It is inadequate for very sudden stops.

1. Glide straight ahead on two skates, with your feet shoulder-width apart.
2. Turn both toes inward and both heels outward so that the toes of the skates face each other in an inverted pigeon-toed (wide and inverted V) position. Keep your hips and shoulders facing straight forward.
3. Scrape against the ice with both skates, using *slight* inside edges. As you scrape against the ice, bend your knees and force your heels still farther apart (figure 8.1). Try to bring up snow with the inside edges; don't try to cut into the ice.

Figure 8.1 Forward two-foot snowplow stop.

Points to Remember

- Keep your body weight on the balls of the feet as you scrape the ice. If you try to scrape the ice with the heels, the inside edges may catch the ice, and stopping will be difficult.
- Keep your shoulders back, your back straight, and your eyes and head up. If you lean forward, you will pitch forward over the curved toes.
- Use *slight* inside edges to stop. If you edge too deeply, the edges will dig into the ice rather than scrape against the ice, making a stop almost impossible.
- Keep the entire blade lengths of both skates in contact with the ice during the stop. Lifting the heels will cause you to pitch forward over the curved toes.

Forward One-Foot Snowplow Stop

The forward one-foot snowplow stop is sometimes used in game situations. For instance, defenders may use it to decelerate in preparation for skating backward, or to slow down or stop gradually. Goalies frequently use the one-foot snowplow stop.

1. Glide straight forward on the flat of the left skate. Keep the left skate centered under your body weight.
2. Holding the right skate somewhat out in front, turn that toe inward (pigeon-toed position) and press the right skate against the ice, using a slight inside edge to scrape against the ice. Scrape the ice with the ball of the foot, not the heel.
3. Concentrate your weight downward over the stopping (right) skate by bending the right knee. Scrape the ice with the right inside edge; the skate should still be in the pigeon-toed position (figure 8.2).

Figure 8.2 Forward one-foot snowplow stop.

4. Repeat, using the left skate to do the snowplow stop. The right skate now glides straight forward.

Note: Except for using the pigeon-toed position and scraping against the ice with one skate rather than two, the stop is performed in the same way as the two-foot snowplow.

T-Stop

The T-stop is often used when players come to the bench or to the face-off circle. This stop is rarely used in situations when explosive, sudden, well-balanced stops are called for. The T-stop uses the outside edge to scrape the ice.

1. Glide straight forward on the flat of the right skate.
2. Lift the left skate and place it behind the right skate, turning the toe outward so that the turned skate is perpendicular to the front (gliding) skate. Your skates should form an inverted T.
3. Place the *outside* edge of the left (back) skate on the ice in this perpendicular position. Apply pressure to the outside edge and simultaneously bend the left knee. Apply gradual but constant pressure to the ice with the outside edge. Use the ball of the foot, not the heel, to press against (scrape) the ice (figure 8.3).
4. Keep your shoulders level to the ice as you lean back. If you lower the back (trailing) shoulder excessively, you will lose your balance and could fall backward.
5. Scrape the ice with the outside edge. If you lean forward, you will be forced to drag the inside edge (figure 8.4), and you won't be able to stop efficiently.
6. Your shoulders, chest, and hips must face forward (the direction of travel) while executing the T-stop.
7. Advanced skaters often do a T-stop on just the back skate; the front skate is actually off the ice (figure 8.5).

Be sure to master both the one-foot snowplow and the T-stop—together, they are the components of the hockey stop.

Figure 8.3 Correct position for the T-stop.

Figure 8.4 Incorrect position for the T-stop.

Figure 8.5 T-stop on one skate.

Hockey Stop

Hockey often demands that players stop on a dime to stay with the play or to change directions as the action shifts. The hockey stop is the quickest and most sudden of all the stops; therefore, it is the stop used in most game situations. In addition to allowing players to stop suddenly, the hockey stop is also a very stable stop (when properly executed). Players must be able to stop in both directions so that they can stop in a position where they are facing the action.

The hockey stop involves turning sideways (90 degrees) to the direction of travel.

1. Skate straight forward. Glide very briefly in preparation for stopping. Now turn your shoulders, chest, hips, knees, and skates sharply to the left (figure 8.6). If this maneuver is done on a straight line, it is a 90-degree change of direction (figure 8.7).
2. As you begin to turn sideways, release your body weight by unbending your knees slightly. Immediately after releasing your weight, rebend your knees deeply and apply your body weight firmly downward toward the ice. This downward pressure combined with the sideways direction of the skate causes the edges to scrape the ice, allowing you to stop. The greater the knee bend and the downward pressure, the quicker the stop.

Note: You must release your body weight before turning and executing a hockey stop. If you don't release your weight, turning sideways becomes almost impossible.

3. Distribute your body weight properly during the stop. The hockey stop is generally executed with the body weight distributed approximately 60 percent on the front (outside) skate and 40 percent on the back (inside) skate, although this guideline may vary with game conditions.

Figure 8.6 Hockey stop to the left.

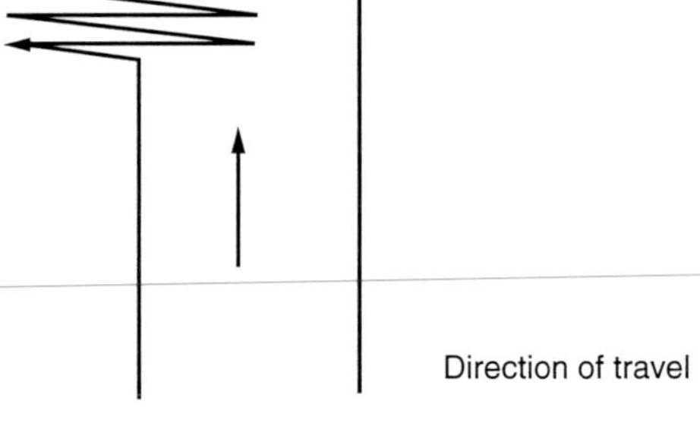

Figure 8.7 A 90-degree change of direction.

4. The front (outside) skate scrapes the ice with its inside edge, while the back (inside) skate scrapes the ice with its outside edge. Scrape the ice with the balls of the feet. Scraping with the heels causes the edges to dig into the ice; this makes stopping difficult.

Note: A sudden stop causes snow to fly. The faster you are going and the more suddenly you press your weight downward toward the ice as you stop, the more snow you will scrape.

5. To stop to the right, mirror the previous procedures.

During the stop, the upper body usually turns sideways along with the hips, knees, and skates. This puts you in an excellent position to use a crossover start to skate forward in the same direction or in the opposite direction.

However, when you stop and then need to start out skating *backward* in the direction from which you just came, use the following variation of the hockey stop: During the stop, keep your chest and shoulders facing forward. Do not turn them fully sideways as you turn your hips, knees, and skates (figure 8.8). The upper body is now prepared to start backward using a backward crossover start (see chapter 7, page 155).

Figure 8.8 Hockey stop: The upper body faces forward.

Points to Remember

- During a hockey stop, the skates should be shoulder-width or even slightly wider than shoulder-width apart. If the skates are too close together, your balance is precarious. In addition, you are in a poor position to shift your weight and push into the upcoming start.
- Keep your back straight, your shoulders level to the ice, and your eyes and head up. The back (trailing) shoulder corresponds to the inside shoulder on a curve; lowering it may cause a loss of balance.
- Keep the entire blade lengths of both skates on the ice during the stop. Lifting the heels will cause you to pitch forward over the toes of your skates.
- You must glide briefly before turning sideways to stop. The glide allows you to release your weight in preparation for stopping. If you don't release your weight, turning sideways will be almost impossible.

One-Foot Stops

One-foot stops are similar in execution to the hockey stop, except that the body weight is concentrated on only one skate. Two variations of one-foot stops are used in hockey—the front-foot stop and the back-foot stop.

Figure 8.9 Front-foot stop.

• **Front-foot stop:** Glide straight forward on the right skate, with the left skate off the ice. To stop, turn your body 90 degrees to the left. Simultaneously bend your right knee and scrape the ice with the inside edge of the right (front) skate. Keep the left (back) skate off the ice during the stop (figure 8.9). Scrape the ice with the ball of the foot, not with the heel. To stop on the left skate, turn your body 90 degrees to the right.

• **Back-foot stop:** Glide straight forward on the right skate, with the left skate off the ice. To stop, turn your body 90 degrees to the right. Simultaneously bend your right knee and scrape the ice with the outside edge of the right (back) skate. Keep the left (front) skate off the ice during the stop. Scrape the ice with the ball of the foot, not with the heel. To stop on the left skate, turn your body 90 degrees to the left.

Note: To stop with the outside edge of the back skate, you need to lean much farther back than in the front-foot stop or hockey stops, but otherwise the stop is executed similarly. If you lower the back (trailing or inside) shoulder, the skate may slip out from under you, causing a fall backward.

BACKWARD STOPS

Backward stops are used for coming to a halt when skating backward. These stops are imperative when playing defense.

Backward Two-Foot Snowplow Stop

This stop is used to stop quickly and efficiently when skating backward.

1. Glide straight backward on both skates, keeping the skates about shoulder-width apart. Rotate the toes of both skates outward while rotating the heels inward. Your feet should be in a wide-based (penguinlike) V position.
2. Push the toes of both skates farther apart. As you do this, the heels will also separate until they are approximately shoulder-width apart.
3. As the toes rotate outward, press (scrape) against the ice with *slight* inside edges.
4. Bend your knees deeply as the inside edges scrape the ice. The more you bend your knees, the more pressure you will exert downward against the ice, and the quicker you'll stop.
5. *Scrape the ice equally with both skates* by keeping your weight equally distributed. Use the balls of the feet, not the heels, to scrape the ice (figure 8.10).

A well-executed backward snowplow stop leaves the player well balanced for the upcoming play as well as prepared to start out skating forward. To thrust off, shift your weight onto the leg that is going to push, dig the inside edge of the pushing skate into the ice, bend the knee more deeply, and skate forward (figure 8.11). Advanced skaters should start on their toes and then skate forward.

Note: When you have stopped, the heels should not be much wider apart than shoulder width. If the heels separate much farther than this, there will be a delay in getting the thrusting leg re-centered under the body in preparation for pushing.

Figure 8.10 Backward two-foot snowplow stop.

Figure 8.11 Stop backward, start forward.

Backward One-Foot Snowplow Stop

The backward one-foot snowplow stop is similar to the backward two-foot snowplow stop except that only one foot executes the stop.

1. Glide straight backward on the flats of both skates.
2. To stop with the right skate, shift your weight over the right skate and rotate the toe of the right skate outward (the heel rotates inward).
3. Bend your right knee deeply and scrape the ice with the right skate, using a slight inside edge. Scrape the ice with the ball of the foot (figure 8.12).

Figure 8.12 Backward one-foot snowplow stop.

Since the stopping skate is centered under the body weight and turned outward in the forward start position, this stop leaves you in excellent position for an explosive forward start. Dig the inside edge deeper into the ice, bend your knee more deeply, and start out forward.

Points to Remember

- To stop when skating backward, lean slightly forward (away from the direction of travel).
- Keep your back straight and your head up.
- Keep your hips, chest, and shoulders facing straight ahead.
- Make sure your toes are turned out (in the wide V position). It is not possible to execute this stop if the skates remain parallel to each other.

DRILLS FOR IMPROVING STOPS

The following drills help players develop the coordination, edge control, and body-weight distribution needed to execute effective stops. These drills can be used to practice both two-foot and one-foot forward snowplow stops. They can also be used for backward snowplow stops. Note that when using these drills for backward snowplow stops, the direction of travel is opposite, and the skate turnout is reversed.

Drills for Snowplow Stops

Stand and Scrape

Basic

Stand in place. Turn the toes of both skates inward (toward each other) and simultaneously turn both heels outward so that the skates are in a pigeon-toed (wide and inverted V) position. Scrape the ice simultaneously with both skates. Use slight inside edges to scrape the ice and bring up snow. Both skates should bring up snow equally. Use the balls of the feet, not the heels, to scrape the ice.

O Drill

Basic

This drill helps players develop the turn-out and turn-in coordination necessary for snowplow stops. For a detailed description of the drill, see chapter 2 (page 18).

Two-Foot Snowplow

Basic to Intermediate

Start at the sideboards and skate forward across the ice. Keep both arms extended and hold the hockey stick horizontally at chest height. This will prevent you from leaning on the stick when stopping. Stop at the other side of the ice using the two-foot snowplow stop. Do not touch the boards.

One-Foot Snowplow

Basic to Intermediate

Repeat the previous drill, but use the one-foot snowplow stop. Alternate using the left and right skates as the stopping skate.

One-Foot Snowplow Stops and Starts

Intermediate

Start from the goal line and skate forward, stopping and then starting again as you reach the near blue line, the center red line, the far blue line, and the far goal line. Use one-foot snowplow stops at each line, alternating left and right skates as the stopping skate. After each stop, start out skating forward again. Start and skate as quickly as possible.

Drills for Hockey Stops

Team-Up Hockey Stops

Basic

If you are just learning the hockey stop, you'll find it helpful to work with an instructor or partner. This allows you to concentrate on learning to coordinate the skates, knees, and hips without having to worry about controlling the upper body. The upper body will be controlled by the instructor or partner.

1. Face the instructor (or partner), holding a hockey stick horizontally at chest height between you. The instructor will skate backward while you glide forward on both skates.
2. On the instructor's signal, do a hockey stop. Turn your hips and feet 90 degrees to the right and bend your knees. Keep the skates parallel to each other as you stop. Scrape the ice with the inside edge of the front skate and the outside edge of the back skate (figure 8.13).
3. Repeat, turning your hips, knees, and skates to the left. Be sure to practice in the direction that is more difficult.

Figure 8.13 Team-up hockey stops.

Hockey Stops on the Whistle

Intermediate to Advanced

1. On a whistle signal, start out quickly (use toe starts) and skate forward from the goal line.
2. On the next whistle signal, do a hockey stop facing the sideboards to your left. Be sure to come to a complete stop.
3. On the next whistle signal, start out quickly and skate forward again in the same direction.
4. On the next whistle signal, stop again, facing the same way.

Do this the entire length of the ice. Coming back down the ice, do the stops facing the same sideboards (now to your right). This way you will work on hockey stops to both sides.

Remember: You must glide briefly to release the body weight in order to turn 90 degrees and execute each hockey stop.

DRILLS FOR IMPROVING STOPS AND STARTS

When hockey players come to sudden stops, they know that they might have to immediately start out again suddenly and explosively. In fact, stops set up the upcoming starts, so the quality of the stop affects the quality of the upcoming start. For example, stopping with the skates too close together limits your ability to shift your weight outward in the desired direction, thereby limiting the distance you can achieve on the first starting strides. Stopping on unbent knees leaves you uncoiled and unable to push into the upcoming start—you are flat-footed and out of the play. Since stops and starts are interrelated, they should be practiced together as well as separately. The following drills combine them. Therefore, these drills should be used when working on stops or starts.

When practicing stops and starts, be sure to stop equally to both sides and to alternate the initial thrusting leg of the start. So, when skating down the ice, perform the stop facing the same sideboards (i.e., to your left) each time you stop. When skating back down the ice in the other direction, perform the stop facing the *same* sideboards (i.e., now to your right). For example, when skating down the ice, you would do the hockey stops facing to your left and then use left-over-right crossovers to start. When coming back down the ice, you would do the hockey stops facing to your right and then use right-over-left crossovers to start. As always, give the weaker side extra attention.

Hockey Stops With Crossover Starts

Stops and Starts on the Lines (Continuing in the Same Direction)

Intermediate to Advanced

1. Start from the goal line using a forward start, and sprint forward to the near blue line. Stop quickly using a hockey stop to the right (see figure 8.6 on page 174).
2. Start out explosively using a right-over-left crossover start, and skate forward in the same direction (figure 8.14, *a-b*). As in all crossover starts, use only one crossover and then pivot forward into a frontal position. The next two steps are the same as those in the forward start. Sprint to the center red line.
3. Stop quickly to the right as before.
4. Do another right-over-left crossover start and sprint forward to the far blue line. Stop to the right.
5. Do another right-over-left crossover start and sprint forward to the far goal line. Stop to the right.
6. Repeat the drill; skate back down the ice, stopping and starting to the left. When starting, you now use left-over-right crossover starts.

Note: In order to start out in the same direction as you were going when you stopped, you must follow this procedure: In the stop (to your right), the outside (front) skate is on its inside edge, and the inside (back) skate is on its outside edge. Quickly change the edges so that the outside (front) skate is now on its outside edge and the inside (back) skate is now on its inside edge. Change your knee bend and body weight accordingly. You are now prepared to do a crossover start in the same direction as you were going when you stopped.

Variation (Intermediate to Advanced)

Repeat the drill, but instead of stopping and starting at the lines, stop and start on whistle signals.

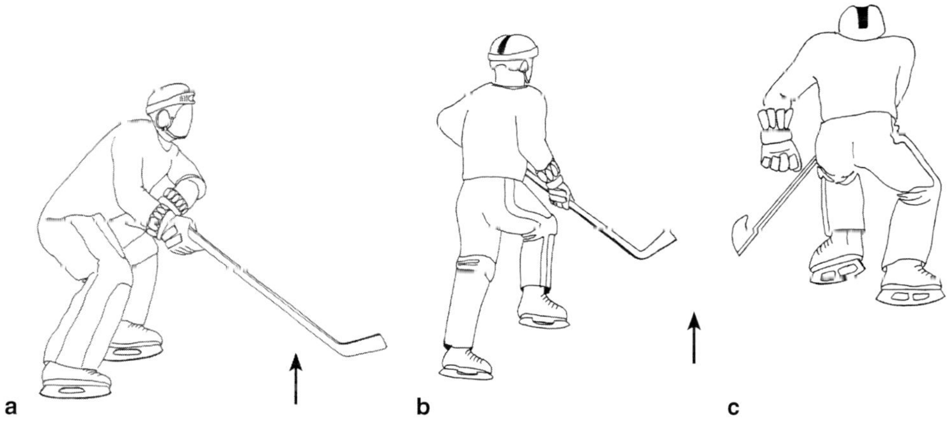

Figure 8.14 Stop and start, continuing in the same direction.

Back and Forth Starts and Stops on the Lines

Intermediate to Advanced

In this drill, all stops and starts are again done facing the same sideboards.

1. Start explosively from the goal line using a forward start, and sprint forward to the near blue line. Stop quickly using a hockey stop to the right (see figure 8.6 on page 174).
2. Start with a left-over-right crossover start (figure 8.15, *a-b*), and sprint forward in the direction from which you came until you reach the original goal line. Stop to the left (facing the same sideboards as in the previous stop).
3. Reverse directions again, using a right-over-left crossover start. Sprint forward to the center red line. Stop to the right.
4. Repeat step 2 using a left-over-right crossover start and return to the original goal line. Stop to the left.
5. Reverse directions, using a right-over-left crossover start. Sprint forward to the far blue line. Stop to the right.
6. Repeat step 2 again using a left-over-right crossover start and return to the original goal line. Stop to the left.
7. Start again using a right-over-left crossover start. Sprint forward to the far goal line. Stop to the right.
8. Repeat step 2 again and return once more to the original goal line. Stop to the left.
9. Repeat the drill, stopping and starting to the other sides (facing the other sideboards).

Variation (Intermediate to Advanced)

Repeat the drill, but instead of stopping and starting at the lines, stop and start on whistle signals.

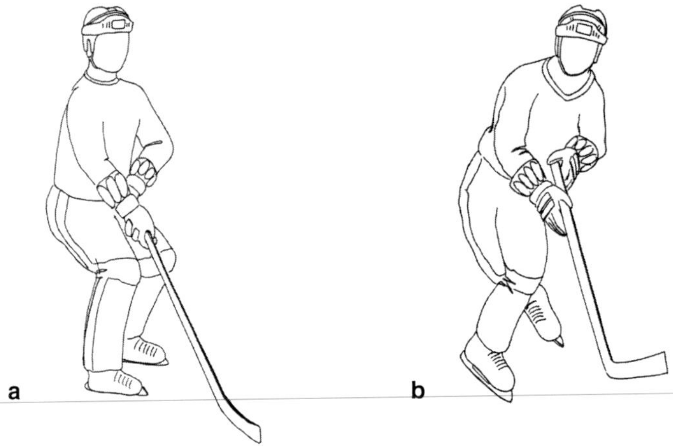

Figure 8.15 Back and forth starts and stops on the lines.

Front-Foot Stops and Starts

Intermediate to Advanced

Skate forward quickly and then do a hockey stop to your left, with your body weight primarily on the inside edge of the outside (front or leading) skate.

1. To continue in the same direction, do the following: After stopping, shift your weight far out to the right so that it is now over the right outside edge instead of over the right inside edge. You are ready to do a left-over-right crossover start. The first push is the stride-push; the second push is the X-push.
2. To skate back in the opposite direction, do the following: When you stop, your weight is over the right inside edge. Keep your weight over the right inside edge.

You have two options:

- Pivot your hips to face forward and do a forward start.
- Do a right-over-left crossover start. As you start to push with the right leg, shift your weight far out to the left until it is over the left outside edge instead of over the left inside edge. Now drive into the crossover start using both the stride-push and the X-push.

Back-Foot Hockey Stops

Intermediate to Advanced

Hockey stops are usually performed with about 60 percent of the body weight over the front (outside) skate. However, there are exceptions to this, as demonstrated in this drill.

Skate forward quickly and do a hockey stop to the left, with your body weight primarily over the outside edge of the back (inside) skate.

1. To continue in the same direction, you can use either a forward start or a crossover start.
    - To use a forward start, first shift your weight from the left outside edge onto the left inside edge. Then quickly pivot your hips to face fully forward, place your skates and legs in the V-diamond position, and do a forward start.
    - To use a crossover start, shift your weight from the left outside edge onto the left inside edge. Continue shifting your weight far out to the right until it is over the right outside edge. Now do a left-over-right crossover start (see figure 8.15).
2. To skate back in the opposite direction, use a right-over-left crossover start. The back-foot stop leaves you immediately prepared to do a cross-over start in the opposite direction. All you have to do before starting is shift your weight farther out over the left outside edge (see figure 8.14 on page 181).

Figure 8.16 Start backward (using the backward crossover start).

Note: When you are stopping on the back foot and starting in the opposite direction, a forward start is also possible. However, a forward start requires that you pivot your hips and chest to face forward before pushing. This takes valuable time and may slow down the starting process.

Forward Stops With Backward Starts

Imagine the following game scenario: You have been skating forward, but the play dictates that you stop. On stopping, you realize that you must now quickly start out backward. In this situation, you should do a forward stop that will prepare you to start backward quickly. You have two choices:

1. One-foot snowplow stop
2. Hockey stop with your weight primarily over the front (outside) skate

In both of these situations, it is advantageous to use a variation of the hockey stop in which your upper body does not turn fully sideways as you stop (see figure 8.8 on page 175). If you use the one-foot snowplow stop, the stopping foot of the snowplow (which corresponds to the front foot of the hockey stop) becomes the initial thrusting skate of the backward start. Similarly, the front foot of the hockey stop becomes the initial thrusting skate of the backward start. The initial push of every backward start is the backward C-cut.

Because the front skate of the forward stop becomes the pushing skate of the backward start, you must keep your weight primarily over the front skate while stopping. Your body weight is then correctly positioned over the pushing (C-cut) skate in order to set up a powerful push (figure 8.16*a*). Too many players stop with their weight almost completely over the back skate; as a result, these players cannot push effectively on the all-important first push of the backward start.

Be sure to use the second push of the backward crossover start (X-push) as well as the first push (backward C-cut) (figure 8.16, *b-d*).

Note: When you start out backward from a hockey stop position, your hips must turn 90 degrees (one-quarter turn) during the start in order to face backward along the new line of travel. The hips must turn during the two pushes, specifically divided as follows: The hips turn 45 degrees from sideways to backward during the first (C-cut) push and another 45 degrees from sideways to backward on the second push (X-push). The 90-degree hip rotation is now accomplished. Do not turn the hips the full 90 degrees on the first push, or the straight backward line of travel will be altered on the second push; you will end up going the wrong way.

Do not turn the hips before the C-cut push because this will delay the start. Do not turn them farther than a one-quarter turn or the new line of travel will be altered; you will travel an S-like pattern rather than straight backward.

Forward Stops With Straight Backward Starts

Intermediate

This drill helps players improve their ability to do forward stops with straight backward starts. I often call this drill glide–stop–C-cut–push–stop. The goal is for the player to get and *feel* the body weight over the front (outside) skate, which is necessary for pushing effectively on the first step of the straight backward start. Since this is a feeling drill, it should be done slowly.

1. Start slowly and skate forward from the sideboards. After taking two or three strides toward the center of the ice, glide forward briefly on the right skate, with the left skate off the ice.
2. Stop to the left on the right skate. This is a front-foot hockey stop.
3. Keeping the left skate off the ice, roll the right skate onto its inside edge and bend the right knee so that the edge and the lower leg form a strong (approximately 45-degree) angle to the ice. Execute a backward C-cut push with your right skate and leg.
4. During the push, shift your weight onto the flat of the left skate and glide straight backward on the left skate.
5. Stop.
6. Mirror the previous procedure, stopping to the right and executing the backward C-cut push with the left skate and leg.

Forward Stops With Backward Crossover Starts

Intermediate to Advanced

This drill helps players improve their ability to do forward stops with backward crossover starts. I often call this drill glide–stop–C-cut–X-push–stop. The goal is for the player to get and *feel* the body weight over the front (outside) skate, which is necessary for pushing effectively on the first step of the backward crossover start. Since this is a feeling drill, it should be done slowly.

1. Perform the previous drill. However, as you execute the backward C-cut push with the right skate and leg, shift your weight onto and skate backward on the outside edge of the left skate (rather than on the flat of the blade).
2. Execute the X-push; push against the left outside edge. As the left (pushing) skate drives under the body, cross the right skate over in front of the left skate. The right skate should take the ice gliding backward on its inside edge (RBI).
3. Stop.
4. Mirror the previous procedure; execute the C-cut push with the left skate and the X-push with the right skate.

Starts and Stops at the Sideboards

Intermediate to Advanced

1. Do a forward start at one sideboard and sprint forward across the ice. Execute the initial push of the start with your right skate and leg.
2. Stop at the opposite sideboards using a hockey stop to the left, and prepare to start out backward.
3. Do a right-over-left backward crossover start, and sprint backward to your original position.
4. Stop at the original sideboards using a one-foot backward snowplow stop with the left skate, and prepare to start skating forward again.
5. Do a forward start and sprint forward across the ice. Execute the initial push of the start with your left leg.
6. Stop at the opposite sideboards, now using a hockey stop to the right, and prepare to start skating backward.
7. Do a left-over-right backward crossover start, and sprint backward to your original position.
8. Stop at the original sideboards using a one-foot backward snowplow stop with the right skate, and prepare to start skating forward again.
9. Keep repeating the drill. Each time you stop, alternate the stopping side and the stopping skate. This also means that you must alternate the skate that performs the initial push of the subsequent forward or backward start.
10. Repeat the drill again. Now each time you begin skating backward, do a straight backward start and skate backward using the straight backward stride.
11. Repeat the drill again. Now use weaving (alternating) backward crossovers to skate backward.

Variation 1 (Intermediate to Advanced)

Repeat the drill; now skate the length of the ice and use whistle signals to command the stops and starts.

Variation 2 (Intermediate to Advanced)

The following drill is diagrammed in figure 8.17. The pattern shown can be used for a variety of drills.

1. Start from one corner of the rink using a forward start. Sprint forward diagonally across the ice to the blue line at the opposite sideboards. Stop.
2. Execute a straight backward start and sprint backward along the blue line across the ice. Stop.
3. Execute a forward start and sprint forward diagonally across the ice to the center red line at the opposite sideboards. Stop.
4. Execute a straight backward start and sprint backward along the red line across the ice. Stop.
5. Execute a forward start and sprint forward diagonally across the ice to the blue line at the opposite sideboards. Stop.
6. Execute a straight backward start and sprint backward along the blue line across the ice. Stop.
7. Execute a forward start and sprint forward diagonally across the ice to the opposite corner. Stop.
8. Repeat the drill, starting from that corner. Perform the stops to the other side and use the other skate to execute the initial thrust of each start.

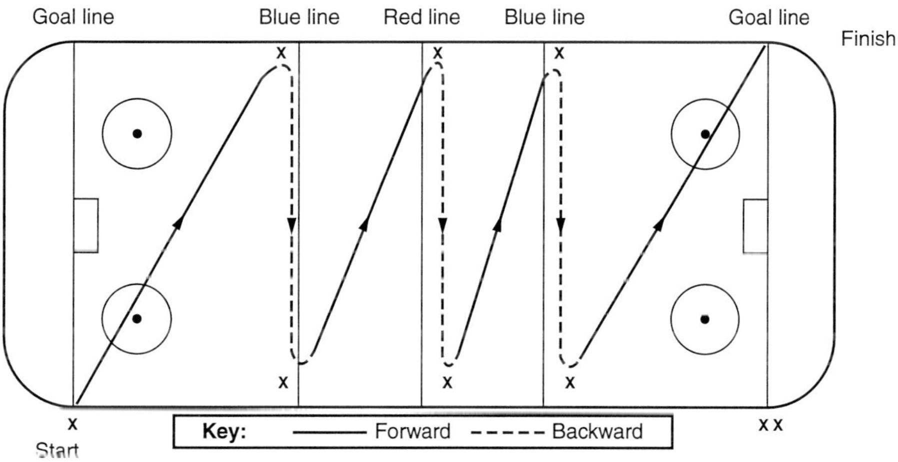

Figure 8.17 Stops and starts: alternating forward and backward skating.

More Variations (Intermediate to Advanced)

1. Do weaving (alternating) backward crossovers each time you sprint backward.
2. Repeat the previous drill using backward crossover starts.
3. Repeat the drill skating forward all the time. Use hockey stops and crossover starts throughout.

Backward Stops and Forward Starts at the Boards

Intermediate to Advanced

1. Repeat the previous drill as follows: Start out from one corner skating backward. Use a straight backward start. Sprint backward; skate diagonally across the ice to the first blue line at the opposite sideboards. Stop, using a one-foot backward snowplow stop.
2. Do a forward start, using the stopping skate of the backward stop as the initial pushing skate of the forward start. Sprint forward along the blue line back across the ice. Stop.
3. Continue in this manner until you reach the finishing corner as described in the previous drill.

Variation (Intermediate to Advanced)

Repeat the drill, but to start backward, use backward crossover starts.

When practicing stops and starts, simulate game situations where you have breakaway opportunities. Stop suddenly and start explosively. This combination is key to beating the opposition!

Note: We've discussed the importance of holding the hockey stick with just the top hand in many skating and game situations. However, when stopping with a puck on your stick, you must hold the stick with both hands. It is very difficult to control the puck if the stick is held with just one hand during a sudden stop. However, before starting, remove your lower hand from the stick. To start out explosively, push the puck well out ahead of you (get it out of your way so you have room to move), angle your body well forward, and swing your arms for additional speed as you sprint forward.

Chapter 9

Turns and Transition for Multidirectional Moves

The ability to turn and change direction instantaneously is critical in today's hockey. Players have to turn around without warning while maintaining and even gaining speed in the process.

The term *turn* refers to the process of changing the body's direction from facing forward to facing backward or from facing backward to facing forward. Turning may or may not involve a change in the direction of travel. For example, players may skate forward down the ice, turn around to face backward, and skate backward down the ice in the same direction they were traveling.

The term *transition* (change) involves a change in the direction of travel but not necessarily a turn from forward to backward or vice versa. For example, players skating forward may transition to a new direction while continuing to skate forward.

Transitional moves are some of the most exciting maneuvers to watch. To be able to transition quickly, players must have BAM—balance, agility, and maneuverability. Transitional situations may require players to do any of the following:

- Change from skating forward in one direction to skating backward in another (sometimes opposite) direction.
- Change from skating backward in one direction to skating forward in another (sometimes opposite) direction.
- Change from skating backward in one direction to skating backward in another (sometimes opposite) direction.
- Change from skating forward in one direction to skating forward in another (sometimes opposite) direction.

PRINCIPLES OF TURNS

Most, but not all, turns require a change of feet during the turn. All turns require an accompanying rotation of the entire body. When properly coordinated with the release of weight, the body rotation allows the player to switch from skating forward to backward or vice versa. Like all skating maneuvers, turns are executed on the edges. Even turns done skating on a straight line require slight edges in order to provide traction.

The upper body and the hips must rotate to fully face the intended (new) line of travel *before* the feet change. The feet step down in the new direction only *after* the body has fully rotated. The result of trying to change feet before totally rotating the body is that the skater ends up stepping down sideways across the line of travel, which usually causes a fall.

Turns require a release of body weight just before turning. Turns are actually minijumps in that the skates slightly release from the ice during the turn. A scraping sound (as in a snowplow scrape or stop) before turning indicates that the body weight did not release. As with a snowplow, the turn will be slowed down.

To stay with or ahead of the action, a player must maintain speed before, during, and after the turn. Skaters who put on the brakes (snowplow) just before turning are unable to stay with the play. It is better to hop or jump into a turn than to scrape the ice.

Players must accelerate after completing a turn. Many players turn and coast. You need to turn and go! Otherwise, you will be out of the play.

Turns are performed while skating on straight lines, curves, and circles. When turning on a straight line, use slight edges. When turning on curves or circles, use deeper edges and deeper knee bend. The sharper the curve, the deeper the edges and the knee bend should be.

Always turn facing the action. A cardinal rule in hockey is that you must never turn your back to the play. When you turn your back to the play, this limits your ability to see what is happening at that moment and to anticipate what the opponent is going to do next.

When turns are performed on curves, the body rotation is sometimes in the same direction as the curve and sometimes in the opposite direction of the curve. Some turns require body rotation toward the center of the curve, and others require body rotation away from the center of the curve (this is the case when the turns are done on outside edges).

For example, when a skater is turning and changing from LFI to RBI, the direction of the curve is clockwise, and the body rotates clockwise as well. When the skater is changing from RFI to LBI, the direction of the curve is counterclockwise, and the body rotates counterclockwise. However, when the skater is turning and changing from LBI to RFI, the direction of the curve is counterclockwise, but the body rotates clockwise. And when the skater is turning and changing from RBI to LFI, the direction of the curve is clockwise, but the body rotates counterclockwise.

Skaters can also turn from backward to forward in the following ways: LBI to RFO, RBI to LFO, LBO to RFI, or RBO to LFI. In these turns, the *direction of the curve* changes when turning from backward to forward. These turns are used in transitional situations (changes of direction).

The key factor in executing any turn is to turn the entire body (head, shoulders, chest, and hips) all the way around *before* changing feet and before trying to step down in the new direction!

Keep your shoulders level, your back straight, and your eyes and head up for all turns. If the inside shoulder drops or if you slump forward or put your head down, you may lose balance and speed.

COACHING TIP

As you exit from a turn or transitional move, the hockey stick should always lead (be ahead of you).

Players should try to master all the turns and transitional maneuvers in this chapter. Practice both directions and give special attention to the weaker side. To practice a turn in the direction opposite the one described, mirror the instructions given.

BASIC TWO-FOOT TURNS ON A STRAIGHT LINE

Two-foot turns on a straight line are the simplest turns to learn. These turns are used in many game situations.

1. **Turning from forward to backward.** Glide forward on both skates. In preparation for turning, bend your knees deeply (90 degrees). Just before turning backward, quickly release your weight (like a minijump) and simultaneously rotate your upper body and hips 180 degrees to face fully backward. The skates will follow your body's rotation and will also face fully backward. On completing the turn, immediately rebend your knees. You are ready to skate backward.
2. **Turning from backward to forward.** Glide backward on both skates. In preparation for turning, bend your knees deeply (90 degrees). Just before turning forward, quickly release your weight (like a minijump) and simultaneously rotate your upper body and hips 180 degrees to face fully forward. The skates will follow your body's rotation and will also face fully forward. On completing the turn, immediately rebend your knees. You are ready to skate forward.

The turns discussed in the following sections are more difficult than the turns just described because they require turning on curves as well as on straight lines. Some of these turns are one-foot turns and others are two-foot turns.

TURNING FROM FORWARD TO BACKWARD ON A STRAIGHT LINE OR CURVE

I call this turn a forward V-diamond (open) turn. It is a two-step turn; a change of feet is required during the turn. When skating a straight line, use slight edges. When skating a curve or circle, use deeper edges. Be sure to turn your upper body and hips *before* turning and stepping onto the new gliding skate.

The following directions are for rotating the body to the right (clockwise), whether skating on a straight line, a curve, or a circle.

Step 1

1. Skate forward on the left inside edge. Hold the right skate behind you and off the ice (figure 9.1*a*). Rotate your upper body and hips to the right (clockwise) and start to bring the right (free) skate in toward the left (gliding) skate.
2. As it draws near the gliding skate, turn the free skate to point backward (toe facing *opposite* the intended line of travel) (figure 9.1*b*). The skates and knees will be in an exaggerated V-diamond position—heels together, knees and toes apart. The toes of the skates will point in almost opposite directions (figure 9.1*c*). The right skate is still off the ice.
3. Keep rotating your upper body and hips until your hips and the skate about to take the ice have turned 180 degrees to face fully backward. The skate that is about to skate backward must point fully backward (toe facing opposite the intended line of travel) before it takes the ice.

Remember: The skate cannot step down backward until the hips have fully turned to face backward.

Step 2

1. Change feet; place the right skate (slight inside edge) on the ice, gliding backward, and simultaneously lift the left skate off the ice. *If you don't lift the left skate quickly during the turn, it will be in the way of the right skate as it steps down backward, and you may trip yourself up.* The turn is completed (figure 9.1*d*). The right skate is now the gliding skate, and the left skate is now the free skate.
2. Push with the right skate and leg (backward C-cut push), and glide backward onto the left skate (figure 9.1*e*).
3. Execute a series of backward C-cut pushes and stride backward.

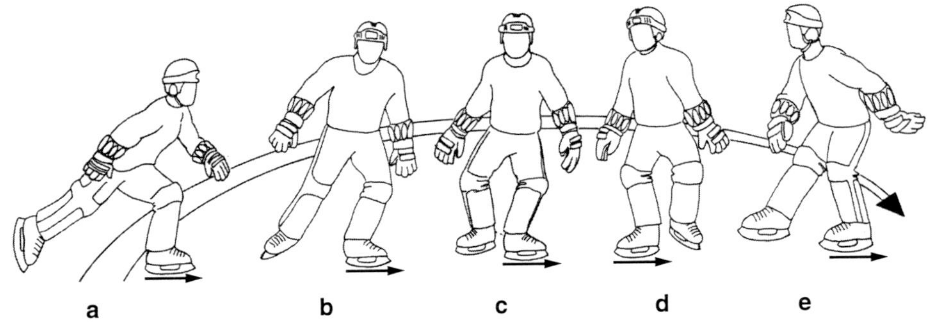

Figure 9.1 Turn from forward to backward on a straight line or curve.

Points to Remember

- You must keep the heels close together in the exaggerated V-diamond position while switching them. If the heels are far apart, your weight will be split between your skates, and the pushing skate will not be centered under your body. You will lose thrusting power and speed. A push is effective only when the body weight is totally over the thrusting skate.
- The use of slight inside edges is imperative when performing the turn. Without the edges to grip the ice, the prerotation of the body would also rotate the gliding skate, causing it to slide and scrape sideways on the ice.
- When you are executing this turn on a curve or circle, each skate must glide on a deep inside edge. The body rotation is such that the chest faces toward the center of the curve.

TURNING FROM FORWARD TO BACKWARD ON A CURVE WITH CHEST FACING OUT OF THE CURVE

Forward-to-backward turns are used both for turning and for transitional situations. For example, a defensive player skates forward into the team's offensive zone, but the opposing team gets the puck and the play changes. The defender must immediately turn from forward to backward (while still facing the play during the turn), and then quickly skate backward into the defensive zone to prevent the opponent from breaking free.

This turn is executed on two skates; it is done as a two-foot minijump. If the turn is done on a curve, the body rotation is such that the chest faces away from the center of the curve. In the following description, the direction of the curve (turn) is clockwise, but the body rotation is counterclockwise (figure 9.2).

1. Glide forward on both skates.
2. In preparation for turning, place 60 percent of your weight over the outside skate (LFI) and 40 percent of your weight over the inside skate (RFO). Bend both knees deeply.
3. Release your weight and simultaneously rotate your entire body to the right (clockwise) until it faces fully backward.
4. Land skating backward with 60 percent of your weight over the outside skate (LBI) and 40 percent of your weight over the inside skate (RBO).
5. You have completed the turn. Do one left over-right backward crossover (C-cut push and X-push).
6. Execute a series of backward C-cut pushes and stride backward.

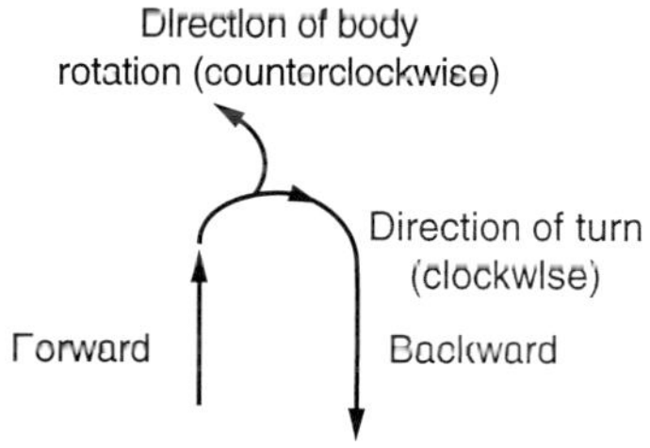

Figure 9.2 Turn from forward to backward with the chest facing out of the curve.

TURNING FROM BACKWARD TO FORWARD ON A STRAIGHT LINE OR CURVE

Two methods are used for executing a backward-to-forward turn. One is the backward V-diamond (open) turn. The other employs a backward crossover before turning. Both methods should be performed and practiced on a straight line (180 degrees), on a curve, and on a circle.

V-Diamond or Open Turn

This is a two-step turn. The following instructions are for skating on a straight line and for rotating your body clockwise (to the right).

Step 1

1. Skate backward, gliding on a slight LBI. Hold the right skate in front of you (trailing your body) and off the ice (figure 9.3*a*).
2. Rotate your upper body and hips to the right (clockwise) (figure 9.3*b*) and simultaneously bring the right (free) skate close to the left (gliding) skate, turning the free skate to point forward. The toe of the free skate should face the intended line of travel as it draws near the gliding skate. Your skates and knees will be in the exaggerated V-diamond position, with the toes pointing in almost opposite directions (figure 9.3*c*). The right skate is still off the ice.
3. Keep rotating your upper body and hips until your hips and the free skate have turned 180 degrees to face fully forward—toward the intended line of travel (figure 9.3*d*).

Note: The toe of the skate about to take the ice *must* point forward along the intended line of travel before taking the ice.
Remember: The skate cannot contact the ice pointing forward until the hips have turned to face fully forward.

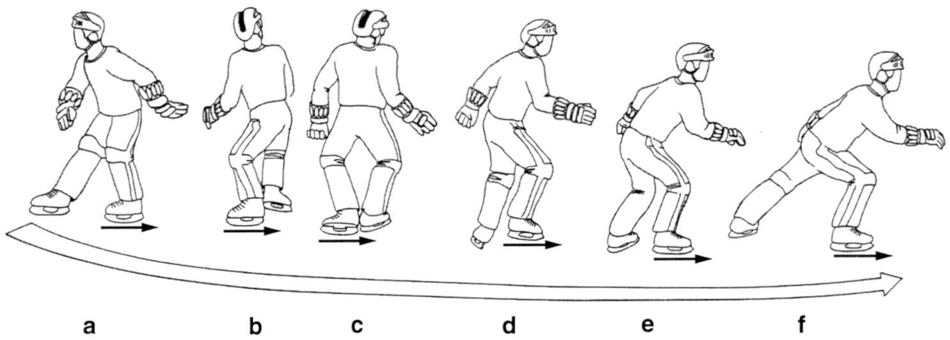

Figure 9.3 Turn from backward to forward (V-diamond or open turn) on a straight line or curve.

Step 2

1. To complete the turn, change feet; place the right skate (slight inside edge) on the ice, and prepare to skate forward (figure 9.3*e*).
2. Push with the left skate and leg as you step forward onto the right skate (forward stride-push) and accelerate (figure 9.3*f*). Sprint forward quickly.

Points to Remember

- To prepare for changing feet, you must draw the skates into the exaggerated V-diamond position.
- Body weight must be totally concentrated and balanced over the engaged skate.
- The V-diamond position prepares you to push powerfully out of the turn. Angle your body forward and keep your weight toward the fronts of the inside edges (similar to a forward start); sprint forward.
- When you are performing this turn on a curve or circle, the body rotation is done with the chest facing toward the center of the curve or circle.
- When performing this turn on a curve or circle, use deep inside edges. Deep edges done with speed create sharp curves and circles.

See figure 9.4 for a guide to forward and backward turns on a circle.

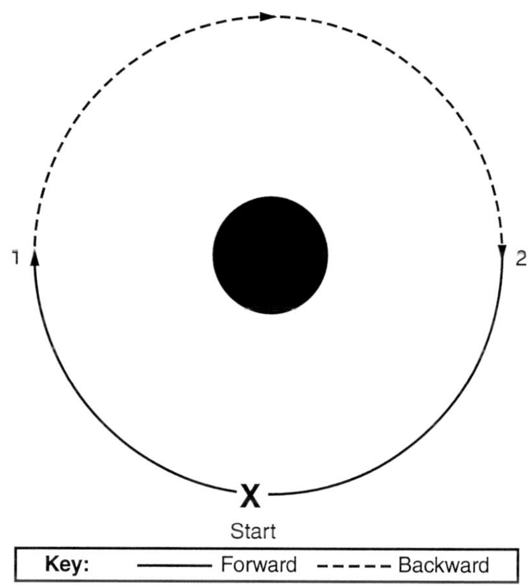

Figure 9.4 Turn from forward to backward on a circle—the body rotates with the chest facing toward the center of the circle: Skate forward on LFI from X, turn backward at 1, skate backward on RBI, turn forward at 2, and skate forward on LFI to X.

Backward Crossover Turn

A backward crossover turn is a three-step turn. The directions given here are for skating right-over-left backward crossovers on a clockwise curve or circle. Although the curve or circle is clockwise, the body rotation (in preparation for turning) is to the left (counterclockwise). The chest faces toward the center of the circle.

Step 1

1. Do a series of backward crossovers and then glide backward onto the LBO. Hold the right skate off the ice and in front of you (trailing your body) (figure 9.5*a* on page 196).

2. Prepare to do a right-over-left backward crossover; start rotating your upper body and hips to the left (counterclockwise).

Step 2

1. Do one right-over-left backward crossover and step down onto the RBI (figure 9.5, *b-c*).
2. While gliding backward on the RBI, continue rotating your upper body and hips to the left (counterclockwise). Your chest will face toward the center of the curve as your body rotates (figure 9.5*c*).
3. Draw the left (free) skate close to the right (gliding) skate in the exaggerated V-diamond position and turn the free skate so that it points forward (toe facing the intended line of travel). Keep the left skate off the ice (figure 9.5*d*).
4. Keep rotating your upper body and hips until your hips and the free skate have turned 180 degrees to face fully forward. The toe of the free skate must point fully forward before it can step down onto the ice.

Remember: The skate cannot point forward until your hips have turned fully forward.

Step 3

1. To complete the turn, change feet; place the left skate on the ice and glide forward onto the LFI (figure 9.5*e*). As you glide onto the LFI, push with the right skate and leg (forward stride-push).
2. Angle your body well forward and keep your weight toward the front of the inside edges (as in a forward start). Sprint forward quickly.

Note: The V-diamond position is extremely important; it prepares the skater to push when emerging from a backward-to-forward turn.

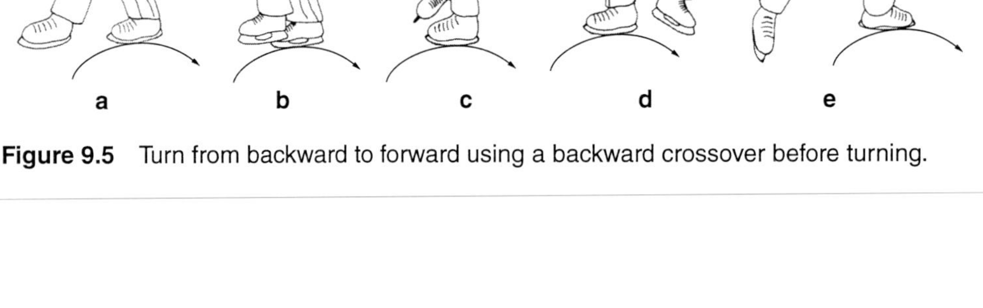

Figure 9.5 Turn from backward to forward using a backward crossover before turning.

Backward-to-forward turns are used in many transitional situations. Here are some examples:

- The player backs up to defend against the opposition—but the play suddenly changes and the puck is now controlled by a teammate. The defending player must quickly change from skating backward to skating forward and then charge toward the offensive zone, which is in the opposite direction.

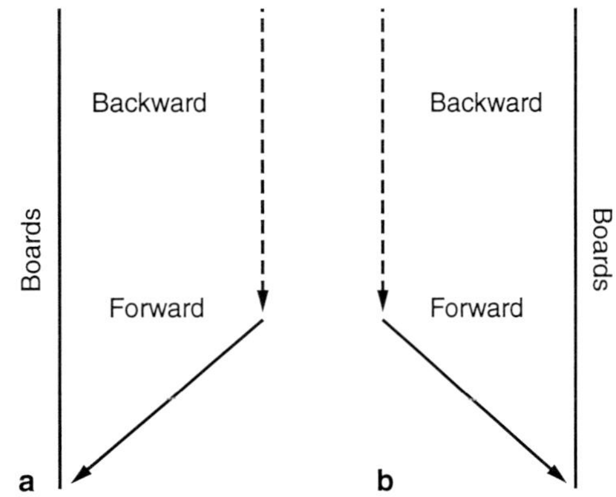

Figure 9.6 Turn from backward to forward on a diagonal line: *(a)* turning to the left or *(b)* turning to the right.

- The player backs up with the puck, waiting for an opportunity to change direction and skate forward toward the offensive zone.
- The defender must accelerate after turning from backward to forward in order to cut off or check the attacking forward at the boards. I call this maneuver diagonal transition.

See figure 9.6 for a guide to turning from backward to forward on a line diagonal to the original line of travel.

Points to Remember

- Use both pushes of the backward crossover to accelerate *into* the turn.
- Be sure the skates are close together and in the exaggerated V-diamond position before changing feet. If the heels separate, your body weight will be split between your skates rather than concentrated and balanced over the thrusting skate. This will result in a loss of thrusting power.
- Keep your knees bent and stay low while you turn. Straightening up throws momentum upward; this will cause a loss of speed.
- While pushing from backward to forward and during the initial forward strides, keep your body weight low and projected forward to accelerate (as in a forward start).

DRILLS FOR IMPROVING TURNS

The following drills are only a few examples of the many available for working on turns. The drills are divided into curve, circle, straight-line, and pattern drills. Mirror the instructions to practice turns in the opposite direction.

Curve Drill

Backward Inside Edges in V-Diamond Position

Intermediate to Advanced

This drill helps players improve their ability to turn and transition from backward to forward by improving their balance on backward inside edges while in the backward V-diamond position. Remember that the backward V-diamond position is needed in order to push when emerging from backward-to-forward turns and transitional moves.

Perform the backward inside edge semicircles drill from chapter 5 (page 89; see figure 2.14*c* on page 25). After each push, bring the free skate and knee into the V-diamond position and maintain this position for the duration of each glide.

Circle Drills

Turn Drill—Body Facing Into Center of Circle

Intermediate

1. After doing a series of right-over-left forward crossovers on a counterclockwise circle, step onto the RFI. Rotate your upper body and hips to the left (counterclockwise); your chest will face toward the center of the circle.
2. After rotating 180 degrees, turn backward, change feet, and step down backward onto the LBI.
3. Do a series of left-over-right backward crossovers on the same circle.
4. On the last crossover, cross the left skate over in front of the right skate, step onto the LBI, and pick up the right skate.
5. While on the LBI, bring the skates and knees into the backward V-diamond position and simultaneously rotate your upper body and hips to the right (clockwise).
6. After rotating 180 degrees, turn forward, change feet, and step down forward onto the RFI.
7. Keep repeating the sequence on the same circle, and perform a series of forward-to-backward and backward-to-forward turns.
8. Mirror the drill on a clockwise circle.

Note: The V-diamond position is an essential position; it prepares the skater to execute backward-to-forward turns.

Turn Drill—Body Facing Out and Facing In

Intermediate to Advanced

In this drill, the first turn requires body rotation with the chest facing away from the center of the circle; the second turn requires body rotation with the chest facing toward the center of the circle. A backward crossover is used in preparation for turning from backward to forward. The following instructions are for skating on a counterclockwise circle.

1. Skate right-over-left forward crossovers on a counterclockwise circle.
2. When your weight is on the LFO, rotate your head and upper body to the right (clockwise) so that your chest faces away from the center of the circle. Turn (flip) around 180 degrees, landing backward on both skates. This turn is like a minijump; both skates come off the ice slightly to turn.
3. Do a backward C-cut push against the left inside edge and proceed to do a series of left-over-right backward crossovers on the same counterclockwise circle.
4. As you begin the last left-over-right crossover (don't forget the X-push) and step onto the LBI, rotate your upper body and hips to the right (clockwise). Your chest will face toward the center of the circle. Continue rotating your upper body and hips to the right (clockwise) until you have turned 180 degrees to face fully forward; then step forward onto the RFI.
5. Change feet so that you are now skating on the LFO. Accelerate using the forward stride-push, and then do a series of right-over-left forward crossovers.
6. Repeat the sequence, skating a continuous circle in the same direction.
7. Mirror the drill, skating in the opposite direction.

Windmill Drill

Advanced

This drill is called the windmill because the skater turns or spins like a windmill. It is an excellent drill for improving BAM (balance, agility, and mobility), especially when performed at high speed. This is a four-step drill that is performed with only one skate on the ice at a time. The body rotations are the same as for the turn drill—body facing out and facing in.

On the first turn—from forward to backward—the body rotation is to the right (clockwise), and the chest faces *away* from the center of the circle. On the second turn—from backward to forward—the body rotation is still to the right (clockwise), but when turning, the upper body now faces into the circle.

The following directions are for skating on a counterclockwise circle.

Step 1

1. Skate right-over-left forward crossovers on a counterclockwise circle to build up speed.
2. Push against the right inside edge (forward stride-push) and step onto the LFO; fully extend the right skate and leg and hold them behind you and off the ice (figure 9.7*a*).
3. Rotate your upper body and hips to the right (clockwise) so that your chest faces away from the center of the circle. At the same time, bring the right (free) skate behind the heel of the left (gliding) skate; the right heel should point backward but should still be off the ice. The body must rotate 180 degrees to face fully backward, and the *heel* of the free skate must point fully toward the intended line of travel (backward), before the right skate takes the ice as the gliding skate.

Note: Make sure the right skate has room to pass behind the heel of the left skate in order to avoid a collision of the skates.

Step 2

1. Change feet to the RBO (figure 9.7*b*), pushing with the left skate and leg (against the left outside edge) as you continue (figure 9.7*c*). This is a seldom-used push that was not named along with the other hockey pushes in chapter 3.
2. Keep rotating your upper body and hips to the right until your chest faces into the circle.

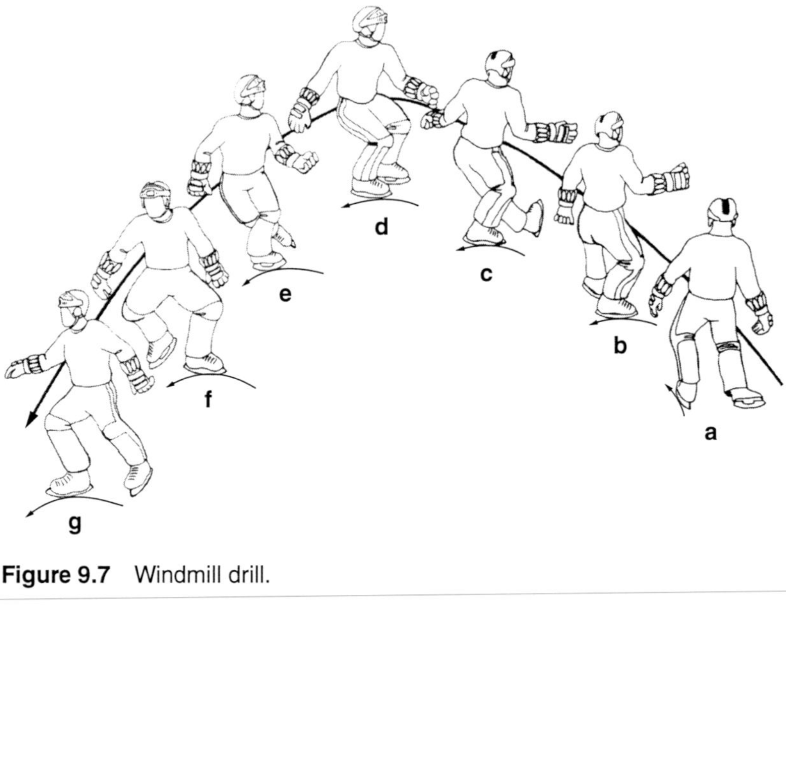

Figure 9.7 Windmill drill.

Step 3

1. Do one left-over-right backward crossover. The left skate takes the ice on its LBI while the right skate and leg push (X-push). After pushing, the right skate becomes the free skate (figure 9.7, *d-e*).
2. Keep rotating your upper body and hips to the right (clockwise, toward the center of the circle) until the entire body has turned to face fully forward. Simultaneously, bring the right (free) skate close to the heel of the left (gliding) skate, turning the right (free) skate so that its *toe* points forward in the intended direction of travel.
3. The skates and knees are now in the exaggerated V-diamond position, and you are prepared to step forward (figure 9.7*f*).

Remember: The toe of the free skate must point fully forward toward the intended line of travel before it steps down onto the ice as the new gliding skate.

Step 4

1. Step forward onto the RFI. Push against the left inside edge (forward stride-push) as you step onto the right skate (figure 9.7*g*). You have completed one sequence.
2. Begin a new sequence: Push the right skate against its inside edge (forward stride-push) and step onto the LFO (figure 9.7*a*).

Repeat the windmill sequence several times on the same circle (counter-clockwise). Then mirror the drill skating in the opposite direction (clockwise). As you become more proficient at this drill, you should push harder, skate faster, and use deeper edges.

Figure 9.8 shows the circular pattern of the windmill drill.

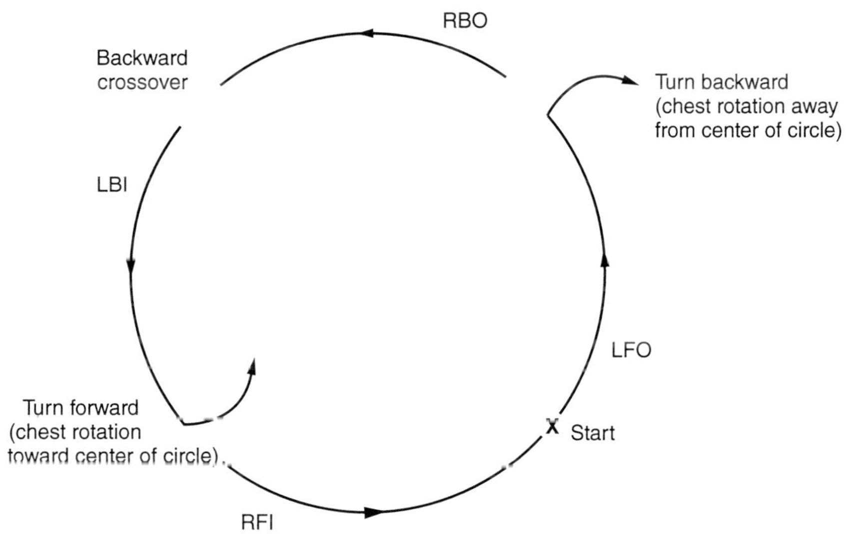

Figure 9.8 Circular pattern of the windmill drill.

Straight-Line Drills

Straight-Line Turns Down the Ice

Basic to Intermediate

Sprint forward from the goal line. At the first blue line, turn from forward to backward (forward V-diamond turn), accelerate, and sprint backward to the center red line. At the red line, turn from backward to forward (backward V-diamond turn), accelerate, and sprint forward to the far blue line. At the far blue line, turn from forward to backward (forward V-diamond turn), accelerate, and sprint backward to the far goal line. Push powerfully to accelerate out of each turn.

Note: Always turn your body toward the same sideboards of the rink. In this way, your turns will be in one direction skating up the ice, and they will be in the opposite direction coming back down the ice.

Variations (Intermediate to Advanced)

1. Do the previous drill on whistle signals.
2. Do the same drill skating on a straight line and using two-foot turns as described for the turn drill—body facing out and facing in (see page 199).

Jump-Turns

Intermediate

This drill emphasizes the importance of rotating the body 180 degrees when turning. It also helps players improve their balance when recovering from situations that involve jumping.

Remember: It is impossible to turn until the upper body and hips have fully turned (180 degrees).

1. Skate forward on a straight line.
2. On a whistle signal, jump up and turn around in the air a full 180 degrees. Land on both skates facing backward. Then skate backward.
3. On the next whistle, jump up and turn around in the air a full 180 degrees. Land on both skates facing forward. Then skate forward.

During each jump-turn, keep your back straight and your head up for balance. On landing, bend your knees deeply to cushion the jolt of the landing. Land with the entire blade lengths of both skates in full contact with the ice. If the heels are off the ice, you will fall forward over your toes.

Pattern Drills

N Drill

Intermediate to Advanced

The pattern of this drill is like the letter *N*. Refer to figure 8.17 (page 187). Perform all turns at the Xs in the diagram.

1. Start from one corner of the rink and skate forward diagonally across the ice to the sideboards at the near blue line. At the sideboards, turn backward (chest facing the end boards on your left). The turn from forward to backward is a two-foot turn with the chest facing away from the center of the curve.
2. After turning, do one right-over-left backward crossover. Then skate backward (C-cuts) across the ice and along the blue line to the opposite sideboards.
3. When you reach the opposite sideboards, turn forward (left-over-right backward crossover turn) with your chest facing the end boards on your right and skate forward. In this turn, your chest will face the center of the curve.
4. Skate forward diagonally across the ice to the opposite sideboards at the center red line.
5. When you reach the opposite sideboards at the center red line, turn backward facing the end boards on your left (two-foot turn with your chest facing out of the curve). Do one right-over-left backward crossover and skate backward (C-cuts) across the ice along the red line to the opposite sideboards.
6. When you reach the opposite sideboards, turn forward (left-over-right backward crossover turn) facing the end boards on your right. In this turn, your chest will face the center of the curve. Skate forward diagonally across the ice to the opposite sideboards at the far blue line.
7. When you reach the opposite sideboards at the far blue line, turn backward facing the end boards on your left (two-foot turn with your chest facing out of the curve). Do one right-over-left backward crossover and skate backward (C-cuts) across the ice along the blue line to the opposite sideboards.
8. At the sideboards, turn forward (left-over-right backward crossover turn) and skate forward diagonally across the ice to the opposite sideboards at the goal line.
9. When you reach the sideboards at the goal line, turn backward (two-foot turn with your chest facing out of the curve). Do one right-over-left backward crossover and skate backward (C-cuts) along the goal line to the opposite sideboards—this is the end point of the drill as well as the starting point for repeating the drill going back down the ice (figure 8.17).

10. Skate back down the ice. Turn facing the same sideboards as described; the turns will now be done in the other direction (right as opposed to left, or vice versa).

Note: Do not decelerate before or during the turns; accelerate when exiting from them. To accomplish these turns with speed and on the sharp curves described, you must be able to balance precisely and use deep edges.

Remember: The two-foot turns are done like minijumps. The jumping action releases the body weight, which is necessary for quick and smooth turns.

Variation (Intermediate to Advanced)

Use backward V-diamond turns instead of backward crossover turns.

Turns at the Lines

Intermediate to Advanced

This drill is diagrammed in figure 9.9.

1. Start from the goal line. Skate forward to the first blue line (1) and turn backward, facing a predetermined sideboard. Skate backward to the far blue line (2).
2. At the far blue line, turn forward (facing the same sideboards) and skate forward to the end face-off circle (3). From there, turn backward (facing the goal crease); immediately execute one backward crossover and then turn forward (4). Skate forward, returning back up the ice to point 5.
3. Repeat the drill. All turns should now face the other sideboards; you will now turn the other way.

Note: Accelerate when exiting from all turns.

Variation (Intermediate to Advanced)

Use backward V-diamond turns instead of backward crossover turns.

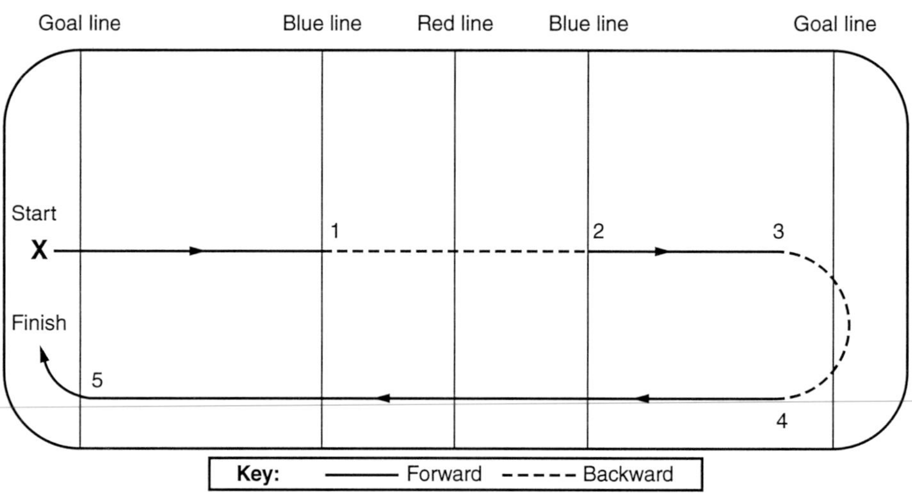

Figure 9.9 Turns at the lines.

Continuous Turns Along the Lines

Intermediate to Advanced

In this drill, only one skate is on the ice at a time, and the upper body stays *sideways* to the line of travel throughout. The drill involves performing continuous turns from forward to backward and from backward to forward, turning 180 degrees and changing feet *as quickly as possible.* The upper body faces the same end of the rink (sideways to the line of travel) throughout the drill.

1. Start from one sideboard at one of the lines. Glide forward along the line on the left skate with the right skate off the ice and behind you. Rotate your upper body and hips so that they face the goal line to your right.
2. Change feet and glide backward on the right skate (still along the line) for a very short distance. Keep the left skate off the ice and behind you; your upper body and hips will still face the same goal line.
3. Change feet and glide forward along the line on the left skate again for a very short distance, keeping the right skate off the ice. Maintain the same body position.
4. Keep turning and changing feet—left skate on the ice when gliding forward and right skate on the ice when gliding backward until you reach the opposite sideboards.

Repeat the drill skating back across the ice. Glide forward on the right skate and backward on the left. To accomplish this, face the same goal line as before.

You may find it helpful to do this drill as follows: Hold a hockey stick with both hands. Hold it horizontally in the air, *parallel* to the line you are skating on and to the goal line you are facing. This stick position assists in keeping the body sideways to the line of travel.

As you get better at this drill, push instead of just stepping from one skate to the other. Remember, when pushing, you must use the edges, bend your knees, and keep your body weight concentrated over the pushing skate and leg.

Note: Each step in this drill lands on an outside edge. However, since the drill is done on a straight line, the edges are very shallow and therefore do not curve.

Turn Out–Turn In Drill

Advanced

This drill includes only two steps. The steps are repeated over and over—at a fast pace (determined by whistle signals) and on a tight circle. The tempo of all steps should be equal. *No gliding and no crossovers!*

The first turn in this drill (from forward to backward) requires body rotation with the chest facing away from the center of the circle (turn out); the second turn (from backward to forward) requires body rotation with the chest facing toward the center (turn in).

1. Skate right-over-left forward crossovers on a counterclockwise circle until you have gained considerable speed. After gaining speed, you will start turning on the whistle signals.
2. On the first whistle, do a forward-to-backward turn (chest facing out of the circle). Body rotation is to the right (clockwise).
3. On the next whistle, do a backward-to-forward V-diamond turn (chest facing toward the center of the circle). Body rotation is to the left (counterclockwise). Land on a deep LFI.

You have completed one sequence.

4. On the next whistle, do a forward-to-backward turn (chest facing out of the circle). Body rotation is to the right (clockwise).
5. On the next whistle, do a backward-to-forward V-diamond turn (chest facing toward the center of the circle). Body rotation is to the left (counterclockwise).

You have completed a second sequence.

6. Turn again from forward to backward and then again from backward to forward.
7. Keep repeating these steps on the same circle.
8. On a command, change directions and do the drill skating on a clockwise circle.

Defensive Turn Drills

In hockey games, defenders are bound to come up against forwards who are racing along the boards with the puck. In this situation, the forward is looking for an opportunity to pass to a teammate or to escape from the defenders and move into scoring position. The next three drills simulate these situations. In each drill, the defender is skating backward and tracking the (imaginary) forward—but at a certain point, the defender must quickly turn, skate forward, and cut off the attacking player. Sometimes the defender cuts off the opponent at the sideboards and sometimes in open ice.

Open (V-Diamond) Defensive Turns

Intermediate to Advanced

Start from the goal line using a backward crossover start and skate straight backward (C-cuts) to the first blue line.

At the blue line, turn from backward to forward (backward V-diamond turn), facing the sideboards to your left. As soon as you have turned forward, accelerate quickly—as in the forward start—and sprint forward on a diagonal path until you reach the sideboards at the center red line (figure 9.10, *a-c*).

Repeat the drill, this time facing the sideboards to your right.

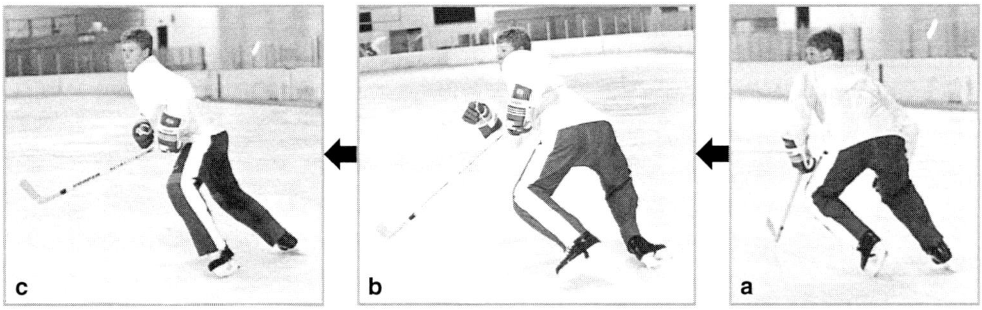

Figure 9.10 Backward-to-forward V-diamond turn to cut off an opponent (to the left).

Backward Crossover Defensive Turns

Intermediate to Advanced

These instructions are for turning from backward to forward to your right. Start in the same manner as in the previous drill. When you reach the first blue line, use one left-over-right backward crossover and then turn from backward to forward (facing the sideboards to your right). Immediately after turning forward, accelerate quickly—as in the forward start—and sprint forward on a diagonal path until you reach the sideboards at the center red line (figure 9.11, *a-g*). See figure 9.6 on page 197 for the patterns of these two maneuvers.

Repeat the drill, this time facing the sideboards to your left.

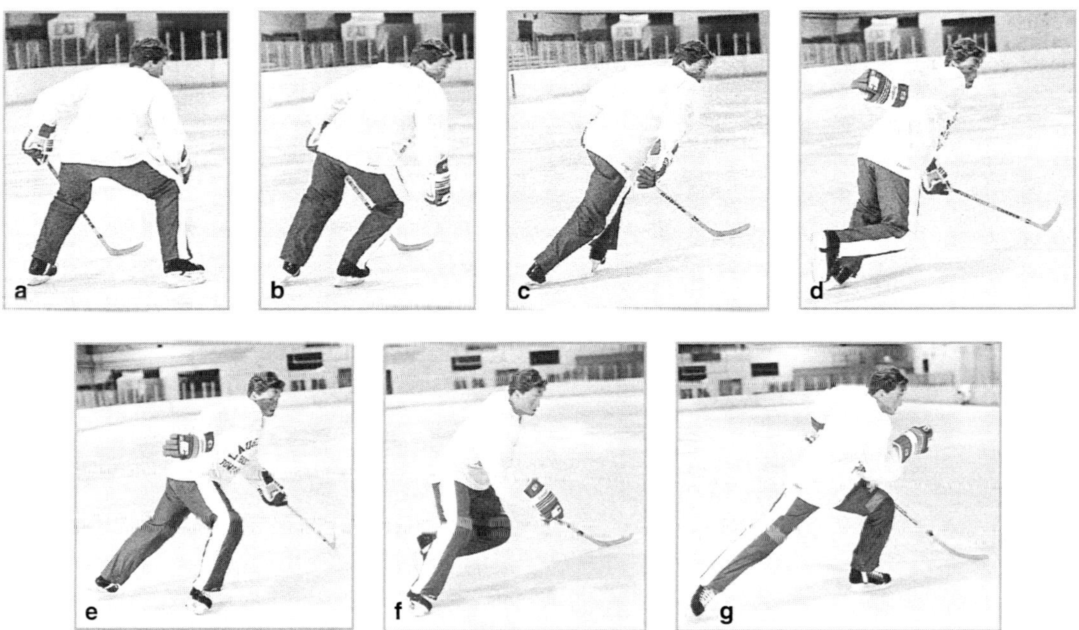

Figure 9.11 Backward crossover turn (from backward to forward) to cut off an opponent (to the right).

Variations (Intermediate to Advanced)

1. Perform the previous two drills, but after turning from backward to forward, drag the toes and touch the heels on every stride until you reach the sideboards. This is the famous drag–touch drill of the forward stride.
2. Repeat the previous variation, but now pull a resisting player. You must still do the drag–touch sequence until you reach the sideboards.

Note: The angle of each of these turns should be approximately 45 degrees.

180-Degree V-Diamond Turns at the Lines

Intermediate to Advanced

Start in the same manner as described for the previous two drills, and skate straight backward to the first blue line.

At the blue line, turn a full 180 degrees from backward to forward using the backward V-diamond turn. After the turn, accelerate quickly—as in the forward start—and sprint forward along the same straight line of travel. Sprint the length of the ice. Alternate the turning side on each repetition.

180-Degree Backward Crossover Turns at the Lines

Intermediate to Advanced

Repeat the previous drill (180-degree V-diamond turns at the lines), but now do one backward crossover before turning from backward to forward. Use both pushes of the backward crossover to accelerate into the turn; accelerate out of the turn as well (forward stride-push).

Transition Drills

All transition drills should be practiced slowly at first, then faster and faster. Practice them first without a puck, then while controlling a puck, and then while controlling a puck at top speed.

Transition From Skating Forward in One Direction to Skating Backward in the Opposite Direction

---

One-Foot Stop–Backward Crossover Start Transition Drill

Intermediate

This drill combines front-foot stops with backward crossover starts. The drill should be done slowly in order to develop proper technique. This drill requires players to make a complete backward C-cut push (the first push of the backward crossover start) as well as to make a complete X-push (the second push of the backward crossover start).

The following instructions are for stopping to the left on the right (front) skate; after the stop, the player starts (while still facing to the left) with a right-over-left backward crossover start.

1. Start from one of the sideboards. Glide forward for a short distance on the flat of the right skate; the left skate is off the ice.
2. Do a front-foot stop facing the end boards to your left. *This is a one-foot stop; keep the left skate off the ice.*
3. Immediately after stopping, start backward using a right-over-left backward crossover start. Skate backward toward the sideboards where you began the drill.
4. Stop.

You have completed one sequence.

Note: In this drill, the backward C-cut push is done with the right skate and leg. The X-push is done with the left skate and leg as the right skate crosses over in front of the left.

Repeat the drill several times, stopping on the same skate. Stop and start so that you always face the end boards to your left. Then practice the drill stopping on the left skate. Now the stops and starts will face the end boards to your right.

In–Out Drill

Intermediate to Advanced

1. Start from one of the sideboards (forward start) and rapidly skate forward to center ice.
2. At center ice, turn backward facing to your left (chest facing away from the center of the curve) and prepare to skate backward in the direction from which you just came.
3. Do one right-over-left backward crossover to accelerate backward, and skate straight backward (C-cuts) to your starting point at the sideboards (figure 9.12).

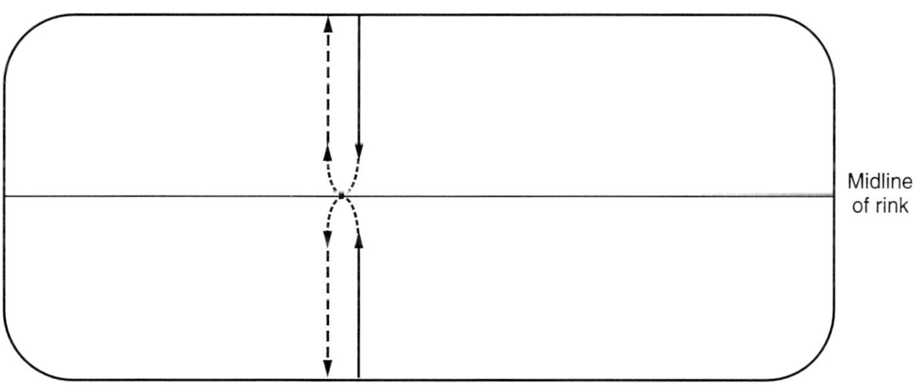

Key: ——— Forward - - - - Backward ········· Transition

Figure 9.12 In–out drill.

4. Stop (using either a two-foot or one-foot backward snowplow stop).
5. Repeat the drill; now turn backward facing to your right and do one left-over-right backward crossover to accelerate backward.

Note: Do not slow down or stop before turning from forward to backward; be sure to accelerate backward.

Transition From Skating Backward in One Direction to Skating Forward in the Opposite Direction

---

Basic U Drill Around Pylons

Basic

This drill trains players to balance on the inside edges long enough for the skates to curve a U-shaped pattern around the pylons. The description is for transitioning from backward to forward to the right (counterclockwise).

1. Start backward from the goal line and skate backward (C-cuts) to two pylons that are placed about 8 feet (2.4 m) apart on the first blue line.
2. Just before reaching the pylons, pick up the right skate and glide backward on the LBI.
3. Dig the LBI into the ice, bend the left knee deeply, and balance over the left skate. Keep the heels and knees in the V-diamond position. The deep inside edge will cause the skate to curve sharply to the right (counterclockwise) and will create the first half of the curve.
4. Continue to balance on the LBI until you reach the peak (apex) of the U (still between the two pylons). Stay between the two pylons.
5. With the heels and knees still in the V-diamond position, change feet. Drive the left skate against its inside edge (forward stride-push) as you step onto and glide forward on the RFI. The curve of the RFI will complete the U-shaped pattern.
6. Sprint forward to the goal line where you started (figure 9.13).
7. Repeat, now transitioning to the left (clockwise). You will now change from the RBI to the LFI.

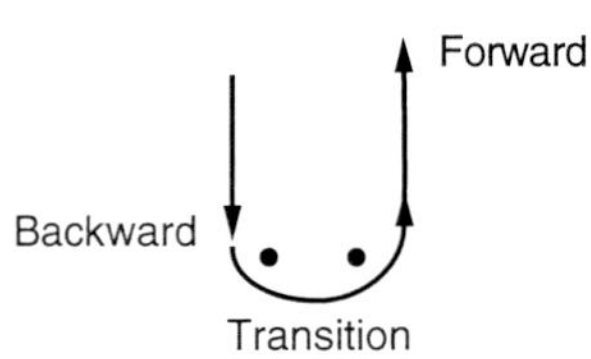

Figure 9.13 Basic U drill around pylons.

Advanced U Drill

Advanced

This drill also requires the use of deep inside edges to create a U-shaped pattern. The description is for transitioning from backward to forward to the right (counterclockwise).

1. Start backward from the goal line using a backward crossover start, and skate backward (C-cuts) to the near blue line.

Entering Into the Transition:

2. At the blue line, pick up the right skate and glide backward on the LBI. Dig the inside edge strongly into the ice and bend the left knee deeply. Balance over the LBI with your heels and knees in the V-diamond position. The deep inside edge will curve you sharply to the right (counterclockwise).

Exiting From the Transition:

3. At precisely the midpoint of the curve, push with the left skate and leg (forward stride-push) and change feet so that you are now on the RFI. The combination of LBI and RFI creates a U-shaped pattern in the ice. Keep the U as tight as possible as you transition from backward to forward.
4. Sprint forward to the goal line where you started (figure 9.14).
5. Repeat, now transitioning from backward to forward to the left (clockwise). You will change from the RBI to the LFI.

Variation (Advanced)

Use one backward crossover before each backward-to-forward transition.

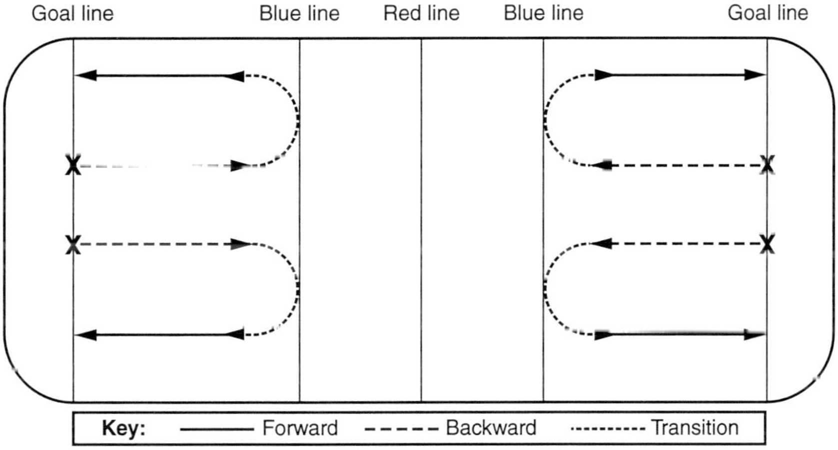

Figure 9.14 Advanced U drill.

Total-Transition Drill

Advanced

This drill combines forward-to-backward transitions with backward-to-forward transitions. The drill is described for turning toward the sideboards on your left.

1. Do a forward start from one goal line and skate forward to the far blue line (figure 9.15).
2. At the far blue line, quickly turn from forward to backward, facing the sideboards to your left (chest facing out of the circle). Do one powerful right-over-left backward crossover and skate backward (C-cuts) in the direction from which you came until you reach the near blue line.
3. At the near blue line, balance over the RBI with your heels and knees in the V-diamond position. Turn from backward to forward, facing the sideboards to your left (clockwise). Exit from the turn on the LFI. Immediately after stepping onto the LFI, sprint forward to the goal line at the far end of the ice. You have completed one sequence.
4. Repeat the drill, turning the other way; all transitions should now face the sideboards to your right.

Note: All transitional moves should be fast, powerful, and smooth. Slow down as little as possible during the transitions; *do not stop!*

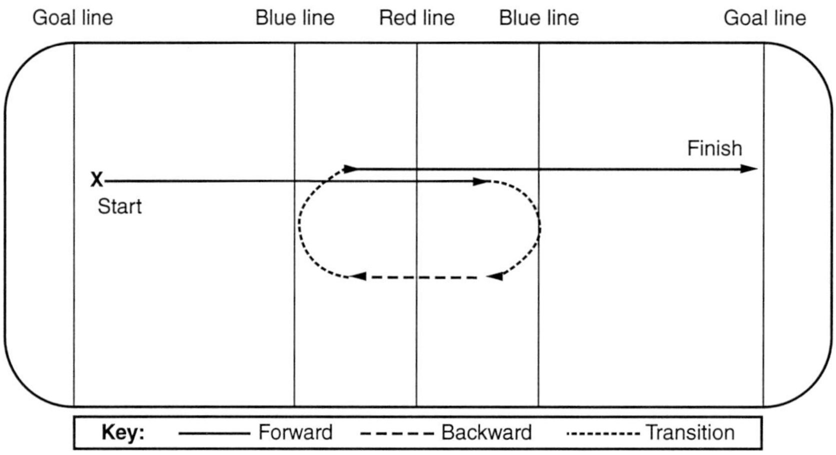

Figure 9.15 Total-transition drill.

Variations

1. Intermediate to advanced. Turn at each line during the drill. For example, skate forward from goal line to center red line, backward to first blue line, forward to second blue line, backward to center red line, and forward down the length of the ice.
2. Advanced. Alternate the direction of turning during the drill. For example, do one set of backward and forward turns facing the sideboards on your left; do the next set of backward and forward turns facing the sideboards on your right.

Basic Z Drill

Basic to Intermediate

1. Glide straight backward on the flat of the left skate.
2. Place the heels and knees in the backward V-diamond position, dig the inside edge of the left skate (LBI) into the ice, and bend your knees. The deep inside edge and knee bend will curve you to the right (counterclockwise) and prepare you to turn from backward to forward.
3. Simultaneously with achieving the backward V-diamond position, rotate your upper body and hips to the right (clockwise) until they face forward diagonally (45 degrees) from the backward line of travel.
4. Push against the LBI and take one stride forward onto the right skate. Stop.
5. Repeat the drill using the opposite skates and turning forward in the opposite direction (figure 9.16).
6. Repeat the drill several times, alternating directions each time.

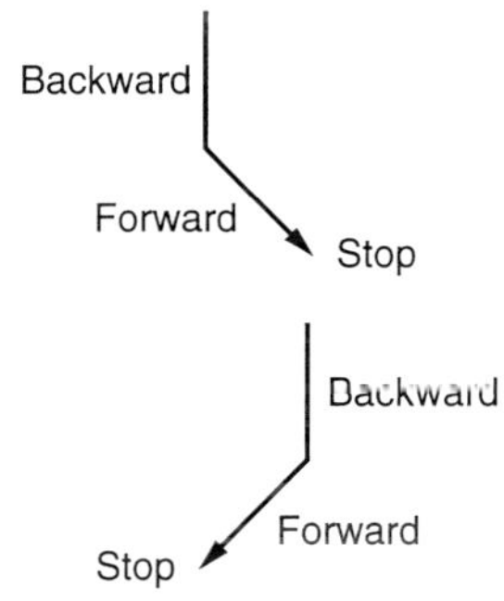

Figure 9.16 Basic Z drill.

Advanced Z Drill

Advanced

This drill is called the Z drill because the pattern described on the ice resembles the letter *Z*. The drill is done skating fast. The following instructions are for turning toward the sideboards on your left.

1. Start backward from one corner of the rink and take two or three rapid backward strides.
2. After the second or third backward stride (when you are gliding on the right skate), pick up the left skate and bring your heels and knees into the V-diamond position. Dig in the RBI, bend your knees, and turn from backward to forward facing the sideboards to your left.
3. Take two or three strides forward and then turn from forward to backward (chest facing out of the curve), still facing the sideboards to your left. Take two or three rapid backward strides, then once again dig in the RBI, bend your knees, and turn from backward to forward facing the sideboards to your left.
4. Keep repeating this sequence until you reach the far corner of the rink, diagonally across from where you started (figure 9.17).
5. Repeat in the other direction. Start backward from the other corner of the rink, and do all turns facing the sideboards on your right.

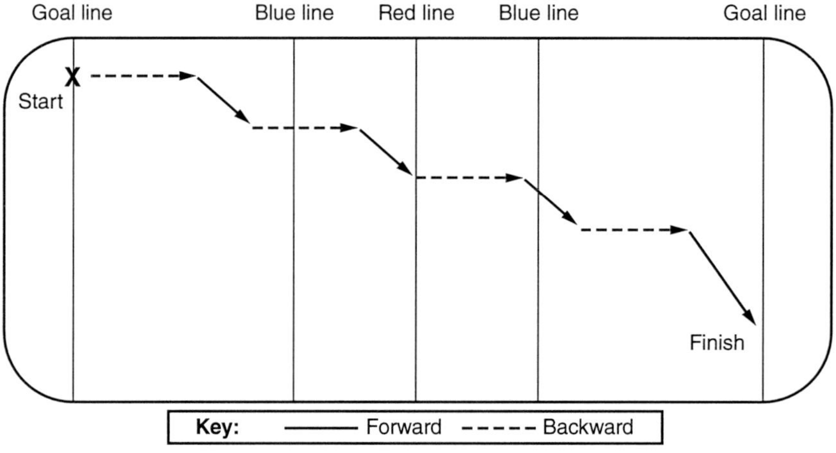

Figure 9.17 Advanced Z drill.

PIVOT (TIGHT TURN)

Wayne Gretzky was a master of the pivot (tight turn). So is Sidney Crosby. They have used it almost magically—in ways that have confounded their opponents.

The pivot is a forward skating move. The skater emerges from the pivot *still skating forward,* but usually in a new direction (figure 9.18, *a-b*). The pivot is a particularly exciting maneuver to watch. It is also an important transitional move because it gives the player many options. This move is particularly effective when trying to fake and elude an opponent. The pivot is also a power move—an attacking player often uses the pivot to ward off a defender while protecting the puck and pushing around and beyond the reach of the defender (bulling).

The pivot consists of two equally divided phases: the entry and the exit. The pivot requires very deep knee bend and strong edges on both the gliding and pushing skates. The skater must also have precise upper body positioning and weight distribution over the skates. The depth of the edges and the downward pressure of the body weight over them determine the sharpness of the pivot.

The tighter the pivot, the more important it is to keep the body weight over the back halves of the blades on the entry phase. Weight on the front halves causes the blades to skid instead of cutting into the ice.

The exit phase requires a powerful and rapid crossover (with the accompanying X-push) in order to accelerate from the pivot.

When executing a pivot, keep your shoulders level to the ice, or even keep the inside shoulder slightly higher than the outside shoulder. This will provide even greater stability. Lowering (dropping) the inside shoulder causes a lean or tilt into the circle, which results in a loss of balance when traveling with speed on a sharp curve.

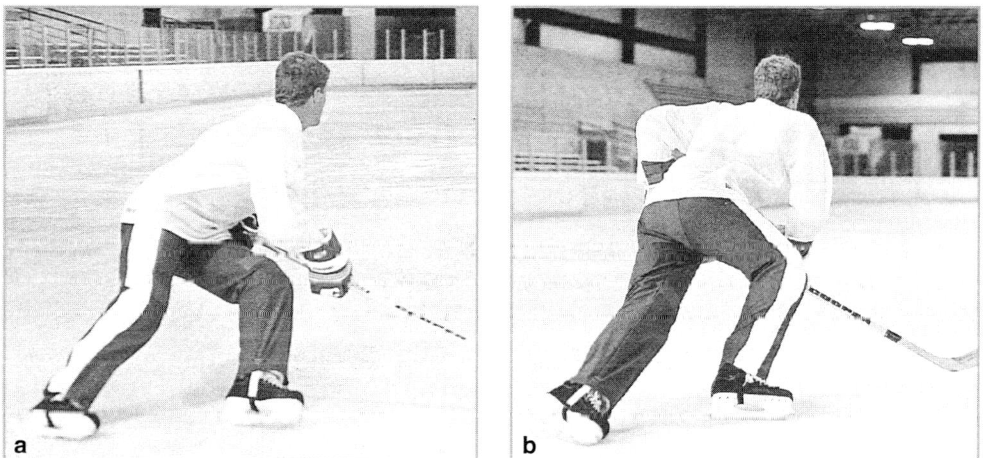

Figure 9.18 The pivot (tight turn).

The following instructions are for executing a pivot to the left (counterclockwise).

Skate forward to a pylon and prepare to pivot around it to the left (counterclockwise) (figure 9.19*a*).

Phase 1: The Entry

The entry phase of the pivot is done with both skates on the ice. The forward C-cut push is used to accelerate into and through the first half of the pivot. The inside skate glides on its outside edge while the outside skate pushes (forward C-cut push) against its inside edge.

1. At the pylon, dig in the edges of both skates and bend your knees deeply (figure 9.19*b*). The left (inside) skate is on a strong outside edge, and the right (outside) skate is on a strong inside edge. Body weight must be concentrated over the outside skate in preparation for pushing.
2. Push (forward C-cut push) with the inside edge of the right (outside) skate. Because you are gliding on a deep LFO, you will curve sharply to the left (around the pylon).
3. During the push, transfer your weight onto the LFO.
4. Keep your hips facing the curved direction of travel. If the hips don't continue to face the curve, you won't be able to finish the pivot.

Phase 2: The Exit

1. At the midpoint of the pivot, do a right-over-left crossover and drive the left skate against its outside edge (X-push). Land the crossover on the RFI. Execute the X-push powerfully and quickly in order to accelerate out of the pivot (figure 9.19, *c-d*).

Note: If the X-push is omitted or only partially done, you will not be able to accelerate out of the pivot.

2. Emerge from the pivot sprinting forward, either in the direction from which you came or in a new direction (figure 9.19*e*).
3. Practice the pivot in the opposite direction (clockwise). The right skate (now the inside skate) glides on its outside edge. The left skate (now the outside skate) drives (forward C-cut push) against its inside edge.

Note: The pivot can be done either with the outside shoulder leading and the chest facing toward the center of the curve or with the inside shoulder leading and the chest facing away from the center of the curve.

Figure 9.19*b* demonstrates step 1 of the pivot performed with the chest facing into the curve; figure 9.20 demonstrates step 1 of the pivot performed with the chest facing out of the curve. Practice both positions.

Regardless of the position, the shoulders must stay level with the ice. It is often preferable to keep the inside shoulder slightly higher than the outside shoulder.

The pivot can be used as a full-circle (360-degree) turn, a three-quarter-circle (270-degree) turn, a half-circle (180-degree) turn, or a turn on any part of a curve or circle that the situation demands. Players who master the pivot can use it to their advantage in many game situations.

Figure 9.19 The pivot: *(a)* preparation; *(b)* entry; *(c)* reaching the apex of the pivot—the hips continuously face the direction of travel; *(d)* exiting from the pivot with a crossover; *(e)* skating forward.

Figure 9.20 Pivot entry with the chest facing away from the center of the curve.

Note: Advanced skaters should attempt to exit from the pivot as if they were doing a crossover start; in other words, they should land the crossover on the toe of the inside edge. This enables skaters to accelerate quickly and explosively as they exit from the pivot.

Points to Remember

- Make pivots as tight as possible.
- Keep in mind that knee bend, edge depth, upper body and hip rotation, and speed determine the tightness of the pivot.
- Keep the inside shoulder slightly higher than the outside shoulder. This balance factor increases in importance with speed and depth of curve.

DRILLS FOR PIVOTS

When performing pivot drills, hold the hockey stick with both hands, keeping the stick blade on the ice and in position to control a puck. Practice first without a puck, then with a puck.

360-Degree Pivots Around Pylons

Basic to Intermediate

Pivot 360 degrees around a series of pylons. After pivoting halfway around each pylon, execute a crossover (and the accompanying X-push). Accelerate through the exit phase of the pivot. Skate to the next pylon and pivot around it in the opposite direction. Alternate the direction of the pivot at each pylon, and stay as close to each pylon as possible (figure 9.21).

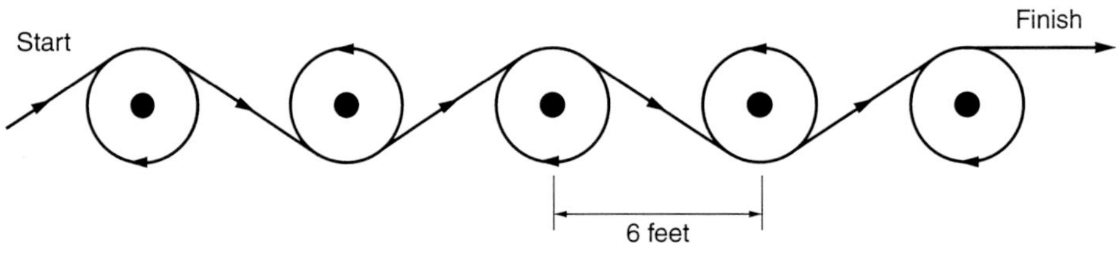

Figure 9.21 360-degree pivots around pylons.

270-Degree Pivots Around Pylons

Basic to Intermediate

Practice 270-degree pivots around a pylon. Skate forward and pivot 270 degrees around the pylon. After the pivot, skate back in the opposite direction from which you came. At the midpoint of the pivot, do one crossover; accelerate out of the pivot.

Figure-Eight Pivots

Intermediate

Set up two pylons and practice 270-degree pivots in figure-eight patterns (figure 9.22).

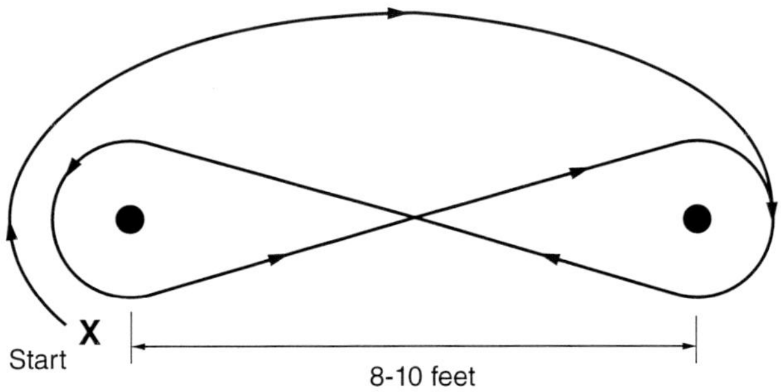

Figure 9.22 Figure-eight pivots.

Pivots at the Red Line

Intermediate to Advanced

Sprint forward from the goal line, staying just to the left of the midline of the rink. Just before reaching the center red line, pivot toward the sideboards on your left. Do not cross the midline of the rink before pivoting. Stay inside (toward the center of the ice) the face-off dots on the left side of the rink as you pivot, cross over, and skate forward to your starting place (figure 9.23).

Repeat the drill; start just to the right of the midline of the rink, and pivot toward the sideboards on your right.

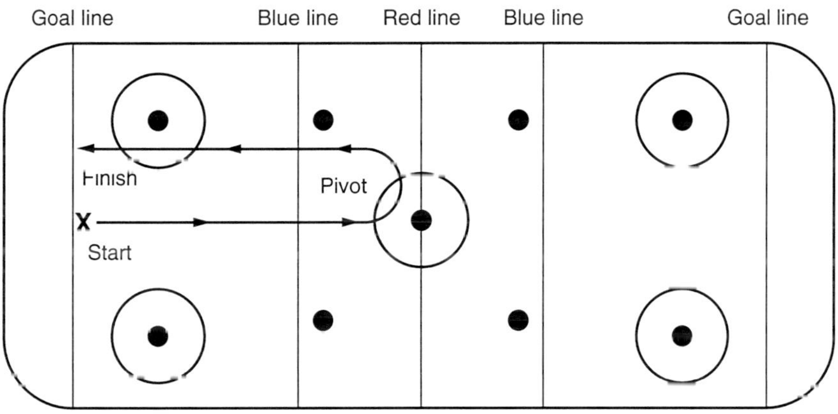

Figure 9.23 Pivots at the red line.

N Pivot Drill

Advanced

Skate forward from one corner of the rink and follow the N pattern diagrammed in figure 8.17 (page 187). Pivot at each X instead of stopping or turning. Complete each pivot with a crossover and its accompanying X-push. Pivot in both directions.

Starts Over Hockey Sticks Combined With Pivots

Advanced

Set up four hockey sticks as shown for the starts over hockey sticks drills (forward and crossover starts) in chapter 7. Start over the sticks (see figures 7.17 and 7.20 on pages 163 and 167) and sprint across the ice to a pylon that is set up about 10 feet (3 m) away from the opposite sideboards. Pivot around the pylon. Use both pushes of the pivot (C-cut to enter the pivot, X-push to exit from it). Accelerate out of the pivot and sprint forward to your starting position at the boards.

Use both forward and crossover starts (both sides) and alternate the direction of each pivot.

Cut and Go

Advanced

In this drill, you need to exit from the pivot in a direction different from the direction you were going when you entered the pivot.

Skate forward. On a signal, do a quick pivot; make a tight turn (figure 9.24, *a-b*). On exiting from the pivot, do one crossover. Land the crossover on the toe of the inside edge, and accelerate forward in the new direction.

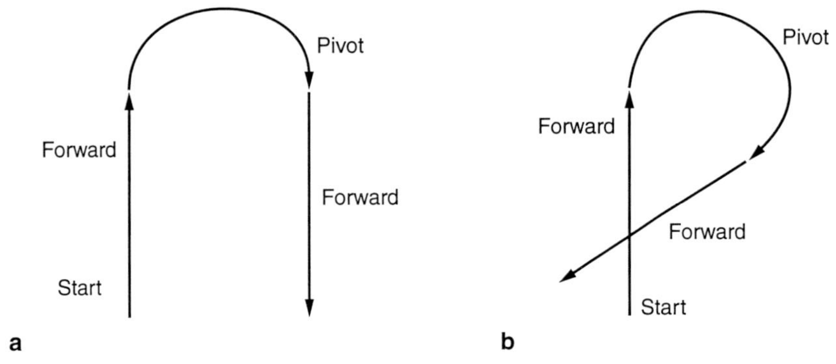

Figure 9.24 Cut and go (two variations).

Turn, Pivot, and Go
Advanced

This drill simulates a game situation in which a player is skating backward with a puck while being chased by an opponent who is skating forward. The backward skater wants to keep the puck away from the opposing player. The drill combines a two-foot turn (from backward to forward) with a pivot.

1. Pair up with a partner. One skater acts as the puck carrier and skates backward with the puck. The other skater acts as the opposing player and skates forward, trying to capture the puck.
2. When the forward skater is about 6 feet (183 cm) away, the backward skater does a two-foot turn from backward to forward (chest facing out of the circle), followed immediately by a pivot. The skater then accelerates explosively in another direction.

Note: Many variations and patterns can be used for practicing pivots. The better the skater, the more challenging the drills should be.

Bulling Around an Opposing Player
Advanced

This is one of hockey's most exciting moves. As an attacking player drives into scoring position, a defending player leans on the attacker, tries to push the attacker off the puck, and at the same time tries to steal the puck. The attacker counters by pushing against the defender (with the inside arm and shoulder) while protecting the puck and doing a variation of the pivot in order to cut around the defender. I call this variation bulling.

Team up with another player. One player acts as the attacker, the other as the defender. The attacker stays to the outside of the defender.

Skate forward to the far blue line, staying abreast of each other. At the blue line, the defender leans on the attacker with the inside shoulder and attempts to push the attacker toward the boards.

To counter, the attacker tries to cut around the defender. The attacker puts his or her back to (faces away from) the defender, with the inside shoulder high and leading. *The upper body must be positioned so the attacker's chest faces away from the center of the curve and away from the defender* (figure 9.25).

Figure 9.25 Bulling around an opposing player.

The attacker uses the inside shoulder, arm, and back muscles to push against the defender while executing a series of consecutive C-cuts with the outside skate and leg. Deep edges and strong C-cut pushes are essential.

While doing the C-cuts, the attacker protects the puck by using his or her reach to keep the stick and puck as far outside the curve and away from the defender as possible. The attacker's objective is to generate power and stability while attempting to keep the puck, gain the lead, and escape from the defender. As soon as the attacker gains the slightest advantage, he or she executes a powerful and quick crossover to accelerate, cut in front of the defender, and escape.

The inside shoulder must be kept higher than the outside shoulder throughout this move. If it is lower (if it drops), the attacker will lose balance (and a step). This is especially true when traveling at high speeds. If the attacker's upper body tilts into the circle a bit too much, the defender can simply back away, and the attacker may land on the ice!

Now practice bulling while holding the hockey stick with just the top hand. Try to protect the puck as you bull around the defender; keep the stick and puck as far outside the curve as possible!

Practice slowly at first and then faster and faster until you can perform these maneuvers correctly, powerfully, and quickly (first without a puck, then with a puck).

Chapter 10

Agility for Maximum Coverage of the Ice

If you can visualize how Pavel Datsyuk skates around and through the opposition, you will understand the importance of agility on the ice. Agility often marks the difference between a mediocre hockey player and a star. It allows a player to outfox an opponent and keep the opponent at bay. Agile hockey players can execute a wide range of moves with dazzling speed and mobility. They can regain their feet and get back into the play quickly after a fall or an unexpected body check. These players seem to be everywhere on the ice; they dominate the action.

The skills and drills in this chapter are designed to improve agility. Goalies should also concentrate on improving agility—it is key to their success in the nets.

Several maneuvers already covered in this book can also be categorized as agility maneuvers—for example, crossovers, turns, transitional moves, and pivots.

As always, practice all agility maneuvers slowly at first, then faster and faster. Practice first without a puck, then while controlling a puck.

DRILLS FOR IMPROVING AGILITY

360-Degree Spin-Around

Basic to Intermediate

Hard checks can send players reeling to the ice. Some skaters manage to stay on their feet and retain their composure after such checks, while others end up out of the play. This drill simulates such a situation. By practicing this drill, you will improve your balance and recovery times in these situations.

The spin-around involves making a 360-degree rotation as rapidly as possible. This move is executed with both skates on the ice during the spin.

1. Skate forward. Pretend you've just been hit with a hard check that spins you around 360 degrees so that after the spin you are facing forward again.
2. When spinning, stay on the flats of the blades with your weight on the balls of the feet. Do not dig in the edges to spin around. If the edges catch the ice, you will have difficulty spinning rapidly.
3. Although this turn is actually a combination of two turns (a forward-to-backward turn and a backward-to-forward turn), try to spin around in one continuous motion.
4. As soon as you have completed the spin-around and you are facing forward again, dig the back (pushing) skate into the ice and push powerfully; sprint rapidly toward the action. After coming out of the spin, you need to accelerate immediately and get back into the play quickly.
5. Keep the hockey stick on or close to the ice as you spin around. Hold the stick with both hands, and bring the stick around as you spin so that it leads you out of the spin. To be prepared for what happens next, you must ensure that the stick is in front of you—close to or on the ice—as you exit from the spin. Many inexperienced players swing the stick high in the air as they spin, or they come out of the spin with the stick trailing behind them. This indicates poor control and upper body instability. It also raises the center of gravity. These factors affect balance, speed, and recovery time. In addition, it is impossible to catch a pass or control a puck if the stick is off the ice or out of position.

Practice the 360-degree spin-around in both directions.

Variations (Basic to Intermediate)

1. Spin around on whistle signals. On the first signal, spin around 360 degrees in one direction. On the next signal, spin around in the other direction. Alternate the direction of each spin to avoid dizziness.
2. Instead of spinning around on whistle signals, spin around at the near blue line, the center red line, and the far blue line.

Inside Edges Around Pylons

Intermediate

In this drill, each skate and leg first glides (for curved direction) and then pushes (for acceleration). Refer to figure 10.1.

1. Skate forward from one end of the rink to the first pylon. When you reach the pylon, curve halfway around it by gliding on the inside edge (45-degree angle) of the outside skate. The knee of the gliding leg must be bent deeply (90 degrees). Keep the free (inside) skate off the ice and close to the gliding skate; the skates and knees should be in the V-diamond position.

2. After curving halfway around the pylon, the gliding skate becomes the pushing skate. Push against the inside edge that you have been gliding on (forward stride-push) to accelerate from the glide.
3. Sprint forward to the next pylon. Curve halfway around the pylon in the other direction; glide on the inside edge of the outside skate. Keep the free (inside) skate off the ice and close to the gliding skate; the skates and knees are in the V-diamond position.
4. After curving halfway around the pylon, push (forward stride-push) against the inside edge that you have been gliding on. Sprint forward to the next pylon.
5. Continue skating to and curving halfway around each pylon until you reach the opposite end of the rink. Change the direction of the curve at each pylon.
6. Repeat the drill skating backward. Each push is now the backward C-cut push.

Note: Keep your back straight and your eyes and head up throughout this drill.

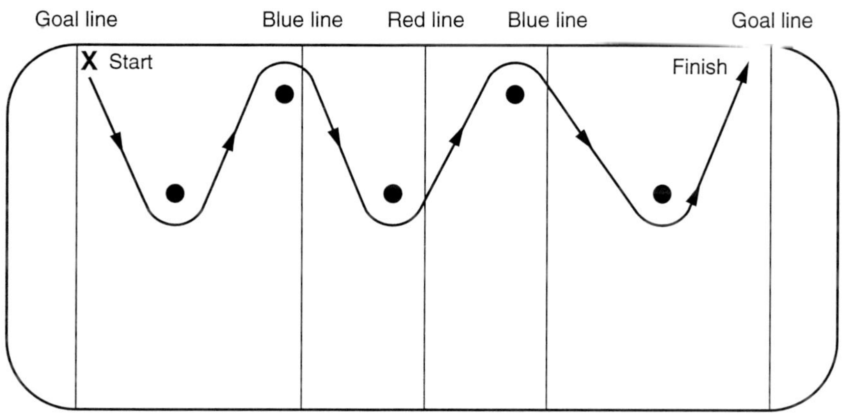

Figure 10.1 Inside edges around pylons.

Outside Edges Around Pylons

Intermediate

Perform the previous drill skating first forward and then backward. However, you will now curve halfway around each pylon by gliding on the outside edge of the inside skate. Keep the free (outside) skate off the ice. After curving halfway around each pylon, push against the outside edge that you have been gliding on (X-push) and do one crossover. Sprint from one pylon to the next. Change the direction of the curve at each pylon.

Note: Be sure to use the X-push to accelerate from each crossover.

Backward-to-Forward Turns Around Pylons

Intermediate to Advanced

This drill is done using the same pattern as in the previous two drills.

Skate backward to the first pylon. Curve halfway around the pylon, gliding on the inside edge of the outside skate. After curving halfway around the pylon, turn forward quickly, push against the inside edge that you've been gliding on, and take two rapid forward strides toward the next pylon. After the second stride, turn backward quickly and skate backward to the next pylon. Curve halfway around the pylon, gliding on the inside edge of the outside skate. After curving halfway around the pylon, turn forward quickly, push against the inside edge that you've been gliding on, and take two rapid forward strides toward the next pylon. After the second stride, turn backward quickly and skate backward to the next pylon. Continue this drill until you reach the opposite end of the rink. Sprint from one pylon to the next, and change the direction of the curve at each pylon.

Note: As you curve around each pylon, keep the free (inside) skate off the ice and close to the gliding skate; the skates and knees should be in the V-diamond position.

All backward-to-forward turns in this drill use the body rotation with the chest facing toward the center of the curve (facing the pylons).

Many variations of the previous drills may be designed, incorporating spin-arounds, full circles around pylons, forward-to-backward and backward-to-forward turns, and so on.

Knee Drops

Basic to Intermediate

Players often have to drop to their knees to block shots. They must be able to quickly return to an upright position and resume skating rapidly in order to stay with the action. When doing the following drills, be sure to drop down gently so that you don't injure your knees. *Those with knee problems should not do knee drops.*

Keep your back straight and your head up throughout these drills.

1. Stand in place on the ice. Hold a hockey stick horizontally at chest height in front of you, with your arms outstretched. Keep the stick in this position during the entire drill. At no time should your hands, elbows, or stick touch the ice.
2. On the first whistle, drop to both knees. On the next whistle, get up. Keep repeating with the whistle signals, which will get faster and faster.

Variation 1 (Basic to Intermediate)

1. On a whistle signal, drop to both knees (figure 10.2*a*).
2. On a second whistle, sit down to one side of your skates (figure 10.2*b*).
3. On a third whistle, get up on both knees (see figure 10.2*a*).
4. On a fourth whistle, get up.

Note: Be sure to practice sitting both ways. Here, too, most skaters favor one side over the other.

Variation 2 (Intermediate)

Skate forward or backward down the ice. On the first whistle, drop to both knees. On the second whistle, get up and get back into stride as quickly as possible.

Variation 3 (Intermediate)

Skate forward or backward down the ice. On the first whistle, drop to one knee. On the second whistle, get up. Keep repeating this on alternating knees (figure 10.2*c*).

Variation 4 (Intermediate to Advanced)

Skate forward. On the whistle, drop to both knees. On the next whistle, get up, immediately turn backward, and skate backward rapidly. On the next whistle, drop to both knees. On the next whistle, get up, immediately turn forward, and skate forward rapidly. This drill can also be done dropping onto one knee. Alternate knees.

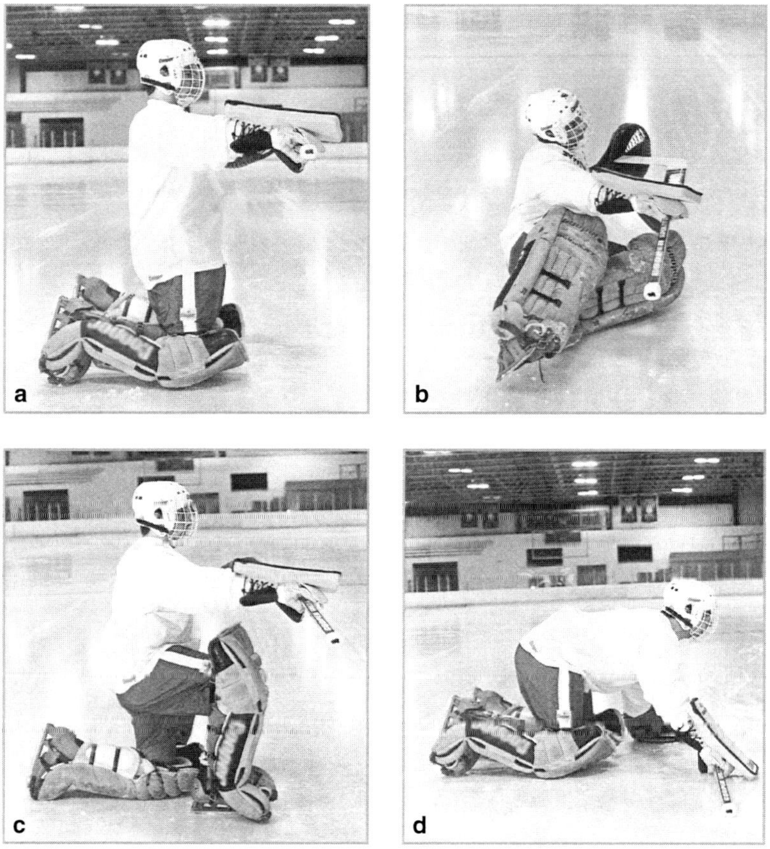

Figure 10.2 Knee drops: *(a-c)* correct form; *(d)* incorrect form.

Points to Remember

- Do not let your hands, elbows, or stick touch the ice at any time.
- When preparing to get up, center the support skate *directly underneath your body* with the entire blade length on the ice (see figure 10.2*c* on page 227). If you place only the front toe of the blade on the ice and lift your heel off the ice, you will not be able to get up.
- Keep your back straight and your eyes and head up at all times. If your shoulders and head slump forward, your weight will pitch over your toes, and you will not be able to get up (figure 10.2*d* on page 227).

JUMPS OVER HOCKEY STICKS

The ability to be airborne, land on one or both skates, and then sprint without losing speed is an example of agility. You never know when you will be thrown into the air by an unexpected body check or when you will have to jump over a fallen player.

To land and resume skating without breaking stride, you must have balance, body control, power, and stability. The use of the knees as shock absorbers is critical.

The following drills are designed to help players improve their balance and recovery capabilities in these situations.

Two-Foot Jumps Over Hockey Sticks

Intermediate

1. Place a hockey stick horizontally over two pylons (the height of the stick must be dependent on the size and ability of the skater).
2. Skate forward.
3. As you approach the stick, glide briefly on both skates and then jump, taking off from both skates.
4. As you jump, lift both knees simultaneously; jump over the stick and land on both skates.
5. On landing, the entire blade lengths of both skates must be in full contact with the ice, and your weight must be over the middle of the blades. If your heels are off the ice as you land, you will end up pitching forward over the curved toes of the skates, and you may fall forward. If you land with your weight too far back (over the heels), you may fall backward.
6. On landing, flex both knees deeply. Keep your back straight, your shoulders back, and your eyes and head up.

Variations (Advanced)

1. Advanced skaters can perform this jump while skating backward.
2. Even more advanced skaters can try these two jumps:

- Skate forward, jump over the stick, turn 180 degrees in the air, and land backward. As soon as you land, sprint backward without losing stride.
- Skate backward, jump over the stick, turn 180 degrees in the air, and land forward. As soon as you land, sprint forward without losing stride.

3. Very advanced skaters can jump and turn 360 degrees in the air (forward and backward).

One-Foot Leaps Over Hockey Sticks

Advanced

Place a hockey stick horizontally over two pylons (the height of the stick must be dependent on the size and ability of the skater). Skate forward. When you approach the hockey stick, take off from one skate, leap over the hockey stick, and land on the other skate.

To leap, drive off powerfully and fully with the back skate and leg. Land on the opposite skate with the takeoff skate still off the ice. Body weight should be on the middle of the landing blade.

Very advanced skaters can leap from one skate, turn in the air, and land backward either on the same skate or on the other skate.

Do not slow down before jumping. To get the height necessary for clearing the stick, you must accelerate into the takeoff.

After landing, sprint immediately. Try not to break stride.

Lateral Crossover Leaps

Advanced

A player skating forward or backward on a straight line who wants to make a sudden lateral move or leap sideways (i.e., over a fallen player) may need to execute a lateral crossover leap. The leap can be compared to doing a crossover start.

This drill is similar to the crossover starts over hockey sticks drill (chapter 7) but with only one stick.

1. Place a hockey stick horizontally on top of two pylons, parallel to the direction of travel rather than perpendicular to it. The height of the stick from the ice must be dependent on the size and ability of the skater.
2. Skate forward until you are alongside and to the right of the stick.
3. Leap over the stick using a right-over-left lateral crossover (figure 10.3*a* on page 230). Drive the left (inside) skate against its outside edge (X-push) to provide thrust through the leap, while simultaneously crossing the right (outside) skate over the left skate. Drive the right (crossing) knee and your body weight as far sideways (to the left) as possible.
4. The right skate must land on the other side of the stick and on its inside edge; the skate blade should be almost parallel to the stick (figure 10.3*b*).

5. As soon as you land, quickly pivot forward and accelerate. Sprint forward (figure 10.3*c*).
6. Repeat the drill. Now leap over the stick starting from the left side and landing on the right side of the stick (left-over-right crossover).

Very advanced skaters can try the same drill from a backward skating position. This is a backward lateral crossover leap.

Figure 10.3 Lateral crossover leap over hockey stick.

Dives

Intermediate

Hockey players quickly learn to expect the unexpected. You never know when you'll take a dive on the ice, but sooner or later you will. When it happens, you must get to your feet quickly and then immediately return to the action. Practicing these drills will improve your ability to recover quickly from such falls.

1. Place a hockey stick horizontally on top of two pylons.
2. Sprint forward.
3. At the stick, belly flop with your hands flat out and your feet outstretched behind you and on the ice (Superman dive). Keep your head up as you belly flop. Dive under the stick, trying not to knock it down.
4. After passing under the stick, immediately get up and resume sprinting.

Variations (Intermediate to Advanced)

- Combine jumps and dives. Practicing these moves will help you gain the agility and quickness needed to jump up, land on your feet, dive, recover, and get back into stride with as little loss of time as possible.
- Design a challenging pylon course. It is particularly difficult to dive, recover quickly, and leap over another stick that is only a few feet away from the stick that you just dove under.

CHECKING AND DEFENDING AGAINST A CHECK

Why can some hockey players check so effectively while others are not as strong when they check? Why can some hockey players remain in front of the net and withstand body checks that would stun other players? Stability is the key to both delivering and defending against checks. Stability refers to the ability to apply the principles of edges, knee bend, and body weight, as well as the ability to get maximum grip into the ice.

Checking: If you are the player delivering the check, you must use the inside edges, knees, leg drive, and body weight to effectively push into the check. If you don't, you will likely bounce off your opponent rather than take him or her out of the play. A proper check works from the skates up—from the edges, then from the knees, then from the legs, and then from the hips. Push into the check, just as you would push into a stride. The push is similar to the forward stride-push, but without a toe flick. The follow-through of the check is accomplished by pushing against the opponent with the upper body (chest and shoulder).

Withstanding checks: Once players reach their desired position, they must stay on their feet and hold their ground. Players with strong edges and deep knee bend are extremely difficult to move. Whether receiving a check or standing in front of the net, you must use the edges and deep knee bends to make it more difficult for a defender to move you out.

As always, the more you dig in the edges and bend your knees, the more stable—and therefore stronger—you become. To defend against (push back against) a check, press down into the ice with as much knee bend as possible and with the maximum grip and leg drive you can apply to the *inside* edges. One of the most common errors is straightening up while being checked. This pulls the edges, knees, and center of gravity up and causes you to lean away from the check. The result of this is often a fall.

1. Work with a partner. Each partner will lean on (check) the other, shoulder to shoulder (figure 10.4).

Figure 10.4 Withstanding a check.

COACHING TIP

Strength on the ice depends on more than just size.

2. Both players must dig the inside edge of the outside (back) skate into the ice. Keep your body weight over the back skate. Both players must simultaneously push against the inside edge of the gripping skate. Try to move each other without giving up ice. If you cannot stand your ground, you are not using your edges, knee bend, or body weight effectively.

Pushing Into a Slap Shot

Advanced

Players must push hard when they are taking slap shots. The push is actually the forward stride-push; the back (outside) skate drives straight out against the gripping (inside) edge. The push finishes with a follow-through and total transfer of weight onto the front (inside) skate.

Push powerfully. Start with your weight on the inside edge of the back skate (windup). Push explosively (release and follow-through) as you shoot. You can actually accelerate and build up speed as you shoot. The acceleration via the push and weight transfer will yield a faster shot.

Very advanced players can try this: When transferring your weight from back skate to front skate, step onto and maintain a deep inside edge on the front skate until the follow-through of the swing is completed. The advantage of stepping onto and maintaining an inside edge is that the grip of the edge into the ice allows for a longer and more complete follow-through (of the swing). This translates into a faster shot.

Tracking an Opponent

Advanced

Partner up with another player. Begin by skating as a forward while your partner acts as a defender. Use crossover steps and leaps in alternating lateral directions, trying to deke (fake) the defender. The defender tracks you by mirroring and following your every move. Whichever way you go, the defender must also go. Reverse roles and repeat the drill.

Repeat this drill with one player skating straight forward and the other skating straight backward. At a moment's notice (for example, on a whistle signal), the forward should make a move laterally. The defender must immediately respond (figure 10.5, *a-b*).

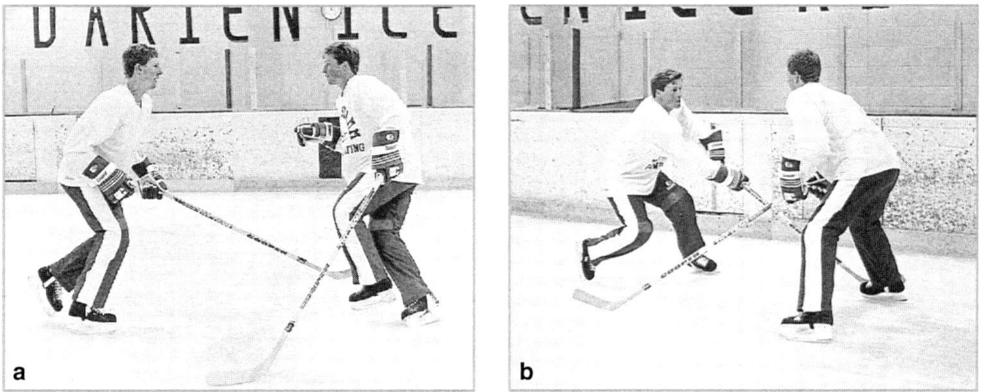

Figure 10.5 Tracking an opponent.

Signal Drills

Intermediate to Advanced

These drills combine a variety of skating skills. The skating maneuvers are performed in a sequence that is not announced before the drill. The purpose is to help players develop agility and instantaneous response.

A particular signal will indicate a specific maneuver. On the signal, you must perform the maneuver as quickly as possible. The moves are done one after the other with no warning about which move will be next. Here are four sample drills:

Drill 1

1. Skate forward.
2. Do crossover leaps to the right.
3. Skate straight backward.
4. Do crossover leaps to the left.
5. Skate backward.
6. Transition from backward to forward (U-turn) and sprint forward.

Drill 2

1. Skate forward.
2. Do crossover leaps to the right.
3. Skate straight backward.
4. Do crossover leaps to the left.
5. Skate backward.
6. Stop and sprint forward.
7. Pivot (tight turn) 180 degrees and sprint forward to the starting point.

Drill 3

1. Skate forward.
2. Do crossover leaps to the right.
3. Skate straight backward.
4. Do crossover leaps to the left.
5. Skate backward.
6. Stop and sprint forward.
7. Turn from forward to backward (chest facing out of the circle) and skate backward to the starting point.

Drill 4

1. Skate forward.
2. Pivot (tight turn) 360 degrees to the right.
3. Skate forward.
4. Drop to your knees, get up, and turn backward.
5. Skate backward, drop to your knees, and get up.
6. Skate forward.
7. Pivot (tight turn) 360 degrees to the left.
8. Skate forward.
9. Pivot (tight turn) 360 degrees to the right.
10. Skate forward and stop. Drop to your knees, belly flop, get up on your knees, and get up on your feet.
11. Skate forward, spin around 360 degrees, and continue skating forward without breaking stride.

Try a game of follow the leader incorporating some of the previous moves. The variations on these drills are endless. Signal drills are excellent for working on technique, and they are also fun.

Maneuvering the Puck With the Skates

Intermediate

To the astonishment of fans, some hockey players control the puck as easily with their skates as they do with their hockey stick. To develop this skill, skate without a stick and control the puck with your skates. Try to move the puck from skate to skate. Don't kick it out in front of you. Keep your eyes and head up; do not look down at the puck.

Other ways to develop this skill include playing one-on-one with another player, free-for-all with several players, or even a regular game with fully equipped goalies. Remember, everyone has only skates for shooting, passing, and puck control—no sticks!

PATTERN AGILITY DRILLS

Pattern Drill 1

Intermediate to Advanced

The tightness of the pattern and the speed in this drill require deep edges, body control, and agility. Skate rapidly throughout. Refer to figure 10.6.

1. Start at X; sprint forward to point 1.
2. At point 1, turn backward with your chest facing into the circle. Perform backward crossovers, left over right, to point 2.
3. From point 2 to point 3, sprint backward (backward C-cuts).
4. From point 3 to point 4, perform backward crossovers, left over right.
5. At point 4, turn forward with your chest facing into the circle.
6. From point 4 to point 1, sprint forward (forward stride).

Variations (Intermediate to Advanced)

1. Skate forward and use forward crossovers only.
2. Skate backward and use backward crossovers only.
3. Turn at point 1 with your chest facing outside instead of inside the circle.

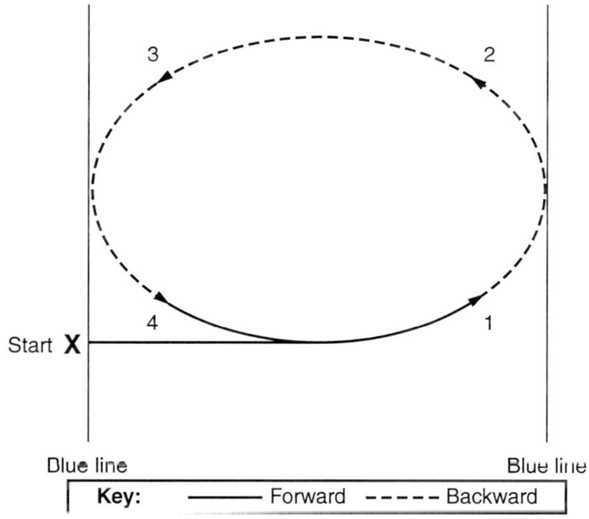

Figure 10.6 Pattern drill 1.

Pattern Drill 2

Intermediate to Advanced

Refer to figure 10.7.

1. Sprint forward from point X to point 1.
2. Turn backward at point 1 and skate backward to point 2, using backward crossovers.
3. Turn forward at point 2 and skate forward to point 3, using forward crossovers.
4. Turn backward at point 3 and skate backward to point 4.
5. At point 4, turn forward and skate to point X, using forward crossovers.

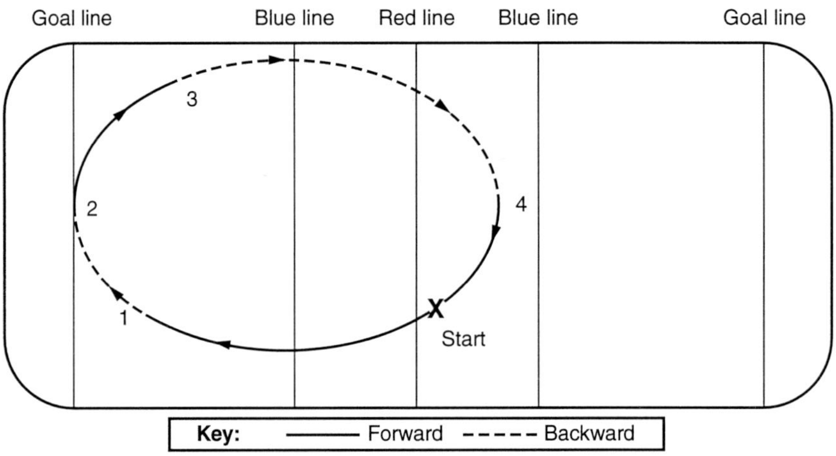

Figure 10.7 Pattern drill 2.

Pattern Drill 3

Intermediate to Advanced

Start from the goal line and follow the circular patterns shown in figure 10.8. The tightness of the pattern and the speed require deep edges, strong knee bend, precise upper body control, and balance. Skate rapidly.

Variations (Intermediate to Advanced)

1. Skate forward using the forward stride on the straightaways; skate completely around each circle using forward crossovers. Alternate direction on each circle.
2. Skate backward using the backward stride on the straightaways; skate completely around each circle using backward crossovers. Alternate direction on each circle.
3. Skate forward from the goal line. Turn from forward to backward at the near blue line, and skate backward crossovers around the first circle. Skate completely around the circle counterclockwise. Turn from backward to forward at the center red line, and skate forward crossovers around the second circle. Skate completely around the circle clockwise. Turn from forward to backward at the far blue line, and skate straight backward to the far goal line. Alternate the drill in order to practice forward and backward crossovers in both directions.
4. Skate forward and perform a pivot at the center red line (counterclockwise). Skate completely around the circle using forward crossovers. On completing the first circle, again pivot at the red line (clockwise). Finish the second circle using forward crossovers. On reaching the far blue line, sprint forward to the far goal line.

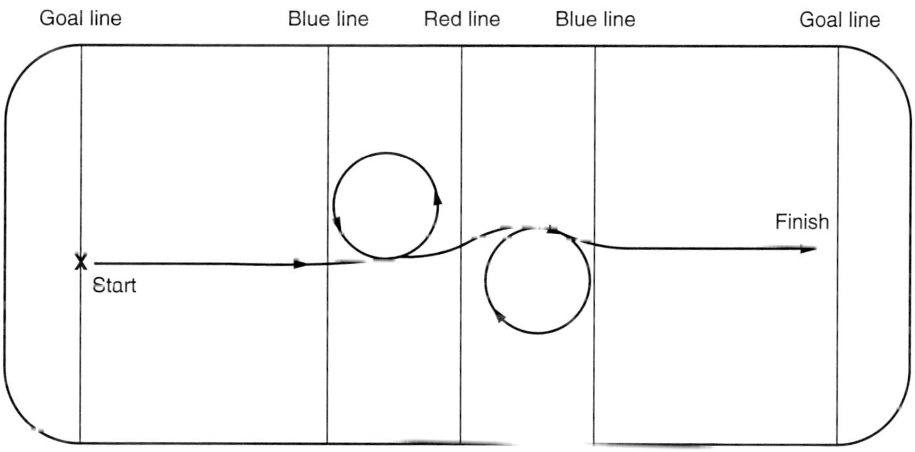

Figure 10.8 Pattern drill 3.

Pattern Drill 4

Intermediate to Advanced

Two players stand at point X; one player is on one side of the rink and the other is on the opposite side of the rink. Both players start to skate simultaneously. Neither player crosses the midline of the rink at any time. Refer to figure 10.9.

1. Skate forward from point X to point 1.
2. Turn backward at point 1, chest facing outside the curve. Sprint backward to point 2.
3. Skate backward crossovers from point 2 to point 3. Turn forward at point 3, chest facing inside the curve.
4. Skate forward crossovers from point 3 to point 4. Sprint forward from point 4 to point X.
5. Repeat, now starting backward. Turn forward at point 1, chest facing outside the curve. Sprint forward to point 2. Use forward crossovers between points 2 and 3. Turn backward at point 3, chest facing inside the curve. Skate backward crossovers between points 3 and 4. Sprint backward from point 4 to point X.

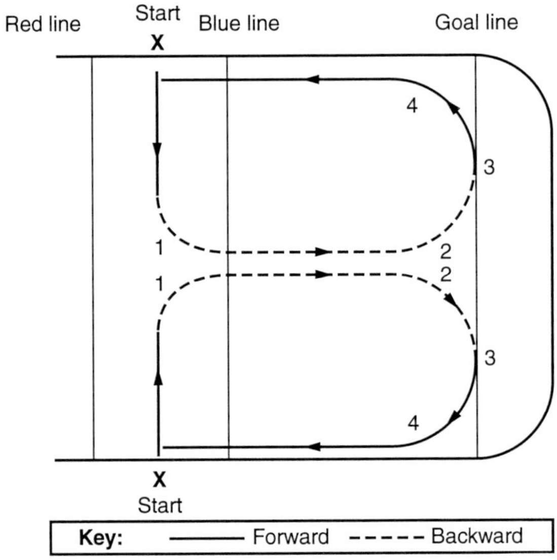

Figure 10.9 Pattern drill 4.

Obstacle Course

All Skaters

Obstacle courses are fun and challenging. They should be modified according to age and ability levels. Refer to figure 10.10.

1. Sprint forward from the X. Between points 1 and 2, skate forward crossovers in and out of pylons.
2. At point 3, jump or leap over the stick. At point 4, dive under the stick. At point 5, jump or leap over the stick again.
3. Between points 6 and 7, perform 360-degree pivots. At point 8, perform a lateral leap over the stick.
4. Between points 9 and 10, execute forward crossovers in and out of pylons. Turn backward at point 11.
5. Between points 11 and 16, perform backward crossovers in and out of pylons. Turn forward at point 16.
6. From point 16 to point X, sprint forward. Perform a hockey stop at the finish.
7. Repeat the course while carrying a puck.
8. It's fun to time players when they are skating obstacle courses. As an incentive to win, you can assess a penalty (.5 seconds) for each stick or pylon that is knocked over.

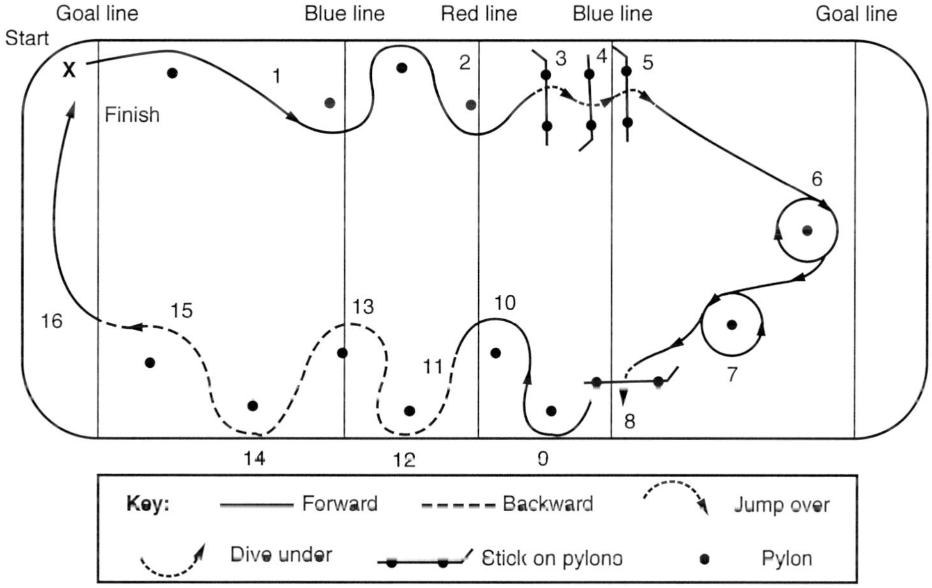

Figure 10.10 Obstacle course.

Chapter 11

Training and Conditioning for Faster, More Powerful Skating

Hockey is a sport involving intense physical and mental work. Games can go almost nonstop and can last up to four hours. Shifts last for 20 to 80 seconds and are filled with explosive bursts that are demanding and depleting. Top hockey players are precisely trained and finely conditioned athletes. Their muscles are honed for power, speed, explosive movement, and agility—and they are capable of working at peak performance even at the end of grueling shifts.

Throughout this book, we stress the importance of correct, powerful, and rapid application of force. As shown, proper skating technique is extremely important for efficient speed and explosive acceleration. But conditioning is also key.

Training and conditioning programs for hockey skating include the elements of flexibility, endurance, strength, power, quickness, and agility. Players cannot skate powerfully or quickly if their muscles are poorly developed, nor can they perform optimally in game situations if their cardiovascular systems are in less than prime condition. Though the training regimen for each element is different, all the elements are interrelated and mutually dependent. For example, agility, which relies on flexibility, also relies on endurance. As fatigue sets in, agility decreases. Strength, power, speed, quickness, and skating technique also suffer as fatigue sets in. Awareness, visual acuity, and reflexes are similarly affected.

Today, coaches and sports scientists recognize that skating technique, as well as explosive speed, improves with proper training and conditioning. In the old days, it was generally accepted that someone could skate or couldn't skate or was born to be fast or slow. Coaches and trainers now better understand the value of training and conditioning in helping athletes reach their potential for speed.

There is no substitute for on-ice workouts. But a well-designed, year-round training and conditioning program—including both on-ice and off-ice work—can help players skate faster than their current speed. These workouts should be designed to meet the needs of each individual, and they should offer enough variety to maintain a high level of interest.

This chapter provides an overview of the fundamentals of training and conditioning specific to hockey skating. For more in-depth knowledge, read and study some of the many sources on training and conditioning programs for hockey. Also learn about subjects such as visualization, mental training, positive self-image, nutrition, hydration, fluid replacement, and proper rest. A few valuable publications are listed in the suggested reading section at the end of this book.

Although skating relies primarily on muscles of the hips, buttocks, and quadriceps, several other muscle groups of the lower and upper body are also used. For example, explosive starts require strong muscles of the feet, arches, ankles, calves, and hamstrings, as well as the quadriceps and buttocks. Full extension requires strong leg muscles, but also strong feet, ankles, and arches for the final push (toe flick). The outward–inward motions in skating call on the adductors and abductors. To keep the back straight and under control, players use muscles of the back and chest. To torque, players must recruit muscles of the waist, chest, and back. Pushing powerfully also requires strong abdominal muscles. The arm and neck muscles must also be strong and flexible. In other words, hockey skating is very much a full-body workout.

WARM-UP AND COOL-DOWN

Hockey is a sport of explosive motions and sudden changes of direction. Muscles *cannot* be called on to perform these movements until they are readied for work. The body must be gradually brought from a state of rest to a state of readiness for work in order to function optimally. This also reduces the likelihood of muscle and soft-tissue injuries associated with sudden movement.

It is easier to stretch muscles that are warm, so light warm-up activities—such as slow skating, walking, or jogging—should be done for 5 to 10 minutes before stretching. After exercise, players should always perform a cool-down. A light skate or slow walk for 5 to 10 minutes followed by 10 to 15 minutes of stretching gradually brings the body from a state of work to a state of rest. Postworkout stretching is very important in order to prevent tightening of muscles and potential injuries.

TRAINING FOR FLEXIBILITY

Improved flexibility brings several specific benefits to a hockey player's performance:

1. Flexibility allows for speedier movement of the engaged muscle groups. As muscles and joints become more flexible, they give less resistance to movement. This allows them to apply force more rapidly and in a greater range of motion. As the speed of applied force increases, power also increases.
2. As flexibility increases, so does agility. Flexible muscles and joints can work more efficiently through their full range of motion.
3. Flexibility delays the onset of fatigue. Increased flexibility reduces resistance as the muscles and joints move through their full range of motion. The amount of energy required is also reduced, so the activity can be prolonged.
4. As flexibility increases, the likelihood of muscle injury decreases. Players who are flexible are generally less prone to injuries.

Flexibility is developed through proper and consistent stretching. Athletes can increase their flexibility by adhering to an *ongoing* stretching program. Flexibility should be valued as highly as technique and strength training.

Stretching serves three functions: (1) to prepare the body for work, (2) to develop body flexibility, and (3) to cool down muscles after heavy exercise. Since ice time is often limited during the playing season, off-ice stretching is recommended unless the stretching exercises are also being used to work on balance. During the off-season, all players should engage in daily stretching sessions.

Because skating uses muscles of both the lower and upper body, you need to do stretching exercises for both areas. Start each stretch slowly and gently, and gradually try to increase the range of motion of each muscle group. Stretch for a minimum of 10 minutes before each workout and 10 to 15 minutes after each workout. Dancers begin each workout by stretching at a bar for about 30 minutes before jumping and spinning on the floor. Keep this in mind when planning your stretching program.

As previously mentioned, warm muscles are easier to stretch than cold muscles. Therefore, some light warm-up activities should precede each stretching routine. Stretch diligently again after each workout. This will help prevent the injuries caused by sudden tightening of muscles when exercise ends too abruptly.

Perform each stretch in a slow, sustained manner to the point that there is light tension (but not pain) in the stretched muscles. Hold the position for about 20 to 30 seconds. Relax and ease off for about 10 seconds. Then increase the stretch to a point of greater tension. Hold this position for another 20 to 30 seconds. Do not bounce, because this may cause injuries.

Nonmoving stretches should be done away from the ice whenever possible. This helps preserve precious ice time for skating-related exercises.

For young people or people who are very flexible, stretching exercises should be quite safe. People who are getting back into shape after an injury or a period of inactivity should be careful not to lock (hyperextend) joints or to put undue stress on the back, hips, neck, or knees.

Here are the key areas to consider when stretching:

- Abdominals
- Abductors
- Achilles tendons
- Adductors
- Ankles
- Arms
- Back
- Calves
- Feet
- Gluteals
- Hamstrings
- Hips
- Neck
- Quadriceps
- Shoulders
- Waist
- Wrists

Change stretches periodically to make the stretching routine interesting and fun. For more information on stretching, refer to *Complete Conditioning for Ice Hockey, Second Edition* by Peter Twist (Human Kinetics 2007) or *Sports Stretch, Second Edition* by Michael J. Alter (Human Kinetics 1998).

TRAINING FOR ENDURANCE

Because of its intensity and duration, hockey requires that players have *exceptional* endurance. Hockey combines explosive speed with punishing body checks, forceful maneuvering, and tough fighting for the puck. Sometimes bursts of speed are short and intense with moments of slower skating or coasting in between. At other times, players skate without relief for entire shifts. Players must be conditioned so that they can recover from these intense work periods during each brief rest period on the bench. Whatever the game situation, players must have sufficient energy reserves to give their all, even toward the end of a long and exhausting game.

The body has two types of energy sources, each yielding a different form of endurance. We will refer to these forms of endurance as wind (aerobic) and explosive (anaerobic) endurance.

Aerobic Endurance

The aerobic (oxygen) system is the body's most efficient—and therefore the most important—source of energy. Aerobic endurance relies on the aerobic system to produce energy and the muscle cells to use that energy. Aerobic fitness is the base for *all* training and conditioning. Strength, power, and speed are impossible unless the athlete has established a strong foundation of aerobic endurance.

When we breathe, we take in oxygen, which the heart, lungs, and blood vessels transport to all parts of the body. Oxygen combines with the nutrients in the cells to produce energy for work. To improve the aerobic system, the heart must be conditioned to pump more blood per beat. As the heart and circulatory system become more efficient, athletes can work harder and longer with less stress before becoming fatigued, and they can recover more quickly to perform at top efficiency.

Aerobic training involves stressing the oxygen system by forcing the heart to beat at a higher rate than normal. This improves its ability to deliver oxygen to the muscles for energy. The improved delivery of oxygen also helps the body recover more quickly from intense work.

The two types of aerobic workouts are *continuous* and *interval*. Continuous aerobic workouts are done at submaximal speeds and are designed to bring the heartbeat to 75 to 80 percent of its maximum rate for 30 to 60 minutes. These workouts are usually done three or four times a week. During work periods, the heart rate is brought to 160 to 180 beats per minute. (The exact number of beats per minute depends on age—the older the athlete, the lower the number of beats per minute.)

In interval training, specific periods of work are alternated with specific periods of rest. Work–rest ratios vary according to the purpose of the specific workout (endurance, strength, power, or quickness) as well as the time of year. Workouts become more intense as the hockey season progresses. Interval workouts can be conducted on dry land as well as on the ice.

Interval aerobic workouts use sets of higher-intensity work (2 to 3 minutes in duration) to bring the heart rate to within 5 beats of its maximum rate. This is followed by 2 to 3 minutes of rest (1:1 work–rest ratio). Interval training builds the aerobic supply and increases the muscles' ability to extract oxygen from the blood.

With aerobic training, the heart, lungs, and blood vessels adapt to the greater demands, and their capacity to transport oxygen is increased. The muscles also adapt, and their ability to use energy improves.

Since aerobic endurance workouts are performed at submaximal speeds, they should usually be done off the ice so that the submaximal speeds do not negatively affect quickness on the ice. Many activities can be used to improve aerobic endurance. Some examples include running (distance and interval), bicycling, dancing, hiking (on hills), rock climbing, swimming, handball, racket sports, basketball, soccer, gymnastics, and in-line skating.

Endurance workouts bring about fatigue. Because fatigue negatively affects skating technique, skating drills in which the top priority is endurance are not recommended for young and developing skaters. Fatigue encourages bad skating habits!

The following on-ice drills are effective for improving aerobic endurance. They can also be practiced on in-line skates. Keep in mind that the submaximal leg speeds used in endurance workouts are not the leg speeds needed for hockey. Players should alternate endurance activities with quickness activities (see "Training for Quickness" later in this chapter).

On-Ice Endurance Exercises

1. Skate continuous laps at half speed for 10 minutes. Skate easily and coast (rest period) for 5 minutes. Repeat. Do this for 20 to 30 minutes.

2. Skate continuous laps, skating at half speed for 20 minutes and skating easily for 10 minutes.
3. Skate laps around the rink, alternately skating slowly, moderately (three-quarters speed), and short sprints (between blue lines). Do this for 15 to 20 minutes.
4. Skate 15 laps around the rink using only four strides for the length of the ice. Skate at three-quarters speed around the corners. Skate easily and coast for 5 minutes. Do this for 20 to 30 minutes.
5. Combine these exercises or create others similar in format. Perform them skating backward as well. Alternate the direction in which you skate around the rink in order to practice crossovers in both directions.

In-Line Skating

In-line skates have wheels that simulate the ice skate blade, but because the wheels do not grip the ground as firmly as edges grip the ice, some ice skating maneuvers are difficult to do. For example, in-line wheels cannot be leaned as extremely as ice skates, so turns have a wider arc. Additionally, it is difficult to make wheels slide sideways along the ground the way skate blades slide sideways on the ice, so stopping is more difficult. However, the principles of edges still apply, and the use of leg drive and body weight is very similar (figure 11.1).

In-line skating can be effectively used for endurance training while incorporating skating-specific muscles in skating-specific motions. However, the weight of in-line skates may encourage leg speeds that are too slow for ice hockey; therefore, they are not recommended for quickness training. Wear full protective equipment whenever skating on in-line skates. Falls on hard pavement hurt and can cause serious injuries!

Figure 11.1 In-line skating can be great off-ice exercise for endurance training.

Anaerobic Endurance

For sudden, intense bursts of power, the oxygen system alone is insufficient to fulfill the energy demands of the body. In these situations, additional energy is supplied by the muscle cells themselves. Nutrients within the cells (stored glycogen) are converted into energy (in the form of sugar) for work in the absence of oxygen. In this *anaerobic* process of energy production, waste products in the form of lactic acid are given off and accumulate in the muscle cells.

The accumulation of lactic acid in the cells causes rapid fatigue and a decrease in coordination, speed, balance, and overall skill. Although the anaerobic energy system is critical to explosive movement, it is not nearly as efficient as the aerobic system in producing large quantities of energy.

Anaerobic training improves the efficiency of the cellular energy system—increasing the system's ability to convert stored glycogen into sugar for energy and to remove waste products from the muscle cells. The more efficient the cellular energy system, the more quickly it can transport waste products back into the bloodstream, thereby reducing the concentration of lactic acid within the cells.

Anaerobic training and conditioning allows players to perform with greater accumulations of waste products in the muscle cells before succumbing to fatigue. Players are better prepared to skate explosively for an entire shift and recover completely during brief rest periods on the bench.

Anaerobic training consists of short bursts of intense activity and slightly longer intense activity. In both cases, the activity must be performed at 100 percent effort. The activity is then followed by a rest period of two to three times the duration of the activity; the rest period allows the body to fully transfer waste products (lactic acid) from the cells into the bloodstream. *Full recovery is essential for optimum performance.*

While training the anaerobic system, you should incorporate exercises that use skating-specific motions and skating-specific muscle groups. Dry-land activities such as in-line skating and slideboard training develop anaerobic endurance while using the skating motion and using muscle groups in skating-specific ways.

The slideboard (figure 11.2, *a-f,* on page 248) was made famous as a training device by Olympic speedskating champion Eric Heiden. It is an excellent device for power training. Use short work intervals such as 20 seconds of work followed by 60 seconds of rest (these are called work–rest intervals). The slideboard also works well for endurance training (use longer intervals such as 40 seconds: 80 seconds). The slideboard is also excellent for practicing the motions of the forward skating stride (technique development). In addition, slideboards are easy to build.

Anaerobic intervals for hockey training involve maximal work for 30 to 45 seconds followed by 1 to 3 minutes of rest (or recovery). A complete rest interval is paramount! The rest period must be long enough to allow complete recovery so that the following work interval can be performed at full intensity. If the quality of rest is sacrificed, the benefits of anaerobic training will be lost.

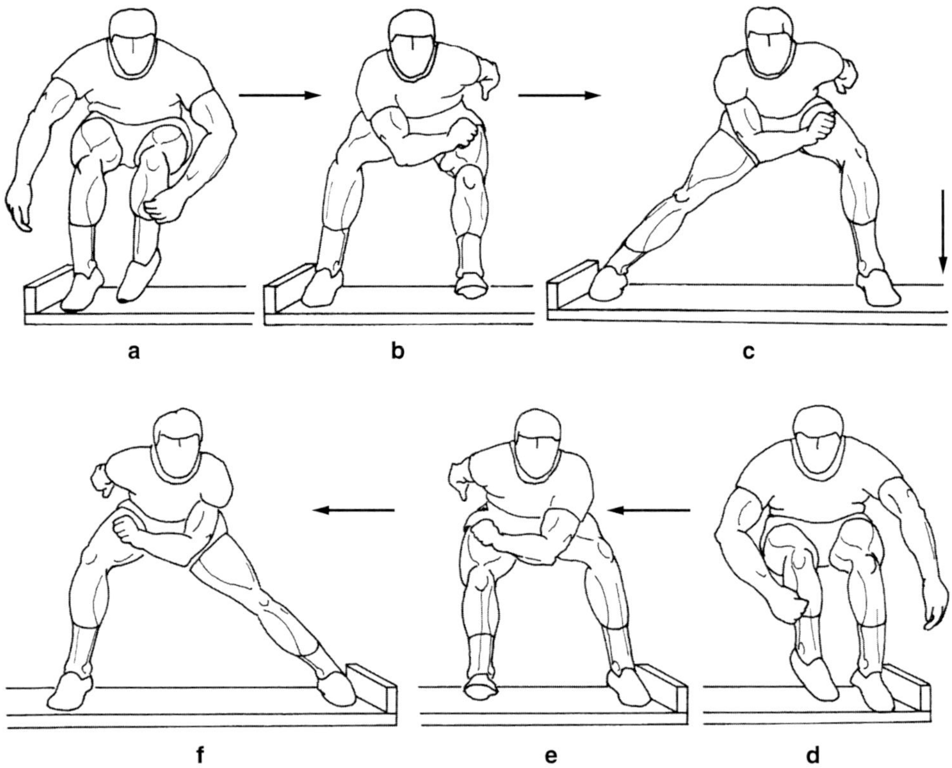

Figure 11.2 Heiden slideboard: Note the similarity to the forward skating stride.

Off-Ice Exercises

Sprint for 50 meters and then walk or jog slowly to rest. Rest two to three times as long as it took to sprint. Do the same for 100, 200, 300, and 400 meters as well as distances in between.

Interval training on a bicycle and hiking (especially on hills) are also effective anaerobic workouts. Use the previously described work–rest intervals for these workouts.

On-Ice Exercises

Train with short, explosive sprints of 5 to 15 seconds followed by slow skating (in order to rest). Also do longer sprints of up to 45 seconds followed by a rest period long enough to allow for full recovery. Use a work–rest ratio of 1:2 (sometimes a ratio of 1:3 is called for). You can also alternate skating intervals as follows:

1. Skate with 100 percent effort for 15 seconds, then skate easily for 45 seconds.
2. Skate with 100 percent effort for 30 seconds, then skate easily for 90 seconds.
3. Skate with 100 percent effort for 45 seconds, then skate easily for 90 seconds.

4. Skate with 75 percent effort for 45 seconds, then skate easily for 90 seconds.
5. Skate with 100 percent effort for 15 seconds, then skate easily for 45 seconds.

Guidelines for On-Ice Endurance Training Intervals

When training for *aerobic* endurance, high-level players generally use intervals with a work–rest ratio of 1:1—skating at three-quarters speed for 60 seconds, then skating slowly (resting) for 60 seconds.

When training for *anaerobic* endurance, players skate with maximum effort, using a work–rest ratio of 1:2—skating all out for 40 seconds, then resting for 80 seconds. When players are performing explosive stops and starts, a work–rest ratio of 1:3 is appropriate—skating at maximum effort for 30 seconds, then resting for 90 seconds.

The top priority on the ice for young (under age 14) and learning skaters is technique, not endurance. On-ice drills specifically designed for anaerobic endurance are counterproductive. As fatigue sets in, these players will necessarily resort to poor skating techniques, and the bad habits developed under these circumstances may be difficult to change. These players should use light aerobic interval training on the ice and should avoid fatigue.

For young players, endurance can be developed by many off-ice activities, some of which have been previously mentioned. On-ice endurance for young players may be developed by the following:

- The sum of all on-ice practice drills (60- to 90-minute sessions).
- On-ice sprints at practice tempo. Keep work periods short enough that fatigue does not destroy skating technique or skill development.

Some endurance workouts should be aerobic in order to build the all-important aerobic base; others should be anaerobic. When planning an endurance program, keep in mind that off-ice activities do not interfere with skating skill. Therefore, these activities offer the most productive opportunity for endurance training.

TRAINING FOR STRENGTH

Developing strength for its own sake is not an appropriate goal for skaters. Their need for strength lies in the ability to apply that strength explosively. When strength is applied properly and explosively, this results in power. Power combined with rapid leg motion results in speed. Strength is, of course, a critical component of power and speed, as well as explosive acceleration and BAM (balance, agility, and maneuverability), so it must be developed.

As discussed in this book's introduction, for prepubescent children, any strength training that is done should involve submaximal resistance, such as one's own body weight, light dumbbells, or medicine balls. Sophisticated and restrictive weight exercises, particularly on machines, are harmful for children with limited strength. Whole-body activities are the most important and beneficial, especially for improving core strength.

For skating, developing players should work on two-leg and one-leg strength training. When players strengthen their legs at a young age, this increases their chances of learning to skate correctly. Skating and leg strength (especially single-leg strength) are synergistic, so they should be developed at the same age. But the training should be fun.

I have taught numerous adolescent players who had recently gone through growth spurts. These players are at the celebrated awkward stage—their muscle strength has not caught up with their bone length. These players look strong, but they can't skate strongly. They can't seem to bend their knees enough, push hard or quickly enough, or skate with agility or explosiveness. These players are too young to engage in heavy strength training programs, but they are old enough to know that this will soon be a necessity.

What many adolescent players don't know is that they need to develop more than just their upper bodies—their primary goal shouldn't be to look good in a bathing suit, but to strengthen the skating muscles (legs and glutes). Strong, flexible muscles are essential not only for power and speed, but also for minimizing injury to soft tissues and joints.

All great skaters have strong quadriceps and gluteal muscles. But they also work on strengthening all the muscle groups used in hockey—these include the muscles of the lower and upper body that are used for explosive skating, as well as those of the upper body that are used for shooting, checking, and withstanding body blows. Whole-body strength workouts are thus a necessity.

The muscles of the lower body to be strengthened for skating are those of the hips, gluteals, adductors (groin), abductors (outer thighs), quadriceps, hamstrings, calves, feet, and ankles. The muscles of the upper body to be strengthened are those of the abdominals, back, chest, shoulders, arms, and neck. Keep in mind that the muscles of the upper body are used for skating as well as for shooting, checking, and so on. For example, the back is used to control excessive upper body movement (balance and stability). The chest and arms are used to create correct and powerful arm swing. The abdominals assist in pushing. Players need to strengthen the muscles on both sides of a joint equally to maintain stability.

Strength training is the process of building muscle mass and recruiting more of the existing muscle fibers for work. Muscle mass can be gained from a variety of workouts that involve working against heavy resistance. Muscle-fiber recruitment is developed by lifting at specific and varying speeds (for example, weightlifting).

In strength training, the muscles to be strengthened must be progressively overloaded. Adhering to the *overload principle* is critical; after being repeatedly forced to work beyond their present capability, muscles eventually adapt to the new work level and perform more effectively. At this point, they must be overloaded again to develop an even greater capability for work. As long as the overload principle is followed, a variety of training methods can be used to achieve the same results. All require the muscles to work against resistance. Calisthenics, isometric training, partner resistance, and weight training are acceptable methods for increasing strength.

Note: Players under the age of 16 should not engage in programs that involve working against *heavy* resistance or weights.

Overloading is achieved in a number of ways—increasing the load to be moved (resistance or weight), increasing the length of each training session, increasing the number of training sessions, or increasing the number of repetitions or sets per exercise. Strength training takes place mostly off the ice.

Calisthenics

In calisthenic exercises, the person's own body weight is used as the resistance to be moved. Exercises include push-ups, sit-ups, leg lifts, trunk raises, side and hip raises, wall squats, chinning, and many others. Young players can do light calisthenics.

Calisthenic workouts are valuable, necessary, and even enjoyable. Most important, they produce positive results. These workouts should be an integral part of every training regimen and should *not* be used to punish. They should be done off the ice to preserve valuable ice time.

Isometric Training

Isometric training involves balanced and opposing equal forces of two or more complementary muscle groups. Use arms to oppose legs, use arms and legs to oppose the central torso, use a given muscle group to oppose a fixed surface, use a partner to resist movement of legs or arms, or just power-flex one group of muscles (such as the abdominals) until sufficient overload is achieved. Isometrics are especially useful when expensive weight training equipment is not readily available. Also, these exercises can be done by young players.

Here is a sample isometric exercise: Lie on the floor with your legs stretched in front of you so that one leg is on either side of a straight-legged chair. Press your legs inward against the chair. This simple exercise strengthens the adductor (groin) muscles. You can also pair up with a partner to perform isometric exercises.

Weight Training

Various devices can be used to fulfill the overload principle by creating resistance when you are walking, running, or skating. Some of these devices include weight belts, weight vests (or weighted backpacks), parachutes (speed chutes), leashes, and bungee cords. In addition, numerous weight training exercises are performed using dumbbells, barbells, machines, or other weight equipment. These are usually performed in a weight room, gym, or open area off the ice.

First off, you must learn to lift correctly to avoid injury. Weight training programs should be designed for each individual and should be supervised by knowledgeable instructors.

Muscles are overloaded by the use of progressively heavier weights. Begin training programs with light weights. Gradually increase the weight to be moved. Vary the weight training routine from session to session in order to work different muscle groups. Weight training for strength development ultimately requires heavy loads.

Remember, strength training exercises tighten muscles. Be sure to warm up, stretch, and cool down gradually before and after each strength training session.

Partner Resistance on the Ice

In this type of training, the overload principle is applied by having one player move (skate) while pulling against or pushing a partner who is resisting the movement. Many skating maneuvers can be practiced using partner resistance (some even by young players), as long as the partner is of similar size, weight, and ability. Partner resistance drills are included in most of the chapters in this book.

TRAINING FOR POWER

Power results when strength is applied explosively. Power accompanied by rapid leg motion results in speed. One way to conceptualize the expression of power is to compare muscles to the pistons in an automobile engine. The power stroke of an engine occurs when the compressed mixture of fuel and air is exploded by a spark; the force of the explosion drives the piston and thus powers the automobile. Leg strength is a necessary component of speed; however, leg strength only enhances speed if the legs apply power correctly and explosively. Efficient and effective speed results when power and quickness are used in the correct skating motion. Watch Scott Niedermayer skate and you will see a superb demonstration of power converted into efficient speed.

Power training, like strength training, requires that *specific* muscle groups be progressively overloaded, but at the same time the athlete must increase the speed of motion (explosiveness) while working against resistance. Power training for skating requires that the muscles specific to skating work explosively in the same range of motion as in skating and at the same speed as (or even faster than) required by the sport of hockey.

Power training workouts should be structured so that the athlete progressively increases the number of repetitions of each set of exercises while decreasing the time needed to work through each set. The athlete must continue working at a fast speed even when fatigued—the goal is to get beyond that threshold of fatigue and reach a new tolerance.

Note: After a certain point, increasing the number of sets or repetitions improves endurance but not power.

A good general rule for using weights for power training is to lift (or push or pull) 50 to 60 percent of *your* maximum weight capability for five sets of each exercise, with five repetitions in each set. Training with maximum loads increases strength, but because the speed is necessarily slow, power cannot be maximized. Training with loads too light produces very fast movement, but the force is too low to develop power.

Each lift should be done with as much speed as possible. Attempt to accelerate all the way through to the *end* of the range of motion on every lift. Acceleration and intensity are key factors. Doing squat jumps while wearing a weighted vest or belt exemplifies the effort to accelerate through the full range of motion. Work–rest ratios for power workouts *must* include a long enough rest period (full recovery time) between sets or exercises so that each set can be performed explosively and with speed. If speed is slow, power is low.

Power training causes fatigue. Complete recovery is essential so that the system can rest, rebuild, and adapt to a new level of work capability and fatigue tolerance. Muscle rebuilding after intense power workouts takes up to 48 hours, so power training workouts should be scheduled at least two days apart. Other types of workouts can be done in between.

Power Training Workouts

As with endurance training, most (but not all) power training should take place off the ice so that it does not affect the quality of skating. Power training that involves relatively heavy resistance is not recommended for skaters under the age of 16.

Off-Ice Workouts

Various methods can be used for power training on dry land, including running (uphill), interval running, slideboards, bicycling (uphill), interval workouts on a stationary bike, calisthenics, plyometric exercises (movements that involve a recoil–spring principle), and partner resistance—all while wearing some weighted device at submaximal resistance levels. In-line skating can also be used for power training. When using in-line skates for power training, skate uphill wearing a submaximal resistance device. Coast down if the hill is slight, and walk down if the hill is steep. Power training on in-line skates is especially useful because the movements are specific to ice skating and in the same range of motion as ice skating; therefore, the skater can also practice ice skating technique (until fatigue sets in).

On-Ice Workouts

Doing some on-ice power training is essential. Skating explosively against resistance is an essential aspect of power training on the ice. Wearing a weight vest or weight belt, skating against partner resistance, using speed chutes and resistance bands, or doing plyometric skating drills are all excellent means of accomplishing this.

Note: Muscles should not be overloaded too much—fatigued skaters inevitably revert to poor skating techniques. Poor skating habits may result and may be difficult to correct.

Interval training is effective in developing powerful leg drive. This type of training is also important for developing leg speed. Use a work–rest ratio of 1:5. For example, skate for 10 seconds, rest for 50 seconds; skate for 20 seconds, rest for 100 seconds. Players 16 years or older can wear weighted vests or belts (with 50 to 60 percent of the maximum weight they can move in strength training exercises).

Plyometric Exercises

One of the most effective means of training for explosive power is *plyometrics* (recoil bounding). Plyometrics links strength and sprint speed. Plyometric exercises involve a quick recoil action that precedes an explosive spring. They involve a coil–uncoil action and a stretch–contract action of the muscles. Examples include bounding, hopping, broad jumping, squat jumps, leaping (forward and backward or laterally) over an obstacle, or jumping up stairs (on two feet or one foot). All of these activities require great spring and agility.

Plyometric training is tough on the joints. This type of training is not recommended for people with medical conditions that limit joint function. Remember that you must establish flexibility and strength around the joints before participating in strenuous plyometric workouts.

Plyometric training works as follows:

1. Recoiling acts as a windup. During the recoil, the muscles are stretched. Stretched muscles and tissues store energy like a rubber band. The stored energy becomes available for use during muscle contraction.
2. When muscles are stretched quickly, they contract actively in a reflex interaction with nerves. This quick stretch–contract interactive pattern makes it possible to recruit muscle fibers in a more powerful manner.

All plyometric exercises involve a deep knee bend, a spring into the air, and another deep knee bend on landing.

Off-Ice Exercises

Hundreds of excellent plyometric exercises are available for working the skating muscles. Most are done off the ice, but there are also many that can be done on the ice. Following are a few off-ice plyometric exercises.

Step Up, Step Down

Step up onto a low bench (about 15 to 18 inches [38.1 to 45.7 cm] high) with your right foot and then with your left foot so that both feet are on the bench. Then step back down with your right foot, then your left foot, so that both feet are on the floor. Keep repeating this sequence rapidly. After several repetitions, switch feet; step up with your left foot first and then with your right foot.

Standing Broad Jumps

Standing broad jumps are one of the most effective plyometric maneuvers when training for skating; they are also an excellent means of practicing front starts on dry land.

Perform continuous standing broad jumps on flat ground and on slight inclines. Do 5 to 30 repetitions. Concentrate on the coil–spring principle and on achieving as much forward distance as possible (figure 11.3, *a-c*).

a b c

Figure 11.3 Standing broad jumps.

Jumps and Hops

Jumps and hops can be done on dry land or on the ice. See chapter 2 for instructions on how to perform these exercises on the ice.

On-Ice Exercises

Following are a few on-ice plyometric exercises.

Inside Edge Jumps

Picture an imaginary axis, or line, along the length of the ice and approximately 20 feet (6.1 m) from the sideboards on your right.

Skate forward from one goal line. After building some speed, glide on the RFI. Aim the glide directly away from the imaginary axis. Maintain a strong inside edge and knee bend during the semicircular glide. The direction of the curve is counterclockwise.

When you have curved a full semicircle (180 degrees), jump off from the right skate. Jump as high off the ice as possible. Land on and then glide on a deep LFI, with the left knee strongly bent. Aim the glide directly away from the axis. Maintain a strong inside edge and knee bend as you glide on the LFI. The direction of the semicircle is now clockwise.

When you have curved a full semicircle (180 degrees), jump off from the left skate. Jump as high off the ice as possible. Land and glide on a deep RFI, with the right knee strongly bent. The direction of the semicircle is now counterclockwise.

You have completed one cycle. Repeat this cycle until you have completed one length of the ice (figure 11.4).

Remember: To balance, you must keep your back straight and your eyes and head up. Keep the free skate off the ice and close to the gliding skate during each jump.

Variations

1. Perform the previous exercise, but skate on, jump from, and land on *outside* edges.
2. Perform the previous jumps skating backward.

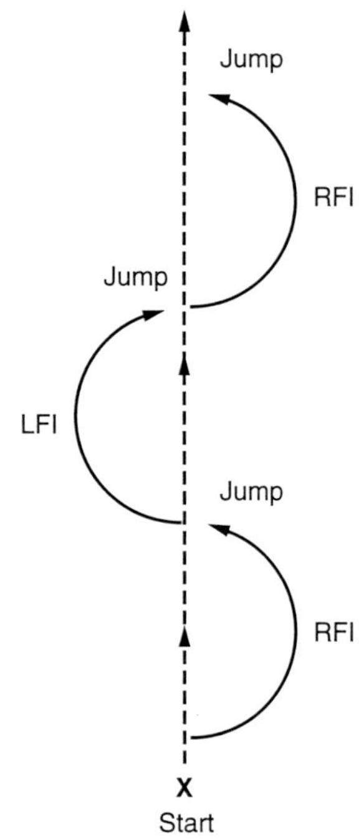

Figure 11.4 Inside edge jumps.

S-Jumps

Refer to the S-cuts drill in chapter 6 (page 117). Like the S-cuts drill, this drill is performed on one skate at a time. You will now jump off the ice in order to change edges on the landing. For example, you will change from the outside edge (RFO) to the inside edge (RFI) or from the inside edge (RFI) to the outside edge (RFO).

Jump as high off the ice as possible. Land on a deep edge with a strong knee bend on the landing leg. Keep the free skate off the ice and close to the gliding skate during each jump. See how many S-cuts you can make before putting the free skate on the ice. Keep your back straight and your eyes and head up. Repeat the exercise on the left skate. Then perform the exercise skating backward on each skate.

TRAINING FOR QUICKNESS

Quickness means fast feet, or rapid leg motion. It also refers to a player's ability to accelerate explosively between point A and point B, either from a dead stop or from slow to fast. Quickness is one of the most important qualities a hockey player can possess. It often determines who gets to the puck first or who gets a breakaway opportunity.

Quickness is enhanced by a combination of factors, including proper skating technique, explosive power, and rapid leg motion. Quickness training involves increasing leg speed while still moving the legs through their full range of motion.

Until recently it was assumed that quickness is an innate quality. Now we know that quickness can be improved with proper training.

The younger a player begins training for quickness, the greater the potential for development. As players get older, they must continue to train for quickness—otherwise, this quality will diminish, just as flexibility, strength, power, and endurance will diminish if they are not continuously trained.

Quickness training requires skating at top speed—without resistance—in all-out, explosive workouts. The bursts are intense and of short duration. Since quickness training forces players into an anaerobic state, long rest periods that allow for full recovery from fatigue are essential so the athlete will be able to perform each repetition optimally.

The principles for achieving explosive acceleration and sprint speed in skating are virtually identical to those in running. The technical differences between the two lie in the differences in the surfaces pushed against; these require that the pushes be executed differently. Figure 11.5 shows the similarities between explosive skating starts and explosive running starts.

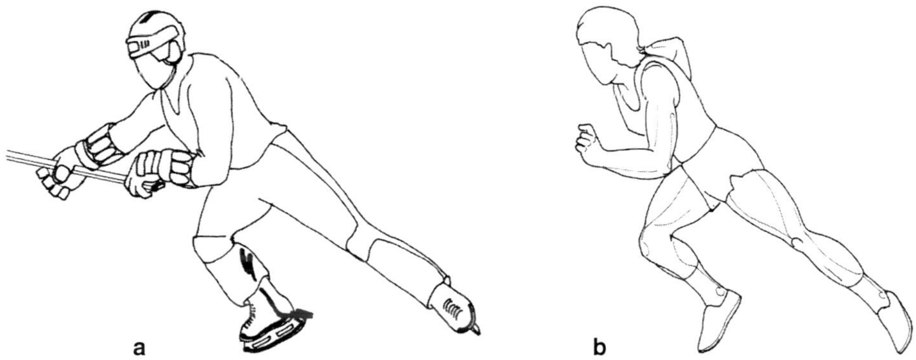

Figure 11.5 Explosive starts: *(a)* skating and *(b)* running.

Quickness Training Workouts

The purpose of quickness training workouts is to develop fast feet and sprint speed. Workouts must be done at top speed at all times, which requires that players be fresh and completely warmed up. Quickness training workouts are nontechnical in nature. They require total concentration and maximum effort. Since the intensity and speed used in quickness training can destroy skating technique, these workouts should be done on dry land until proper technique is established. Because workouts involve no resistance, they can be performed daily with alternating workout intensities. Perform light workouts one day and heavy workouts the next. Movement must be fast paced; slow movement trains slowness. Quickness training does not focus on conditioning, although improved conditioning is a by-product.

Work intervals should be short, and rest intervals should be long. A work–rest ratio of 1:5 or 1:10 allows for total recovery. This long rest period is necessary for each repetition to be performed with full intensity and optimum effort. For example, sprint at maximum speed and effort for 10 seconds, rest for 50 seconds; sprint for 5 seconds, rest for 40 seconds; sprint for 8 seconds, rest for 40 to 80 seconds. The same applies for skating sprints.

Note: Quickness workouts should never be done after strength or power workouts, or when fatigued.

Off-Ice Workouts

Hockey players can perform quickness training off the ice by running or biking using sprint intervals. This is a highly recommended form of training because skating technique is not affected while a player is in the process of sprinting at full speed. Slight downhill sprints are another means of quickness training on dry land. Because of their weight, in-line skates are not recommended for quickness training.

Workouts for developing overall speed include running a 30-meter dash, a 60-meter dash, or a 100-meter dash. Leave enough time between sprints for complete recovery (work–rest ratio of 1:5).

Explosive starts can be practiced on a track, on sand, or on grass. Explosive acceleration on the first five steps is of primary importance. To work on starts, run 20-meter sprints. Run from a standstill. Start from both forward and sideways positions. Standing broad jumps (figure 11.3 on page 255) can help you develop the falling feeling experienced in explosive starts. Performing racing-style dives in a pool simulates the same feeling.

Here are some other variations of quickness training on dry land:

- Sprint 20 meters, cut sharply to the side, sprint again, then cut sharply to the other side.
- Incorporate crossovers, lateral leaps, sprints up and down slight inclines, and running backward. Do different combinations of these moves at top speeds (even out-of-control speeds).
- Swing a bat and run to first base. This simulates the lateral weight shift and outward-falling feeling necessary for explosive crossover (side) starts.

Another aspect of quickness is BAM: balance, agility, and maneuverability. Exercises that require coordination and flexibility are good for improving BAM. These exercises may include tumbling, rolling, jumping, hopping, juggling, doing gymnastics moves, dribbling balls with the feet, running obstacle courses, or performing moves with no previous knowledge of the moves (all while moving fast).

Remember: Quality, intensity, and top speed are essential for quickness workouts. When you're tired and quality is suffering or when you're not accomplishing anything, switch to another kind of workout. If muscles are sore, delay quickness work until the soreness is gone.

On-Ice Workouts

On the ice, the player's goal is to develop the fastest possible leg rhythm while still moving the legs correctly, powerfully, and through their full range of motion. Since skill and quickness on the ice are developed while skating, most on-ice skating drills should be geared toward skill and speed development rather than endurance development. Once correct skating techniques are established, on-ice sprint intervals may be the most important aspect of a player's training program. With or without the puck, the point is to perform everything at *top speed.* In game situations and even in practices, players rarely skate as fast as they would if they were being timed. Players slow down to carry the puck, receive passes, or wait for the play. In practices, players inadvertently slow down, fearing a fall or the loss of the puck in front of their coach or teammates.

When training for quickness, players must avoid fatigue because fatigue inhibits the ability to move the legs at top speed. Quickness intervals therefore involve short sprints followed by long rest periods that allow for full recovery. The recommended intervals when training for quickness are 1:5 or 1:10 (work–rest ratios).

The neuromuscular system can be likened to a computer: It records everything you do (whether fast or slow, correct or incorrect) so that this information can be used for future performance. If you practice skating technique only at slow speeds, the neuromuscular system will pass that information on, and you will learn to skate correctly but slowly. You *must* learn to skate correctly, then learn to skate correctly *fast* (Blatherwick 1986). Training to become a great hockey skater is a long and methodical process. You must first learn to execute correctly (technique training); then correctly and powerfully; then correctly, powerfully, and quickly; then correctly, powerfully, and quickly with the puck; and finally, correctly, powerfully, explosively, and quickly with the puck in game situations and under lots of pressure.

Following are some guidelines for quickness training off and on the ice:

1. Sprint or skate at maximum speed and effort for 10 seconds; rest for 50 seconds.
2. Sprint or skate at maximum speed and effort for 5 seconds; rest for 40 seconds.
3. Sprint or skate at maximum speed and effort for 8 seconds; rest for 40 to 80 seconds.

One excellent way to improve quickness on the ice is by skating to music of varying (ever more rapid) tempos.

Overspeed Training

Another aspect of quickness training is overspeed training. This type of training requires players to perform skating maneuvers at ever-increasing speeds. At a certain point, the player must practice the maneuvers at leg speeds that are out of control and out of the player's current comfort zone. This training is nontechnical in nature. Players are expected to fall; they will surely mess up. During overspeed workouts, it is better to fall or lose the puck than to slow down just to avoid mistakes or avoid losing control. In fact, players should push themselves to speeds that *cause* mistakes. This is called getting out of your comfort zone.

Out-of-control skating maneuvers must be repeated again and again until players become comfortable at the *new* speed. Then players must go beyond that speed to a new out-of-control speed, again making mistakes as they practice until they are comfortable at that new level of speed. Overspeed training can also be done to music (i.e., fast music). Music makes the training more fun.

When combined with slower drills used to learn and improve technique, these overspeed sprints increase the player's ability to perform difficult maneuvers at top speed while *in control*. Strive for progressively greater speed, increased quickness, more agility, and the three Cs—*control, composure,* and *comfort* (Wenger 1986). Players who achieve the three Cs have attained the ability to perform intricate maneuvers at top speed in game situations.

The off-ice exercises previously described for overspeed training on dry land can also be done on the ice. Keep the on-ice sprints short (20 to 100 yards or meters), leaving time for full recovery between repetitions. Other dry-land exercises can be used on the ice as well: tumbling, jumping, hopping, juggling, dribbling pucks with the feet, skating obstacle courses, and performing a variety of skating moves with no previous knowledge of the moves. Resistance bands can be used for overspeed training in the following way: Skate as fast and hard as you can against the resistance. When your partner releases the bands, this will force you to move your legs overly fast just to stay on your feet.

Remember, when training for quickness, all moves must be performed while skating fast.

Mental Quickness

Another aspect of quickness training is mental quickness, or mental preparedness. The ability to anticipate, make quick decisions, and respond instantly to changing conditions can be learned and enhanced by awareness training. Players must learn to know where others are and what others are doing while they themselves are performing intricate maneuvers at great speed. Players who master this awareness are able to anticipate, read plays, react, and move quickly in games. Mental quickness was one of Wayne Gretzky's greatest attributes.

Awareness and Visual Acuity

More than ever before, players are using training techniques to improve their awareness and visual acuity. Here are some ways you can train yourself to improve these important skills.

Be aware of teammates and opponents as much of the time as possible. Try to know where everyone is! This awareness can be increased considerably by developing peripheral vision. Practice by focusing on a point directly in front of you. Concentrate on seeing out of the corners of your eyes. Mentally list everything you see. Practice determining color and spotting movement at the corners of your vision. Have someone hold up various colored objects off to one side and then the other. Keep your eyes focused straight ahead as your partner brings the objects slowly into your field of vision from behind you and off to the sides. Call out, "Now," followed by the color as soon as you can see the movement. With practice, you can more quickly spot pucks, sticks, and players—and also determine the colors of jerseys. Many techniques can be used for training the eyes to move quickly. This type of training is essential for all hockey players, but it is especially important for goalies.

DRY-LAND TRAINING FOR SKATING TECHNIQUE

With ice time as precious as it is—and with the overwhelming amount of skill work that must be covered in limited practice sessions—players should take advantage of dry-land training as a method for developing and practicing correct skating movements.

Using dry-land skating for technique training offers several advantages:

- Skaters can practice the exact motions and body positions of the skating strides (forward, backward, crossovers, starts, and so on) in a slow, exaggerated manner.
- Coaches can give instruction, have discussions, and answer questions away from the ice, freeing up ice time for implementing and practicing skating moves.
- As previously discussed, slideboards and in-line skates are very effective for simulating skating strides and practicing skating technique off the ice. The activities are different, but the motions and muscles used are similar. (Figure 11.2 on page 248 illustrates the use of a slideboard.)

When used for developing and practicing correct skating techniques, dry-land training should initially be conducted at low levels of speed and resistance. This enables players to feel, act, see, and think (FAST) about executing each segment of the skating move. In the learning stages, each movement should be exaggerated, and each stride and position should be executed as perfectly as possible. Technique and fitness should *not* be trained together—there is a time to concentrate on developing correct technique, just as there is a time to concentrate on conditioning.

Remember: Fatigue destroys technique! As the correct motions and body positions become ingrained, the speed of execution should be gradually increased until each skating maneuver can be performed correctly at top speed.

Some dry-land exercises that can be used to practice skating technique are shown in figures 11.6 through 11.10 on page 262 and 263. When performing dry-land skating exercises, apply the principles of body weight, knee bend, and the push–recovery sequence of the specific stride being practiced.

MAINTAINING THE LEVEL OF CONDITIONING

When players are involved in a heavy schedule of competition, it is impossible for them to continue a rigid conditioning program. To hold the training effect at a high level while also avoiding the fatigue that accompanies heavy training

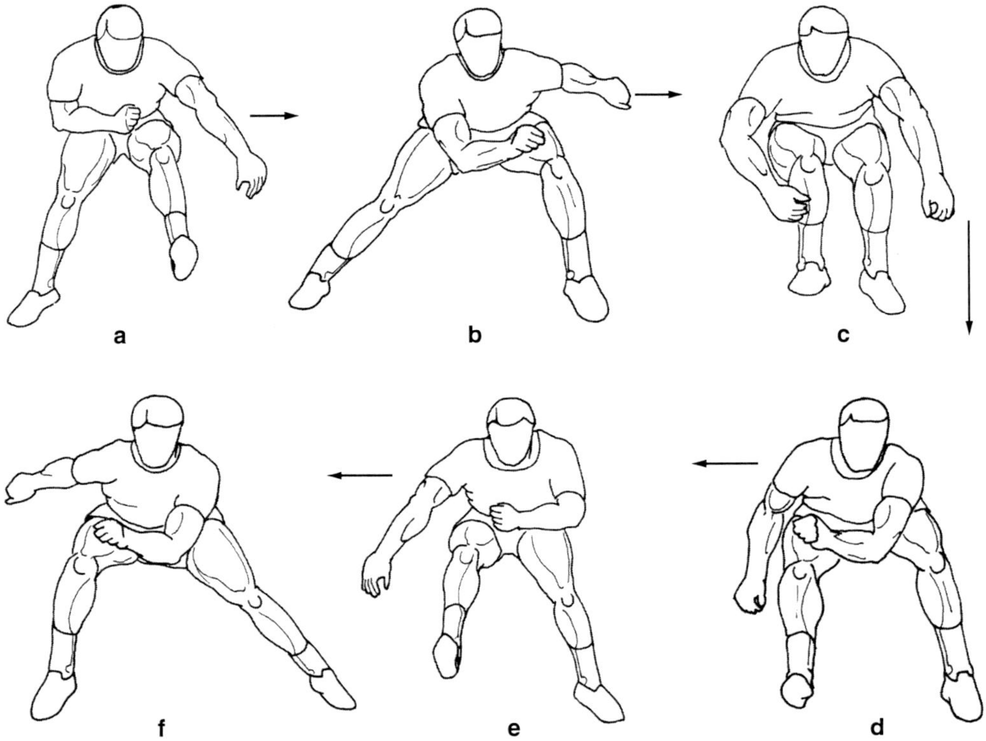

Figure 11.6 Lateral skating: Make skating motions from side to side rather than forward; note the knee bend of the support leg.

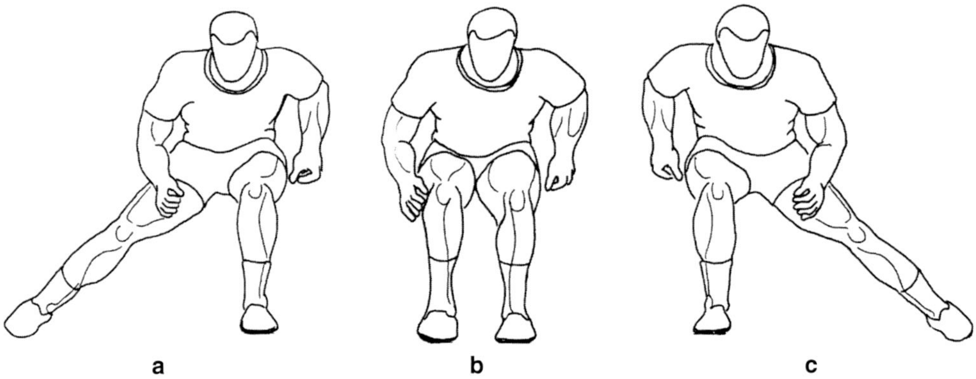

Figure 11.7 Side steps: Push to the side; return the feet together, using the same leg to push each time; maintain a deep knee bend as the leg returns.

a b c

Figure 11.8 In-and-out jumps: Jump out in a splitlike position; return the legs under the body, maintaining the knee bend as the legs return.

Figure 11.9 Crossovers: Practice crossover moves; note the full extension of the pushing leg under the body.

a b c d

Figure 11.10 Sprint starts: Practice sprint starts on a track, starting both from a frontal and side position.

during these times, hockey players should use a maintenance program. For a maintenance program, decrease the duration of training sessions but keep the intensity high. Also decrease the number of workouts to once or twice a week or as scheduling allows.

At all times, you must be sure to get enough rest, follow a high-quality diet, and drink lots of water before, during, and after skating, playing, or working out.

OTHER SPORTS

Hockey requires a lot of hard and intense work—players need to relax and take a break once in a while. During the off-season, other sports provide variety, and they are excellent supplements to hockey-specific training. Sports that involve running—such as basketball, soccer, track, and racket sports—use the leg muscles in different motions than skating, but these sports help develop overall coordination, strength, quickness, agility, and endurance. Sports such as rowing, paddling, swimming, and wrestling develop and improve upper body strength and power. Jumping rope (on a cushioned surface) is great for developing balance and quickness. Dancing and lateral or backward running are excellent for improving balance, coordination, and agility. Cycling, in-line skating (especially on hills), and walking or running on an inclined track are excellent workouts for the quadriceps.

Points to Remember

- Use proper warm-up and cool-down activities.
- Stretch conscientiously before and after workouts.
- Use a combination of on-ice and dry-land training methods to improve skating.
- Overload for strength and power.
- Underload for quickness and agility.
- Vary work–rest ratios and intensities in interval work in order to develop aerobic and anaerobic endurance.
- On the ice, combine correct skating technique with power, quickness, and agility—the formula for speed.
- Use on-ice sprint intervals to develop the ability to apply power in a rapid skating motion.
- Use high-quality skating drills that combine speed work with technique work. These are the most important ingredients of training to be a great hockey skater.
- Understand that repetition guarantees that learning will be permanent—but only *correct* repetition guarantees that learning will be *correct* and *permanent.* Only perfect practice makes perfect, so practice perfectly.

Afterword

The legendary Anatoli Tarasov once said, "You will not get far using old skates, using old tactics, skill, and techniques." That statement was true when he coached his Soviet teams to nine world championships, and it is especially true in today's fast-paced game. Superior skating is essential for success to players and teams.

Fortunately, skating is a skill that can be developed through proper training and technique. NHL stars weren't born with their amazing skating ability; they mastered the fundamentals, then worked many hours to refine their movements and to become more powerful on skates. In many cases they've benefitted from the lessons of an expert skating instructor, providing them special insights and tips to gain that split-second advantage over the competition.

In this book, Laura Stamm offers you the same special technical advice and drills that have made her such a popular skating instructor. If you believe you can skate better, she will show you how. I highly recommend this book to all players and coaches.

Herb Brooks
Coach, 2002 U.S. Olympic Men's Ice Hockey Team
Coach, 1980 U.S. Gold Medal Olympic Team
Member of U.S. and International Hockey Hall of Fame

Glossary

abductor muscles—The muscles of the outer thigh, used to push the leg away from the center of the body.

adductor muscles—The muscles of the inner thigh and groin, used to draw the leg inward toward the center of the body.

aerobic—In the presence of oxygen.

anaerobic—In the absence of oxygen.

angle of blade turnout—The angle (direction) that the blade (pushing or gliding) faces on the ice.

center of gravity—An imaginary circle approximately 3 inches (7.6 cm) in diameter, located at the midsection of the body (just above the waist). For effective power generation in skating, every push must be initiated from beneath it.

centrifugal force—An apparent outwardly directed force that acts on a body rotating around a central point. This force is the pull on the body that is directed away from the center of the circle. It is equal in magnitude but opposite in direction to the centripetal force.

centripetal force—An inward force that bends the normally straight path of a body into a circular path. This force is the pull on the body that is directed inwardly—toward the center of the circle.

counter area—The reinforced arch support of the skates.

crossover—The two-step sequence used to maneuver and gain speed on a curve.

deke—Fake.

edge of the blade—The knifelike parts of the blade. The function of an edge is to cut into the ice. There are two edges on each blade. The following abbreviations are used throughout the book to describe the edges used to perform skating maneuvers:

RFI—Right foot skating forward on the inside edge

RFO—Right foot skating forward on the outside edge

RBI—Right foot skating backward on the inside edge

RBO—Right foot skating backward on the outside edge

LFI—Left foot skating forward on the inside edge

LFO—Left foot skating forward on the outside edge

LBI—Left foot skating backward on the inside edge

LBO—Left foot skating backward on the outside edge

flat of the blade—Both edges engage the ice simultaneously. The skate glides in a straight line.

flexibility—The ability to move a muscle group through its full range of motion.

free foot, skate, hip, leg, shoulder, side—The parts of the body that correspond to the skate that is off the ice.

full extension—The finish of the stride. The knee of the gliding leg is well bent, and the thrusting leg is locked and stretched as far away from the body as possible.

gastrocnemius—The large muscle in the back of the calf.

gliding skate—The skate (foot) on which the body weight is situated while gliding. Also known as the skating foot.

gluteal muscles—The muscles of the buttocks.

groin muscles—The muscles of the groin area (the crease at the junction of the thigh and the trunk).

hamstring muscles—The long muscles in the back of the upper leg.

inside edges of the blades—The blade edges closer to the insides of the boots.

inside foot (skate)—When skating a curve, the foot (skate) closer to the center of the circle or curve.

inside shoulder—When skating a curve, the shoulder closer to the center of the curve.

leg turnover rate—The rate at which the legs or feet alternate when skating.

lower body—The body from the hips down (hips, buttocks, thighs, knees, calves, ankles, and toes).

outside edges of the blades—The blade edges closer to the outsides of the boots.

outside foot (skate)—When skating a curve, the foot (skate) closer to the outside of the curve.

outside shoulder—When skating a curve, the shoulder closer to the outside of the curve.

plyometrics—Movements or exercises involving recoil-bounding (coil–spring) actions.

quadriceps (thigh muscles)—The muscles at the front of the upper leg.

quickness—The rate at which a skater moves the legs.

rock of the skate blade—The convex curvature of the blade.

rockering the blade—Creating a specific convex curvature of the blade during the sharpening process.

skating foot, hip, leg, shoulder, side—The parts of the body that correspond to the skate that is engaged on the ice.

thrusting foot (skate) or pushing foot (skate)—The foot (skate) that thrusts (pushes) against the ice to propel the skater.

toe of the blade—The extreme front of the inside or outside edge of the blade that provides the final push.

torque—A turning or twisting force.

transition—A change in the direction of movement on the ice. Transitional moves may or may not involve a turn of the body from forward to backward or from backward to forward.

traveling on a curve or circle—Traveling (moving) in a clockwise or counterclockwise direction.

turn—Changing the body position from skating forward to skating backward, or from skating backward to skating forward. Turns may or may not involve a change in the direction of travel.

V-diamond position—The skating position in which the heels are together and the knees are apart.

V-diamond or open turn—A two-step maneuver used to turn from forward to backward or from backward to forward with the skates and legs in a V-diamond-like position prior to turning and changing feet.

Bibliography and Suggested Reading

Alter, M.J. 1998. *Sports stretch.* 2nd ed. Champaign, IL: Human Kinetics.

American Academy of Pediatrics. 2000. Intensive training and sports specialization in young athletes. *Pediatrics* 106:154-157.

American Sport Education Program. 2001. *Coaching youth hockey.* 2nd ed. Champaign, IL: Human Kinetics.

Blatherwick, J. 1986. *Team U.S.A. year round training.* Colorado Springs, CO: Amateur Hockey Association of the United States.

Bloom, B. 1985. *Athlete development: Phases of the learning model.* Colorado: USA Swimming.

Bompa, T. 2000. *Total training for young champions.* Champaign, IL: Human Kinetics.

Borms, J. 1986. The child and exercise: An overview. *Journal of Sports Sciences* 4:3-20.

Clifford, C., and R. Feezell. 1997. *Coaching for character.* Champaign, IL: Human Kinetics.

Endestad, A., and J. Teaford. 1987. *Skating for cross-country skiers.* Champaign, IL: Leisure Press.

Faigenbaum, A., and W. Westcott. 2000. *Strength and power for young athletes.* Champaign, IL: Human Kinetics.

Foeste, A. 1999. *Women's ice hockey basics.* New York: Sterling.

Hockey Canada. 2002. Hockey Canada safety manual. General Principles of Conditioning. Calgary.

Holum, D. 1984. *The complete handbook of speed skating.* Hillside, NJ: Enslow.

Minkoff, J., G. Varlotta, and B. Simonson. 2006. *Ice hockey.* Baltimore, MD: Williams and Wilkins.

Ozretich, R.A., and S.R. Bowman. 2001. *Middle childhood and adolescent development.* Oregon State University.

Powell, M., and J. Svensson. 1993. *In-line skating.* Champaign, IL: Human Kinetics.

Publow, B. 1999. *Speed on skates.* Champaign, IL: Human Kinetics.

Siller, G. 1997. *Roller hockey: Skills and strategies for winning on wheels.* Indianapolis, IN: Masters Press.

Small, E. 2002. *Kids and sports.* New York: Newmarket Press.

Sports Coach. 2004. *Coaching young athletes.*

Twist, P. 2007. *Complete conditioning for hockey.* 2nd ed. Champaign, IL: Human Kinetics.

Wenger, H. 1986. *Fitness: The key to hockey success.* Victoria, British Columbia, Canada: British Columbia Amateur Hockey Association.

About the Author

© Erik Hill

Internationally renowned power skating coach **Laura Stamm** has been coaching hockey players for more than 38 years. She is recognized as the pioneer of modern power skating in North America. The first woman ever to coach a major league professional hockey player, Stamm showed the hockey world how important skating technique is to a hockey player's success.

Stamm has taught at hockey schools throughout the United States and Canada. She has worked with college and youth hockey players, U.S. Olympic team members, and professional players, including many NHL stars. Several of her former students went on to become NHL coaches and general managers. Laura has also taught thousands of minor league pro and amateur players how to increase their speed, agility, and efficiency on the ice.

Stamm has worked with the Los Angeles Kings, the New York Rangers, the New York Islanders, the New Jersey Devils, and the Atlanta (now Calgary) Flames. Her power skating system has been employed by prestigious hockey teams around the world.

Stamm has conducted power skating clinics throughout the United States and Canada since 1973. She has personally trained and certified her own team of instructors who teach her power skating system worldwide.

In addition to authoring three books and numerous articles on hockey skating, Stamm has been a frequent speaker at coaches' symposiums, camps, and conventions around the world. In 2006 she was the featured presenter at the USA Hockey Level 5 Coaching Certification Symposium.

In January 2007, Laura was featured in *USA Hockey Magazine* as one of the top women working in hockey. In 2009, Laura was nominated for induction into the U.S. Hockey Hall of Fame.

A champion athlete in ice dancing and tennis, Stamm majored in physiology at Cornell University and taught high school biology and physics. In 1971 she became a power skating coach at a summer hockey school directed by then-NHL stars Rod Gilbert and Brad Park. She went on to coach rookie New York Islander star Bob Nystrom. Her enormous success with him led to coaching assignments with other teams in the NHL and WHA (World Hockey Association), thus beginning her long career in hockey.

Stamm lives in Anchorage, Alaska.